The Odyssey of China's Imperial Art Treasures

Jeannette Shambaugh Elliott

with David Shambaugh

A SAMUEL AND ALTHEA STROUM BOOK

The Odyssey of China's Imperial Art Treasures

UNIVERSITY OF WASHINGTON PRESS

SEATTLE AND LONDON

This book is published with the assistance of a grant from the Stroum Book Fund, established through the generosity of Samuel and Althea Stroum.

Printed in the United States of America

Design by Ashley Saleeba

12 11 10 09 08 07 06 05   5 4 3 2 1

UNIVERSITY OF WASHINGTON PRESS

P.O. Box 50096, Seattle, WA 98145

www.washington.edu/uwpress

Library of Congress Cataloging-in-Publication Data

Elliott, Jeannette Shambaugh.

The odyssey of China's Imperial art treasures / Jeannette Shambaugh

Elliott with David Shambaugh.—1st ed.

p. cm.

Includes bibliographical references and index.

ISBN 0-295-98522-4 (hardback : alk. paper)

1. China—Kings and rulers—Art collections.   2. China—History—Qing dynasty, 1644–1912.

3. China—History— 20th century.   4. Art—Political aspects—China.   5. Art, Chinese.

I. Shambaugh, David L.   II. Title.

N8846.C6E44   2005   2005002224

709'.51— dc22

Contents

Foreword: The Saga of China's Imperial Collections

Descriptions of the art collections assembled by the rulers of China throughout the past two millennia enhance the image of a cultural heritage characterized by extraordinary richness and—it must be admitted—by periodic wanton destruction. The partial or total loss of those imperial collections is a recurring theme in China's cultural history. In light of the upheavals marking China's recent history, it is remarkable that the art collection assembled by the Qing dynasty rulers has remained virtually intact. Equally remarkable is the fact that the Qing imperial collection, of unparalleled richness and variety, should have been assembled by the Qing emperors, who were Manchus rather than Chinese, and who controlled China for less than three centuries (1644–1911).

Although the Qing rulers' zeal in art collecting was part of a calculated effort to enhance the legitimacy of their dynasty, there is no denying that the Qing imperial collection set new standards in sheer quantity. The Qianlong Emperor (1711–99, r. 1735–96), who devoted an impressive amount of time and energy to his art holdings, is also remembered for having commissioned catalogues of portions of the collection.[1] Those catalogues remain important research documents, especially for the judgments of the compilers who inform us of traditional Chinese connoisseurship.

The most dramatic period in the history of the Qing imperial collection, or, as it came to be known, the Palace Museum collection, began with the abdication of the Xuantong Emperor (1906–67, r. 1909–12)—usually referred to in the West as Pu Yi—followed by the establishment of the Palace Museum in 1924 and the opening of portions of the imperial compound to the public in 1925. For the first time there was an complete inventory of the contents of every building in the Beijing palace and an effort to reevaluate the authenticity of each art object.

It is to the credit of the staff members of the newly established Palace Museum that they were successful in carrying out their duties in spite of all the problems that arose. Many of those people devoted their entire lives to the study and preservation of the collection, whether in Beijing, Nanjing, Shanghai, in southwestern China, or, after the establishment of the Communist regime in 1949, on both mainland China and Taiwan. From 1949 to the present, since there have been two Palace Museums, just as there have been two rival regimes, leaders of both governments repeatedly have cited their possession of portions of the imperial collection as being symbolic of their mandate to rule all of China.

So many people deserve recognition for their role in the preservation of the treasures in the imperial collection that it would be impossible to name all of them. Inevitably, the more colorful personalities emerge most clearly: people such as Shaoying, a Manchu prince, and Luo Zhenyu, a Qing loyalist, who represented the interests of the Manchu household in negotiations with the Nationalist government;[2] Yi Peiji and Ma Heng, early directors of the Palace Museum in Beijing; Huang Binhong, the artist who offered controversial opinions on some examples of calligraphy and painting in the collection, when questions were raised about their authenticity; and Yeh Gung-chao (George K. C. Yeh), former ambassador of the Republic of China to the United States, who succeeded, with admirable subtlety, in resolving the sensitive question of how to express differing opinions regarding the attributions of several paintings included in the 1961–62 loan exhibition.

For specialists in Chinese art, the availability of the treasures in the Palace Museums and the opportunity to discuss them with museum curators offer invaluable opportunities to learn more about traditional connoisseurship. Several generations of students and scholars have benefited from the generosity of those curators who have shared their expertise, just as they have recounted their experiences when traveling with the collection in China and abroad.

Anyone who had the good fortune to spend time with people like Chuang Yen and Na Chih-liang—both of whom had joined the Palace Museum staff shortly after it was established—will remember their unfailing courtesy and unassuming expertise, as well as their enthusiasm for every aspect of the collection. To listen as Chuang Yen discussed the connoisseurship of Chinese painting and calligraphy, together with his informative comments regarding the artists' selection of ink and paper, as well as the placement of seals, was to experience the awesome complexity of Chinese culture.

Na Chih-liang's animated description of how he stood on a chair and directed visitors to the exhibition galleries on the opening day of the Palace Museum, in 1925, captures a crucial moment in China's cultural history. Na's thoughtful analyses of Chinese jade reflect a lifetime of having examined and written about one of China's most characteristic art forms, just as his two volumes, *Thirty Years of the Palace Museum (Gugong Bowuyuan Sanshinian Zhi Jingguo)* and *Forty Years of the Palace Museum (Gugong Sishinian)*, attest to the author's erudition—tempered by his endearing wit. These two publications are required reading for anyone seriously interested in learning more about the history—and the idiosyncrasies—of the Palace Museum.

In this study, Jeannette Shambaugh Elliot and David Shambaugh provide an informative background for understanding Chinese imperial collections in general, and they introduce the personalities and events that have shaped the two contemporary Palace Museum collections. For several years Jeannette traveled extensively in the United States, Europe, and Asia to gather information about the Palace Museum collection and to talk with people who were familiar with its history. Her enthusiasm for the project was infectious and it was a pleasure to listen as she discussed her progress during the period she was assembling the various elements of the story.

It is unfortunate that Jeannette was unable to bring her manuscript to completion during her lifetime. Nonetheless, David, her nephew and an accomplished China scholar, has done yeoman's service in editing Jeannette's manuscript, adding the final chapters, with his judicious evaluations of the political ramifications of the imperial antiquities, and bringing the story up to the present. Their collaboration enables all of us to appreciate more fully the intricacies of the acquisition and preservation of the treasures in the Palace Museum collection. Their book also provides an eloquent tribute to Chinese creativity and endurance.

Thomas Lawton
WASHINGTON, D.C.
JANUARY 2005

Prologue

My late aunt Jeannette Shambaugh Elliott, known affectionately to her friends and family as "Nini," spent the last decade of her life working on this study of the saga of China's imperial art collection. Unfortunately she did not live to complete the project. After her passing in 1996, I decided to try and bring the manuscript to fruition and publication. Given the amount of time, energy, research, and passion she devoted to the study, as well as the importance of this understudied subject, I believed that it would be a tragedy if the manuscript (and her effort) died with her.

While much of what Jeannette had written required editing, reorganization, tracking down incomplete footnote citations, and adding some factual information, fortunately most of the text had been drafted. Jeannette had not, however, finished chapters 5–7, and there were some gaps in earlier ones as well. Chapter 6, on the history of the Palace Museum (Gugong) during the period of the People's Republic of China (1949–), required the most work. Although I am not a scholar of the arts or culture of modern China, as a specialist on post-1949 China I was intrigued by— and thought I could bring some expertise to—completing this chapter. As my aunt had discovered with earlier periods, I found that the museum and imperial collection not only had its own distinct history during this time, but also was a microcosm of broader political and social events transpiring in China. It was fascinating to dig into, and it opened up a whole new field of inquiry in studies of contemporary China for me. I was able to collect unique materials recently published in China about this period in the history of the imperial collection and was able to interview several individuals who either worked at, or had retired from, the museum. Dr. Alfreda Murck was also of enormous help after I finished drafting this chapter, as she graciously shared her own knowledge, interviews, and research on this period. I also delved into the periods and gaps of earlier chapters, particularly chapter 3 on the Republican period. In all, I did my best to complete, fine-tune, and improve the manuscript while endeavoring to retain my aunt's original voice and primary authorship.

My efforts alone, however, would not have been sufficient to bring this book to fruition. I would like to express deep appreciation to three of the world's leading scholars of Chinese painting and arts: James Cahill, Thomas Lawton, and Alfreda Murck. All three were close personal friends and colleagues of my aunt, and all offered support and considerable constructive assistance during her and my work on the project. All three undertook numerous careful readings of various drafts of the manuscript, offering countless suggestions for improvement and modification, for which I am most grateful (and I know my aunt would be as well). One could not ask for more knowledgeable or helpful peer reviewers. I am also most grateful to Dr. Lawton, former director of the Freer and Sackler Galleries of Art of the Smithsonian Institution, for contributing the book's foreword. The three (anonymous) peer reviewers commissioned by the University of Washington Press also offered generally positive and constructive evaluations, which helped to sharpen the narrative and improve the overall text (including suggestions for illustrations). To all, I am most grateful. All believed that this was an important story in modern Chinese history as well as in the history of Chinese art, which needed to be told and made available in the scholarly and public domain. This conviction and their support were instrumental in bringing the project to completion. I am also grateful to all of the institutions that contributed the illustrations for inclusion in this volume. It was not easy to locate these artworks, but they hopefully provide richer context for the study.

My aunt's three daughters—Susan Elmendorf, Nancy Seasholes, and Carol Stein—all gave great support and provided specific input on various parts of the manuscript. Madelyn C. Ross brought her professional editing expertise to the original text. My wife, Ingrid Larsen, a Chinese art historian at the Freer and Sackler Galleries of the Smithsonian Institution, was also very helpful in tracking down obscure references, in completing the bibliography, in helping to acquire the illustrations, and in offering various suggestions on the manuscript. I am also most grateful to Michael Duckworth, executive editor at the University of Washington Press, for his support and for sponsoring the manuscript for publication, to Julie Van Pelt for her expert copyediting, and to Marilyn Trueblood for shepherding the manuscript through production to publication.

This undertaking has been a long time in preparation. It was begun by one person and finished by another. My work on this study was often delayed by my own projects, and I am grateful for the patience of my aunt's family in this respect. In the end, I think she would have been very pleased with the final product and we can all be grateful to her for initially exploring this absolutely fascinating topic. While not an exhaustive assessment of the subject, we have endeavored to draw together substantial information on the history of the collection and to contribute an accessibly written study that can serve as the basis for more detailed scholarly work in the future.

This study is lovingly dedicated to the memory of Jeannette Shambaugh Elliott (September 11, 1912–April 2, 1996).

David Shambaugh
WASHINGTON, D.C.
JANUARY 2005

The Odyssey of China's Imperial Art Treasures

1

China's Imperial Art Treasures
from Early Times to the Twelfth Century

China's imperial art treasures represent far more than exquisite artistic craftsmanship. Historically they served several important functions. The earliest imperial treasures were valued largely for their quasi-religious powers. Later treasures were valued as a conduit for the transmission of morality and social conduct. Eventually, imperial treasures became an expression of an emperor's individual taste and discrimination. Yet even as moralizing messages gave way to aesthetic considerations, the imperial collections retained their importance as a means of confirming political legitimacy—something that continues to the present day.[1]

Thus, to trace the history of China's imperial art treasures is to trace a key source of political power and legitimacy in China over the centuries. This remains the case today, as the division of the imperial collection—between the Palace Museum (Gugong) in the People's Republic of China (PRC) and the National Palace Museum in the Republic of China (ROC) on Taiwan—symbolizes the political division of the nation, while exemplifying the cultural continuity of a singular Chinese civilization.

CHINA'S EARLIEST IMPERIAL TREASURES

China's dynastic histories make mention of rulers from as early as the second millennium BC. They record a succession of dynasties: the Xia

(c. 2000–1600 BC) was replaced by the Shang (c. 1500–1050 BC) which was replaced by the Zhou (c. 1050–256 BC). Although this ancient chronology is still questioned by modern historians, the possibility that it was founded on more than myth was confirmed by a series of stunning archaeological discoveries in the late nineteenth century.

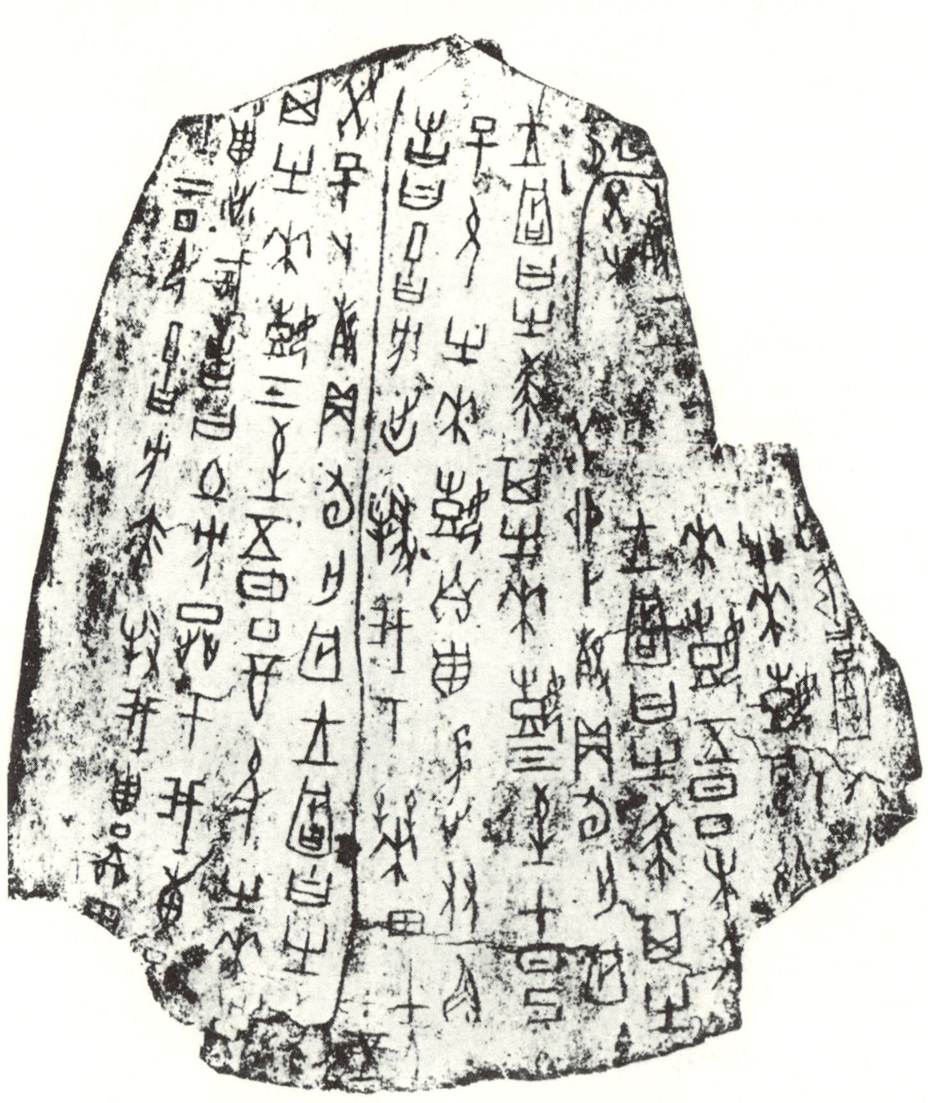

Shang dynasty oracle bone. From Keightley, *Sources of Shang History*, fig. 14, after Lo, *Yin-hsu shu-ch'I ching-hua*, 2.

One such discovery occurred in 1898, when some "dragon bones" sold in Chinese apothecary shops in Beijing were recognized by a scholar "as no less than inscribed bones with a primitive Chinese script."[2] They lend credence to the existence of the legendary Shang dynasty, with evidence that no one had possessed since the early Han dynasty (c. 202 BC–AD 220). Buried in and around royal tombs, the "oracle bones" symbolize the power of languages transmitted through writing.

Bronze Vessels as a Source of Power

China's earliest rulers became associated with certain treasures considered the precursors of the later imperial collections. During the Bronze Age (c. 1050–200 BC), the most prized imperial treasures were ritual bronze vessels. As these vessels came to symbolize the reservoir of political power, a key to sustaining power became control over their production—the mines, labor, and casting technology. Bronze vessels with inscriptions have helped verify historical chronologies and formerly mythical personalities. These vessels—actually composed of a combination of tin, lead, and copper—were provided in more than thirty different varieties.[3]

Early in the second millennium BC, exquisitely cast bronze vessels were used by rulers in life for worship and at death were relegated to perpetual use in the tomb. The imperial collectors of later dynasties also treasured these ancient bronze v essels, which added political confirmation and legitimacy to each successive dynasty.[4]

The well-known myth of the Nine Tripods reflects the supreme importance of a particular set of bronze tripod vessels. According to the myth, a virtuous ruler in China's earliest dynasty, the Xia, ordered indigenous metal from every region of the country sent to the imperial court in the capital. From the collection, nine bronze vessels were cast in the form known as *ding*, or tripod, each bearing the image of animals of those regions. These bronzes became symbols of the state, representing fealty to Xia authority and symbolizing a harmonious relationship between heaven and earth. The divine tripods were said to appear when a ruler rose to power and to disappear when a ruler fell from grace.[5] Without the tripods, the legitimacy of the dynasty or tribe would be lost. According to legend, the Nine Tripods were transferred to three successive ruling clans and then were to pass to the virtuous founder of the successor dynasty, the Shang, on the supposition that the last king of the Xia would be licentious and wasteful, and thus not deserving of inheriting the Mandate of Heaven. The Nine Tripods were passed down from one Shang ruler to the next for six hundred years, from the sixteenth to eleventh centuries BC. As the last Shang king descended into debauchery and misrule, the tripods went on to the founder of a new, virtuous dynasty, the Zhou.

King Wu of Zhou is said to have seized the nine tripod vessels and moved them to the Zhou capital, near the present-day city of Xi'an. King Wu then held a great ceremony to establish their function. By this time the tripods had come to represent a special authority, like a crown, throne, or scepter in the West.[6]

Almost a millennium later, the power inherent in the Nine Tripods was still of vital interest to King Zheng, who eventually conquered all of the territory of the various warring states into which China had fragmented. He ruled as the first emperor of the Qin dynasty from 221 to 206 BC—but, somehow, the Nine Tripods had been lost before he came to power. Some said that after King Zheng's father defeated the last of the Zhou dynasty, he had thrown them into the River Si. To reinforce his claim for legitimacy, historical lore has it that King Zheng stopped by the River Si in 219 BC and ordered his men to dredge for the tripods. It is said that the men hooked one of them, but as it came to the surface a dragon appeared, bit the rope, and the tripods disappeared into the river forever. This loss of the historic symbol of legitimacy was said to be an inauspicious omen for the new Qin dynasty, foreshadowing its brief reign.

In addition to the bronze tripods, the founder of each new dynasty had to claim control of the production of ritual vessels, jades, and other items in order to receive the Mandate of Heaven and to be fully accepted by the officials of the displaced ruler. To ensure smooth succession, passing of the Mandate of Heaven also had to be confirmed by the appearance of various omens. If auspicious, these omens signified the source of authority from Heaven; if of evil portent, they signified deteriorating political conditions. The emperors themselves were the first to take advantage of omens,

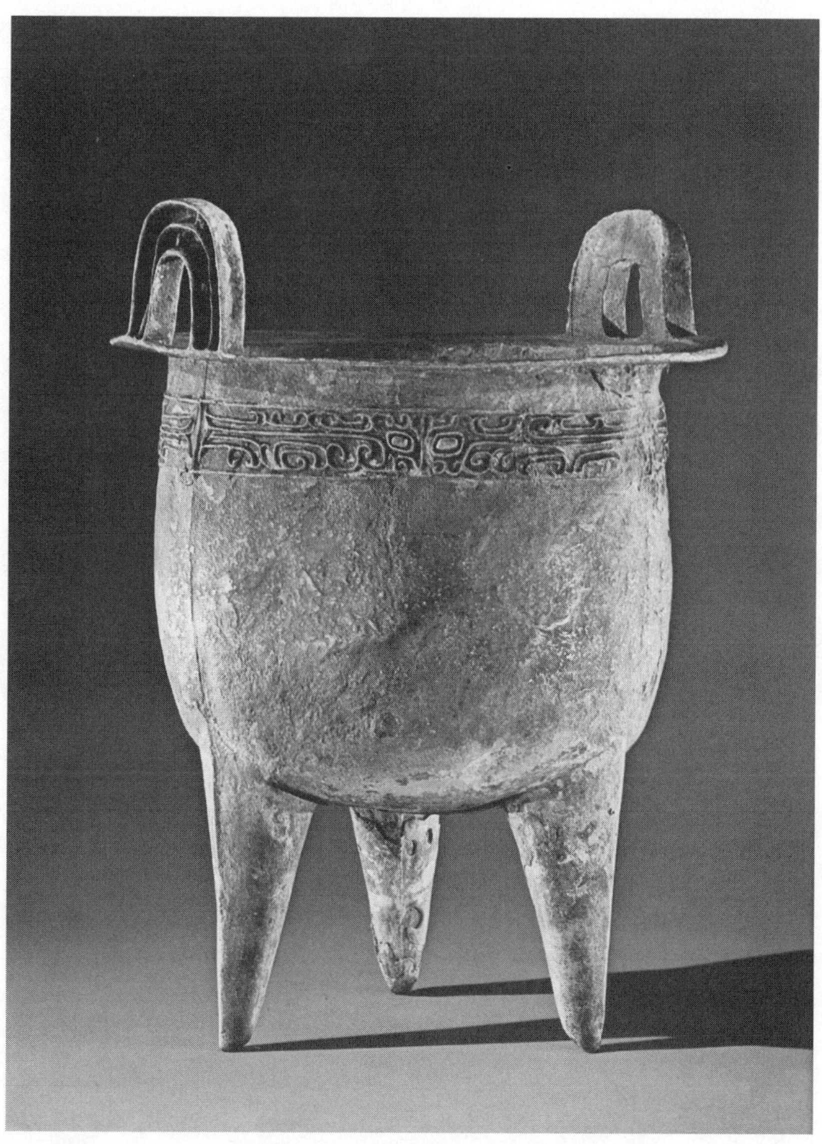

Bronze tripod, mid-second millennium BC. From Fong, *Great Bronze Age of China*, pl. 4.

claiming auspicious interpretations of reported finds ranging from rare plants and animals to the unearthing of an ancient bronze vessel. The Han dynasty founder Liu Bang (r. 202–194 BC), was of humble origins and had no family ties to previous ruling families. To assert his legitimacy, Liu Bang needed to link himself with the sage emperors of antiquity and with

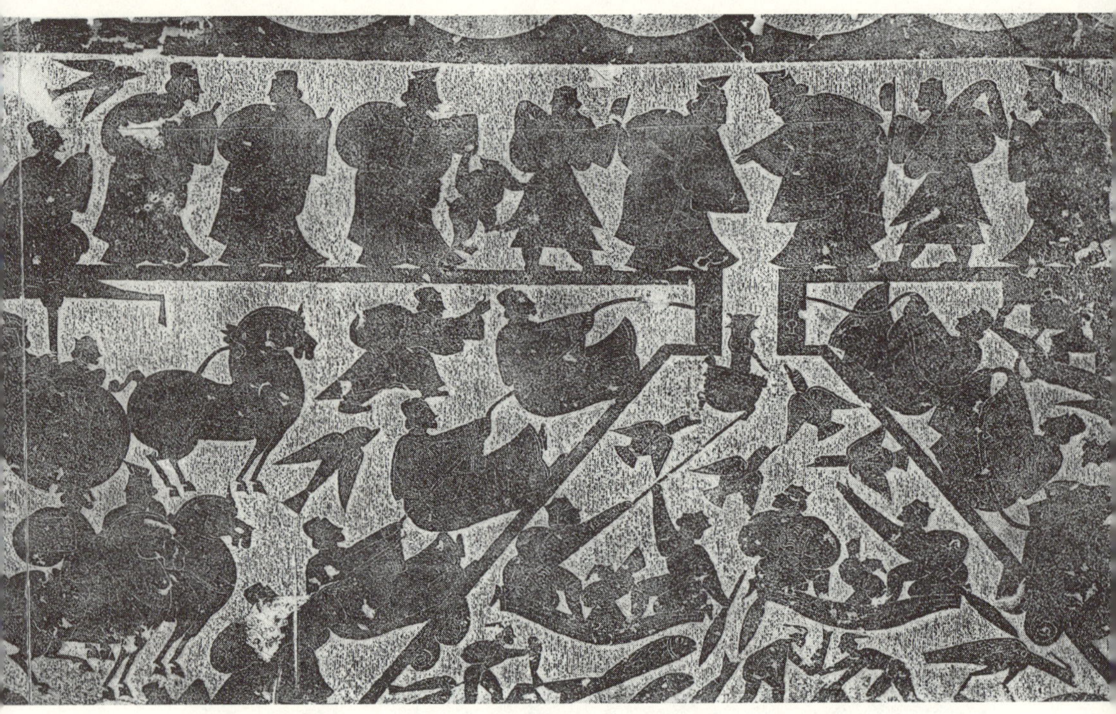

The first Qin emperor's unsuccessful search for the tripod. Ink rubbing from Chavannes, *Mission Archaeologique*, vol. 2, pl. 59, no. 121.

the Mandate of Heaven. This was accomplished by an increase in sightings of propitious omens such as a dragon and other quasi-mythical beasts. A later Han emperor, Wudi (r. 141–86 BC), when alerted that a large tripod had been unearthed, journeyed to meet the vessel and claimed to have been enveloped in a cloud of imperial yellow upon witnessing it.[7]

Other ritual objects mentioned in ancient texts as essential to the assumption of power and legitimacy were astrological charts, population registers, scrolls (which could be records or paintings), and imperial seals of office. These objects were handed down from Xia to Shang, Shang to Zhou, Zhou to Qin, Qin to Han, and successively to later dynasties.[8]

During periods of dynastic change, a newly victorious ruler would seek to acquire these trappings of legitimacy—the ritual vessels, charts, seals, documents, and paintings—from the previous dynasty. This process was often violent and destructive, as successor regimes sought to seize the contents of the palaces and storehouses, only to be resisted by imperial guards of the moribund ancien régime. As a result, items of the imperial collection were frequently destroyed or lost.

Sima Qian, known as the Grand Historian, described how the forces of Han dynasty founder Liu Bang captured the Qin dynasty capital of Xian-yang in 202 BC: "All the generals rushed to the storehouses and fought with each other over the Qin goods and treasures. But Xiao He entered ahead of them, gathered up all the maps and official records . . . and stored them away."[9] Liu Bang went on to establish the Han dynasty and become Emperor Han Gaozu. His success in legitimizing the new dynasty was aided by acquiring the charts, registers, and documents; by having the imperial seals surrendered to him; and by taking possession of what remained in the imperial storehouse.

China's early governmental history can thus be documented with these maps, records, seals, scrolls, and bronze vessels.[10] They also reveal much about social and cultural life, economic and technological development, and environmental conditions at the time.

BUILDING THE IMPERIAL COLLECTION

Art sponsored by the emperor and his court gradually began to broaden the development of the imperial art collection. Beginning in the early Han dynasty, court-sponsored art was used to convey lessons to the ministers and members of the court. Generic "portraits" of eminent literati or heroes, in which portraiture individuality was suppressed, were commissioned for "the propagandistic glorification of the state."[11]

Numerous shrines were built during the Han dynasty. Some included an offering place at which nobles and officials were required to offer sacrifice to the Han founder each year. The walls may have been decorated with portraits of meritorious officials, Confucian literati, and historical episodes.[12] The greatest of the Han emperors, Wudi, built a gallery to display the portraits of famous ministers and generals in the company of an auspicious unicorn. Portraits of former officials were also displayed in provincial meeting halls to give both advice and warning. Their selection was highly political; the emperor appointed the most famous contemporary Confucian scholars to select acceptable exemplars from the Confucian classics.[13] The effect of these portraits was described by the son of the famous General Cao Cao, founder-hero of the Three Kingdoms (AD 220–265):

> Of those who look at pictures, there is not one who beholding the mythical emperors of the past would not look up in reverence, nor any that before a painting of the Three Decadent Rulers (each one the last ruler of the earliest dynasties—the Xia, Shang and Zhou) who would not be moved to sadness. There is no one who, seeing a picture of usurping ministers stealing a throne who would not grind his teeth; nor any who, contemplating a fine scholar of high principles would not forget to eat, or who would not avert his eyes from the spectacle of a licentious husband or a jealous wife? From this you may know that paintings are the means by which events are preserved to serve as models for the virtuous and as warnings to the evil.[14]

The portrait tradition held interest at court for many centuries. Zhang Yanyuan, the great art critic and historian of the ninth century, emphasized the importance of visual imagery in conveying moral messages. The purpose of portraits, he claimed, was "to preserve appearance and to make known the deeds of the virtuous."[15] In his record of famous painters, Zhang wrote emphatically and prophetically that "pictures and paintings are the great treasures symbolizing Empire . . . They are the strands and leading ropes which can regulate disorders."[16]

An early painting that demonstrates the function of the portraiture is a well-known handscroll in the British Museum, attributed to Gu Kaizhi (c. 345–c. 406).[17] Although the actual date of the painting has been the subject of serious scholarly debate, it presents a series of moralizing vignettes entitled *Admonitions of the Court Instructress to Palace Ladies (Nushi Zhen).*[18] Each scene carries a particular lesson in propriety for the ladies who attend the emperor. For example, in one scene, the emperor is seated on a canopied traveling chair carried by four bearers into which the exemplary lady has refused to enter for fear of distracting the emperor's attention from affairs of state.

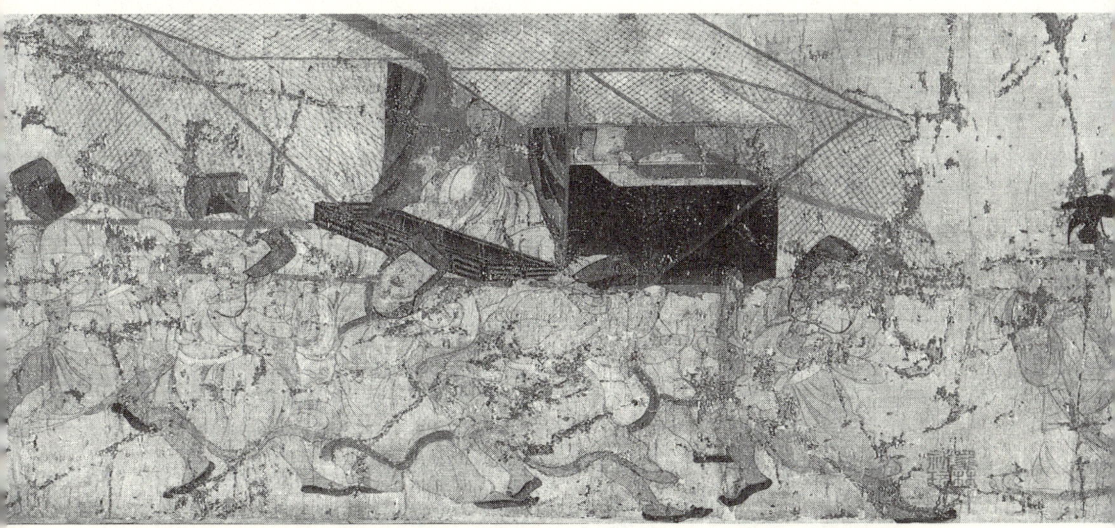

Attributed to Gu Kaizhi, *Lady Ban Declines to Ride with the Emperor,* section of *Admonitions of the Court Instructress to Palace Ladies.* Handscroll, ink and color on silk, Tang dynasty copy of a fourth- or fifth-century painting. British Museum, London.

A second handscroll from the Gu Kaizhi tradition depicting virtuous women is entitled *Biographies of Eminent Women (Lie Nü Zhuan).* This message was intended primarily for palace women.[19] In these paintings, people demonstrate proper deportment based on subjects popularized in the Han, several centuries before Gu Kaizhi's time. These didactic scenes follow naturally from portraits designed to inspire awe, found in the halls of the Han rulers of the second century BC.

As the older symbols of magico-religious power, such as the stylized monsters on ancestral vessels, lost their importance, they were replaced by austere and didactic portraits of literati scholars, worthy officials, and past rulers. These in turn were supplanted by intricate designs and scenes of hunting and feasting that conveyed the richness of court life.

Art in the Age of Disunion

The four centuries of the Han were followed by four centuries of political disunion during the Three Kingdoms period (220–265) and the Southern and Northern dynasties (420–581). However, this era was marked by a cultural flowering in all of the arts: poetry, philosophy, architecture,

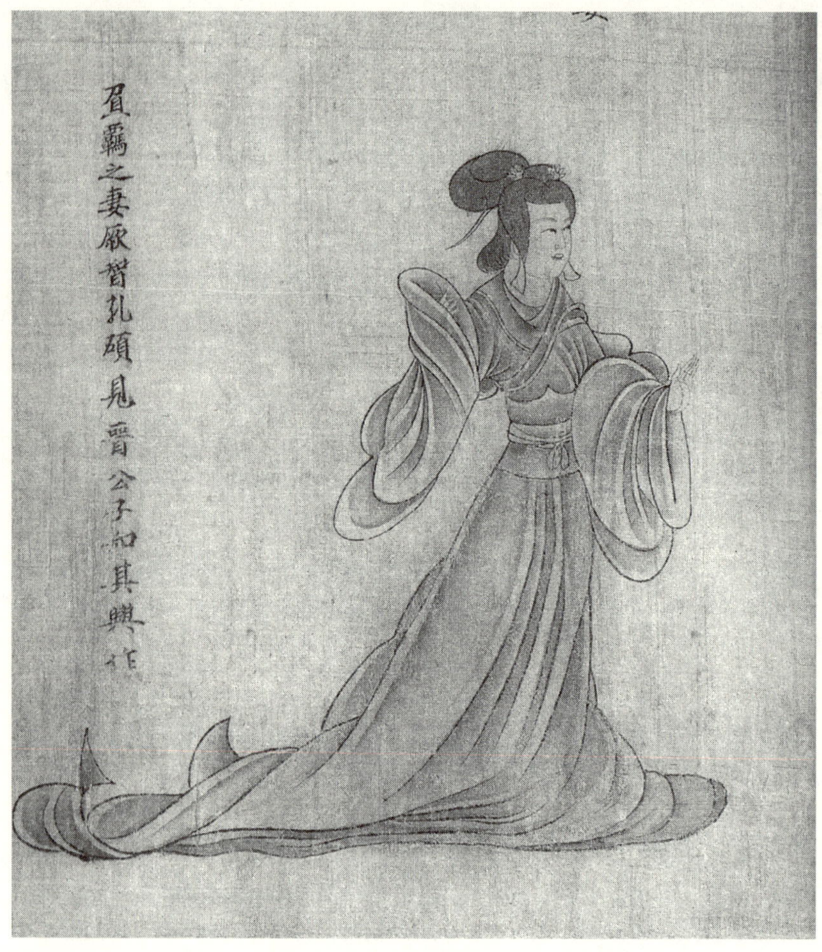

Attributed to Gu Kaizhi, *Wise and Benevolent Woman*. Handscroll, ink and slight color on silk, Song dynasty copy of a fourth-century painting. Palace Museum, Beijing.

sculpture, garden design, calligraphy, and painting. Several local rulers of small kingdoms acquired art collections, but only the topics of paintings and names of painters survive. The destruction of palace treasures that accompanied the civil wars during this age help to explain why no original works by famous artists, of that time and before, exist today.

Among a succession of unspeakably cruel rulers who found pleasure in art are two of special interest from the early sixth century. Emperor Wu Di (r. 502–534), who murdered his way to the throne during the late Northern Wei dynasty (386–534), was truly a great patron of the arts and of Buddhist and Confucian learning. He himself was a noted painter. Absorbed by his studies and sponsorship of a center of learning, Wu Di neglected his city's defenses and the city fell to conqueror Hou Jing. When fire broke out in the occupied palace, books and pictures filling several hundred chests were destroyed. A well-educated general managed to save eighty thousand scrolls from Wu Di's enormous library.[20]

Emperor Wu Di's descendant, Liang Yuandi (r. 534–549), who eventually overcame the conqueror Hou Jing, also became devoted to his inherited collection—so much so that he was not willing to turn it over to the eventual conqueror of his kingdom. Instead, when Liang was forced to surrender, he ordered more than two million scrolls of famous paintings, fine calligraphy, and classical texts gathered into a pile and set on fire. Liang tried to throw himself into the fire, but ladies of the palace dragged him back by his robe. Some four thousand scrolls of calligraphy and painting were reportedly salvaged from the embers.[21]

Soon after this great loss of art, China was reunited under the Sui dynasty (581–617). Sui Wendi (r. 581–604), the founder of the dynasty, gained control by murdering many members of the Liang ruling clan, although he also initiated reform measures described as creative and energetic. In his later years Sui Wendi became irrational and violent, and is said to have been put to death by his son and successor, Sui Yangdi (r. 605–617).

Upon assuming power, Sui Yangdi immediately sent for the contents of the palace storehouse and found more than eight hundred scrolls.[22] At age thirteen he married a young princess from an art-collecting family, which strengthened the emperor's interest in art. He had two towers built at the capital of Luoyang, one to store books and the second for paintings and other treasures.[23]

Sui Yangdi became obsessed with his collection of fine paintings and calligraphy. According to one account, "When he went on a riverboat journey, he took all of the paintings with him, and when one of his boats capsized on the way, the greater part of [the paintings] sank to the bottom and were lost."[24]

Eventually Emperor Yangdi was assassinated, and Li Yuan (r. 618–626) succeeded him and established the Tang dynasty. Also known as Gaozu, he took possession of the works that had been stored in the two towers. These were loaded onto boats and transported up the Yellow River (Huanghe) westward to Chang'an, Li Yuan's new capital. As they were passing some rocks, the boats carrying the paintings were suddenly swept away, and no more than 10 or 20 percent of these works were saved.[25]

Court Patronage in the Tang Dynasty

The variety of art in the peaceful and prosperous Tang dynasty (618–907) reflected the cosmopolitan nature of the empire. Surrounding countries continually sent tribute to the court, adding material substance to the symbolic hegemony China held over her neighbors. This gave rise to the structure of imperial China's relations with peripheral states, known subsequently as the Tribute System. Paintings of this imperial wealth were used to record and extol the importance of the deference paid by peripheral states to the imperial court.

Court patronage provides a window on how art came into the Tang imperial collections. Portraits, which had been used to glorify the state and offer paragons of virtue since the third century BC, reached a new height of excellence in the Tang. Lawrence Sickman and Alexander Soper describe this period as "a long procession of great artists [who] built a tradition of figure painting, both religious and secular . . . which dominated that special sphere of art throughout the rest of Chinese history."[26]

Court art flourished under a series of significant figure artists who popularized the genre of intimate scenes from the lives of court women. Two noted court artists, Zhou Fang (c. 730–800) and Zhang Xuan (c. 714–742) painted figures of nobles with gossamer-fine lines and consummate skill. No one but the emperor was allowed in the harem; thus the intimate scenes of women in court life were presumably commissioned by the emperor or a high court official. Though these artists' work is mostly known from good copies, a painting attributed to Zhou Fang shows two elderly and portly palace women concentrating over a game board, one impatiently snapping her fingers at her opponent. Another portrayal of court life is Yan Liben's (d. 673) handscroll of Emperor Xuan and his courtesans.

Other subjects favored by court painters reflected sporting activities such as polo playing, soccer, and riding. Horses were a favorite motif. A tenth-century painting *Eight Gentlemen on a Spring Outing* shows a group of elegantly dressed courtiers, all on sprightly mounts but one, who is beating a stubborn nag. The background of rare eroded stone, exotic trees, and an elegant fence with angled railing denotes that the outing is at court, not in the untamed world of nature.[27]

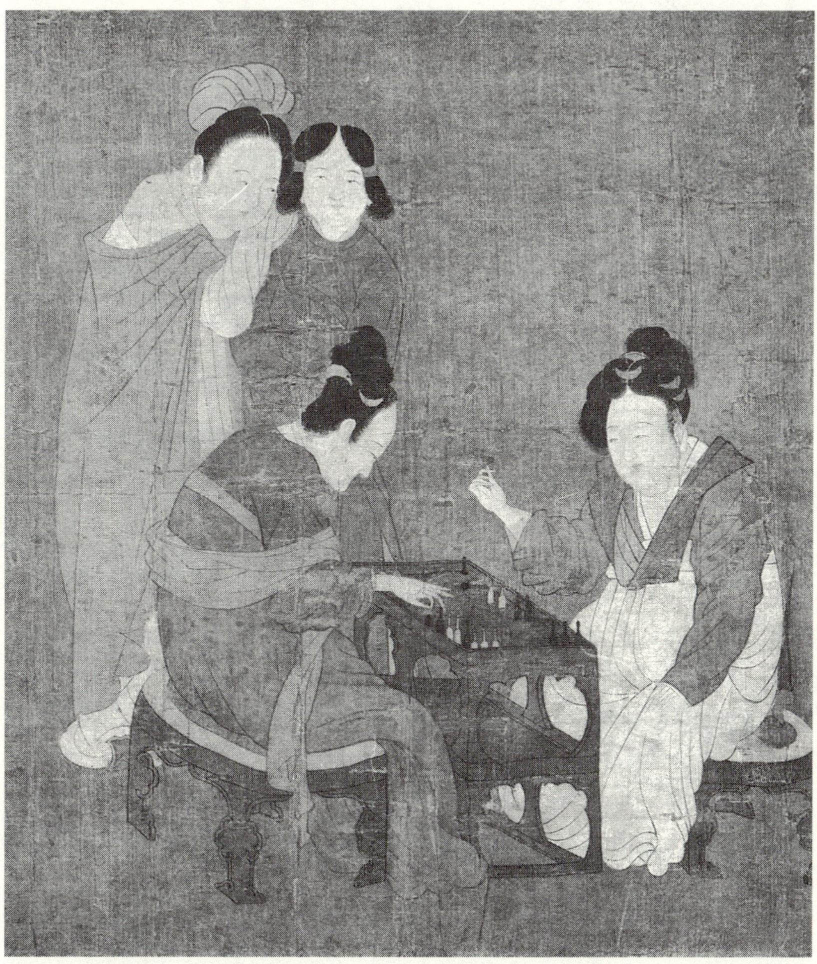

In the style of Zhou Fang, section of *Ladies Playing Double Sixes*. Handscroll, ink and color on silk, Song dynasty, tenth to eleventh century. Freer Gallery of Art, Washington, D.C.

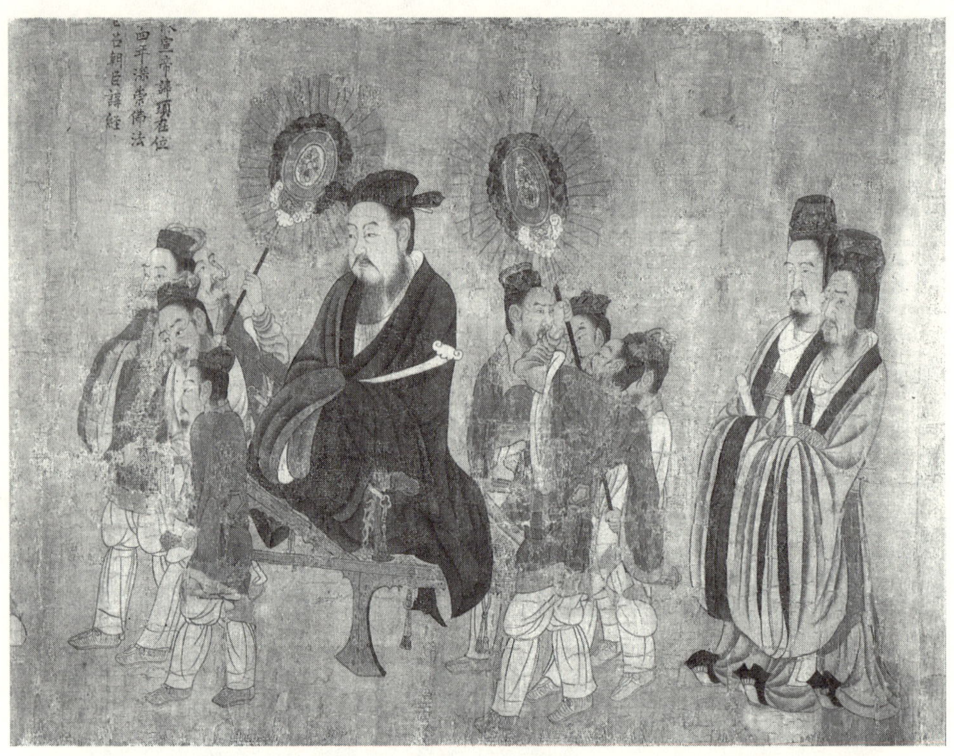

Attributed to Yan Liben, section of *Emperor of the Successive Dynasties*. Handscroll, ink and color on silk. Museum of Fine Arts, Boston.

Artists of the Tang were also commissioned to paint religious themes: Daoists grew in numbers and influence and large Buddhist sculptures for new temples were created. Empress Wu (r. 684–705) sponsored many Buddhist buildings, which created a growing demand for Buddhist frescoes, portrait painting, and sculpture. Countless sculptures and paintings were destroyed during the period of proscription of Buddhism in China (842–845), which was a reaction against the wealth and power of various Buddhist sects at the time. The art of both Daoism and Buddhism, sponsored by the imperial workshops, had a continuing importance in later dynasties.

Excavations of Tang tombs have also revealed original wall paintings of the period (many can be visited today, outside of Xian). Tomb art was undertaken by royal commission, the work of highly skilled journeymen different from the more refined court paintings.

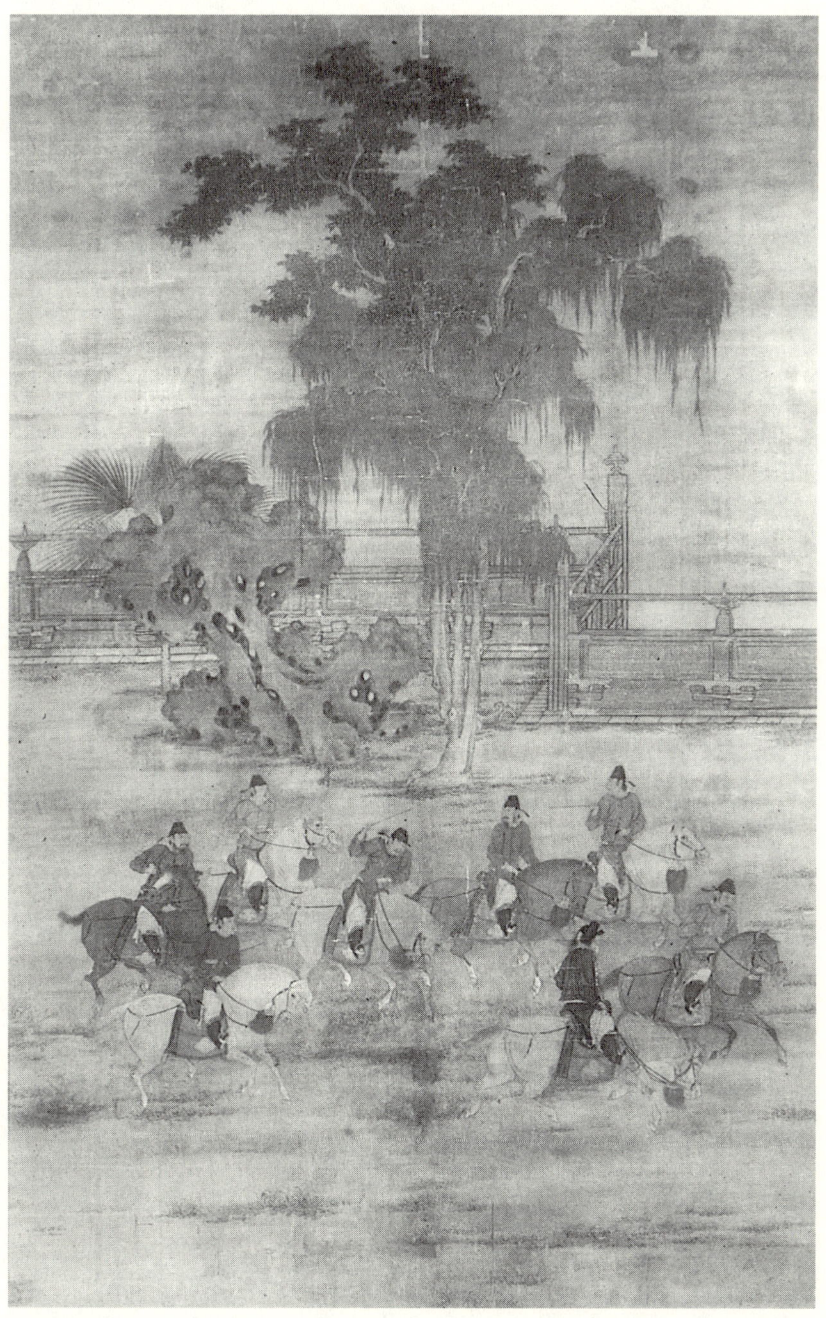

Attributed to Zhao Yan, *Eight Gentlemen on a Spring Outing*. Hanging scroll, ink and color on silk, tenth century. National Palace Museum, Taipei.

The Special Role of Calligraphy

Calligraphy has long played a very special role in Chinese imperial art. A profound change in focus for imperial collectors began during the third century AD, when calligraphy began to be collected for its aesthetic qualities rather than its written content. Calligraphy thus became the first art form treasured primarily for aesthetic reasons in imperial Chinese collections. By the fourth century, handwritten pieces entered the palace collections as works of art, soon followed by paintings. The aesthetic qualities in paintings and calligraphy gradually became more highly valued than either the magical powers and views of the afterlife seen in the bronze tripods or the moral guidance found in portraits and figurative scenes. However, imperial art selected for aesthetic excellence served the same legitimizing function as those magical bronzes and other treasures collected by China's earliest emperors.

The two Sui emperors, Sui Wendi (r. 581–604) and Sui Yangdi (r. 605–617), who reunified China after three centuries of division, made calligraphy an instrument of political authority. These father and son emperors were military usurpers from the north who had conquered the cultivated southern regions, home to the conservators of China's oldest cultural heritage. The northern regions had favored a style of calligraphy suited to stone engraving, vigorous strokes within a grid pattern.[28] In the south, the style of fourth century calligrapher Wang Xizhi (307–365) and his son Wang Xianzhi (344–388) had become the most admired model, with its elegant brushwork and delicate characters flowing freely from one to the next. To consolidate their rule over the culturally diverse realm, the two Sui rulers imposed a unified style of writing. They chose this southern style of calligraphy to unify the north and south, and perhaps to offset their own less refined origins.

Tang emperor Taizong (r. 626–649) also imposed the calligraphic style of Wang Xizhi during his reign and took special pleasure and interest in art. The emperor's main goal of collecting was to acquire for the imperial storehouses every single original by this famed calligrapher. Tang Taizong's collection of Wang Xizhi's writings is said to have numbered nearly 2,300 pieces, suggesting that not all the works were original.

Among Wang's many writings was his memorable account of a gathering of friends in 353 for annual spring absolutions at the Orchid Pavilion (Lanting). A descendent had given this precious manuscript to a certain monk named Biancai, who kept it secretly hidden, but word of its existence was passed to the emperor. Three times the emperor asked the monk to "submit" the scroll to the imperial collection. In reply the monk claimed it had been lost. So the emperor devised a ruse. He dispatched a learned man named Xiao Yi, disguised as a traveler and armed with other scrolls by the great calligrapher. After gaining the monk's confidence the emissary in disguise offered to show him a rare scroll of the master. The monk took the bait and fetched his own prize scroll to show the visitor—the Orchard Pavilion scroll. The emperor's emissary pretended that he thought the scroll was a fake, which so dismayed the monk that he hurriedly ran from the house. The emissary snatched the scroll, leapt on his horse, and then revealed his identity to the monk—who fainted straightaway. The emperor became so infatuated with the piece that he ordered it to be buried with him.[29]

This emperor's infatuation with one calligrapher was to have "lasting repercussions on the history of calligraphy . . . The position of Wang Xizhi as China's greatest calligrapher went unchallenged for more than a millennium."[30] Other possibly fine calligraphers may have been lost to posterity because they did not have the imperial cachet.

The Five Dynasties

After the fall of the Tang dynasty in 906, disunity characterized the tenth century. The north was dominated by the Liao dynasty (916–1125) under the militarily strong Qidan people. Their tombs have yielded opulent artifacts and excellent wall paintings. The central plain was home to a succession of five states that gave rise to the historical designation "Five Dynasties." Another ten short-lived states controlled the south, where culture flourished under relative political stability. Of great consequence for the arts was the development of blockprinting, which became commercially successful in Luoyang, Kaifeng, Chengdu, Hangzhou, and Nanjing. Judging from the fine objects found in tombs in the Nanjing region, the economy of the Southern Tang state also supported the production of luxury goods. In Nanjing, Li Jing (r. 943–961) built a grand capital and patronized the arts, attracting artists from all regions. His son, Li Yu, who was the Southern Tang's last ruler (thus called Li Houzhu), was a fine poet and, like his father, a generous patron. More than a dozen prominent painters worked at his court, including Dong Yuan, the Buddhist monk Juran, and the Confucian scholar Li Cheng, all of whom would become important figures in painting history.

THE INFLUENCE OF THE SONG DYNASTY

History shows that an emperor's interest in establishing a palace collection was often both egocentric and exocentric. That is, it served equally to satisfy a ruler's cravings as a collector and to reinforce his prestige and political power. A good example of such a collector is the penultimate ruler of the Northern Song dynasty, Huizong.

The Collection of Song Huizong

The arts flowered during the Northern Song dynasty (960–1126), and Huizong (r. 1101–1125) was the most brilliant imperial artist, collector, and patron of the era. He amassed more than 7,000 paintings and calligraphies (of which only approximately one hundred are extant).[31] If he was a man of contradictions, described sometimes with adulation and admiration, elsewhere as being weak and superstitious, he was also a man who mastered a broad range of artistic and religious practices and who could adroitly use culture to political ends.[32] One thing on which almost all historians agree is his precocious interest in many forms of art and art collecting.

As a young prince, Huizong is said to have shown an interest in collecting old calligraphies and paintings.[33] Upon inheriting the imperial mantle at the age of seventeen, following the death of his brother, Huizong immediately directed the Privy Library to send the painting and calligraphy collection of his deceased father to his own residential palace.

Early in his reign, numerous auspicious omens were reported—a red

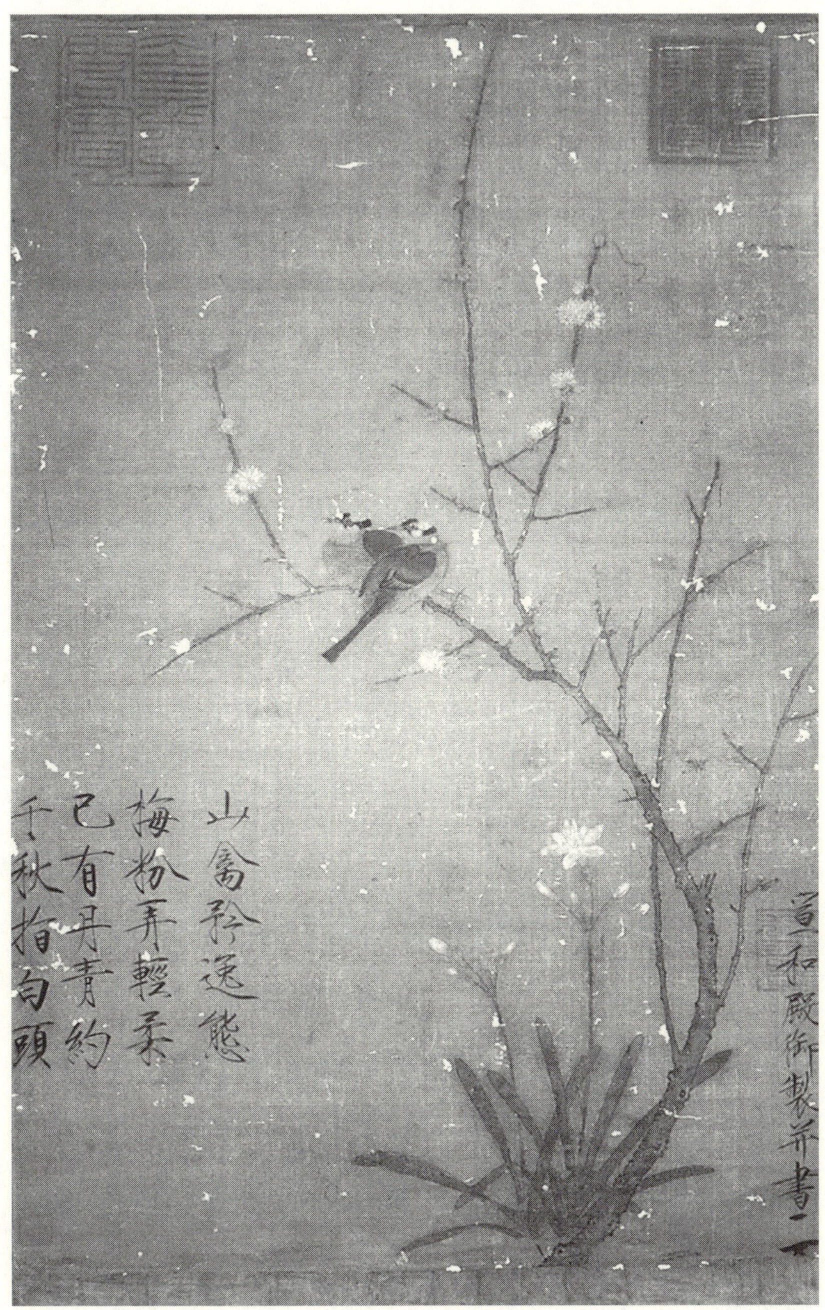

Emperor Huizong (1082–1135; r. 1101–25), *Birds in a Blossoming Wax-Plum Tree.* Hanging scroll, ink and color on silk. National Palace Museum, Taipei.

crow, a heavenly deer, a white magpie, rare fungi sprouting in the palace, and double bamboos. Not surprisingly, all were interpreted as signs of Huizong's virtue as a ruler.[34] In the peaceful first two decades of Huizong's rule, paintings of these good omens were assembled and mounted into albums—some with prose commentaries—until by 1115 there were more than one thousand volumes of such omen paintings.[35]

The young emperor also placed great store in the creation of an imperial hunting park. Long a privilege of Chinese rulers, these imperial parks were important not only for the emperor's private enjoyment and recreation, but also for their cosmic significance. Many in China believed that by making a replica one could wield power over the real object. Such replication was carried out by furnishing imperial parks with every plant and animal of the realm, even some imported from foreign lands, in order to create a mandala of the universe, symbolic of the emperor's control of his domain. Huizong's garden was unique in its lavish use of stones to create, on the flat plain around the capital of Bianjing (Kaifeng), an elabo-rate landscape with mountains, cliffs, chasms, rivers, and exotic imported flora, each area replicating a region of the empire.[36] The realization of Huizong's garden paradise placed a major burden on the state treasury and on thousands of corvée laborers for two decades.

Calligraphy and painting, however, were Huizong's favorite objects and his interest extended far beyond acquisition for the imperial collec-tion. The catalogues of Huizong's collections, which still exist in some-what mutilated form, are a unique record of his tastes and interests.[37] The catalogue of bronze vessels was produced in 1107, while catalogues of cal-ligraphy and paintings were produced in 1120. The Xuanhe era calligraphy catalogue (*Xuanhe Shupu*) contained chronological examples of calligra-phy by Chinese emperors, followed by a discussion of the various styles of calligraphy and biographies of the artists. Huizong's own calligraphy, called Slender Gold style, exhibits an elegant beauty that has always been admired. More than 6,000 paintings are listed in the Xuanhe era catalogue of paintings (*Xuanhe Huapu*), divided into several categories: Buddhist and Daoist, human figures, architecture, foreigners, dragons and fishes, land-scape, animals, birds and flowers, bamboo, and vegetables. Each category has an introduction followed by biographies of the artists; though without information about signatures and seals, the text is of limited usefulness to scholars.[38]

Early in his reign Huizong raised the status of the court painter. In 1104, he reorganized and upgraded the famous Imperial Painting Academy, with highly competitive selection of artists, and his court commissioned many paintings. The espoused ideal was realism based upon the well-developed tradition of form-likeness. The emperor himself painted hundreds of plants and birds in small format.[39] The few bird paintings known to be by his hand exemplified his beliefs: careful and minute observation of nature coupled with great brush dexterity.

Other arts also flowered during Huizong's reign. The great imperial kilns in Henan province, south of Kaifeng, produced exquisite wares with celadon glazes, and the textiles of this period may have never been equaled. The discovery of six ancient bronze bells in 1104, early in Huizong's reign, provided a catalyst for archaeological research. The emperor became interested in correcting the dynastic rituals and encouraged the study and performance of ritual music at court ceremonies. Huizong's interest in ancient bronzes made him attach great importance to the myth of the Nine Tripods, discussed earlier in this chapter, and he ordered replicas to be cast. As they were being installed in a special building, a momentous omen reportedly occurred: tens of thousands of cranes flew over and reappeared the following day when Huizong was inspecting the tripods. The next year when the music for the rites was inaugurated, ten cranes again appeared, circling and crying. Huizong himself wrote in the records, "After this, every time the [ritual music] was played the cranes would appear—a mutual calling between music and cranes."[40]

The Fall of the Northern Song Dynasty

Huizong's refined court came to an end as the cultural riches and prestige of a preeminent Chinese dynasty once again lured the northern nomadic people to forcibly enter China. Years of skirmishes with tribes on the northern frontier weakened the Song's rule, and the dynasty gradually failed to hold off barbarian pressures. Several groups of nomadic conquerors held sway over the northern regions after the tenth century and eventually encroached on the Song dynasty. In the far north, the Qidan and their Liao dynasty were challenged by the Tangut Xixia, who in turn were displaced by the Ruzhen tribes of the Jin, or Gold, dynasty (1115–1234).

In 1127, Kaifeng, the capital of the Northern Song, fell to the armies of the Jin.[41] As the Jin scaled the walls of the city, the Song defenders threw away their weapons, killed their commanders, and plundered the city. The gentry families dressed their wives and children in the clothing of poor people and hid in their homes.[42] The imperial family, dressed in the blue cloth of common folk, were led out of the city after it had been thoroughly looted and were taken into captivity. Huizong's empress and empress dowager had never ridden horses, so the soldiers lifted them up by the arms to mount the beasts. Before long Empress Zhu reportedly died of exhaustion, at the tender age of twenty. After ten years in captivity the retired Huizong died at age fifty-four. The empress dowager survived to be repatriated to the court of the Southern Song dynasty, along with the bodies of Huizong and the young empress, after a peace treaty was signed in 1142. This solemn event was commemorated in a sumptuous court painting, *Welcoming the Imperial Carriage*, which today survives in the collection of the Shanghai Museum.[43]

Having routed the imperial armies, the Jin confiscated the imperial collection and the fruits of two hundred years of collecting and carried it all off to Beijing in 2,050 carts. The Jin invaders had little appreciation of what they had confiscated, giving half of it away.[44]

The Jin were intent on garnering further dynastic legitimacy, which proper ceremonials and rites could provide, imitating as closely as possible prestigious Song court rituals. To this end, two months after Kaifeng fell, "the Jin demanded the ceremonial regulations of the sacrifice to Heaven, plans, and records; the next day they demanded the musical instruments and the ceremonial paraphernalia from the Court of Sacrificial Worship. Likewise the seals of state, clothing and imperial headgear, chariots and sedan chairs, instruments of sacrifice, the large musical instruments, charts and maps—in sum, everything needed for a sovereign."[45]

Without understanding their antiquity and importance, the Jin also took away the famed Stone Drums of Qin. Engraved with a particular script dating from the fifth century BC, these stone drums had been brought to Huizong's court after their discovery. In 1126–1127 the Jin loaded them, without protection, into an open cart with other booty and transported them to the Jin capital in modern-day Beijing. Because the calligraphy on the drums had been gold filled, they were given a place of honor in the courtyard of the Imperial Painting Academy in Beijing.[46]

The penultimate Jin emperor, Zhangzong (r. 1190–1209), the fifth generation of his clan, wished to emulate and rival his predecessor Song Huizong as an art collector, educator, creator of an imperial garden, and calligrapher. Zhangzong lived in the Jin dynasty's new palaces, described by a diplomat from the old Song court as having walls hung with tapestries of embroidered dragons; beams and girders were wrapped in embroidery extravagant beyond measure.[47] His calligraphy closely resembled Huizong's Slender Gold style, and Zhangzong's imperial treasures included paintings from Huizong's great collections,[48] some of which were later incorporated into the Mongol imperial holdings. But in 1234, after little more than one hundred years, the Jin dynasty fell before the most powerful of all the northern nomad tribes, the Mongols led by Genghis Khan.[49]

The Southern Song Dynasty

Despite these depredations in the north, a branch of the Song dynasty continued to rule in southern China through 1279. The ninth son of Huizong, who posthumously became known as the emperor Song Gaozong (r. 1127–1162), had escaped capture by the Jin in 1127 and had established a splinter dynasty, which became known as the Southern Song. For 150 years this splinter dynasty preserved and promoted the essence of high Song culture.

The problem of legitimacy was complicated, however, since Gaozong was forming a government in exile. The former Song capital of Kaifeng, and all the lands north of the Huai River, were now controlled by the northern nomads. The legitimate Song dynasty heir, Emperor Qinzong (1101–1161; r. 1126–1127), was alive and being held captive in the north by the

Jin along with Gaozong's father, the recently retired Emperor Huizong. Gaozong therefore determined to create his own imperial art collection to earn legitimacy and prestige in the eyes of the Confucian bureaucrat-officials who had followed him to the south.

In 1138, Gaozong established a new capital, naming it Lin'an (temporary peace). The name implied that his troops would recapture Kaifeng in the north, but that effort was abandoned in 1142. Palaces were built in the new capital, civil service examinations reinstated, and official sacrifices offered.[50] Cultural and artistic activities were prominent in the new court, and the Painting Academy was reinstated, incorporating some of Huizong's criteria. A leading artist in Gaozong's Painting Academy was the venerable Li Tang (active c. 1120–1140). He was a crucial figure in redirecting the landscape style during the transition from the Northern to Southern Song dynasties. As a landscape painter from Huizong's court, Li Tang was particularly noted for his abrupt brush technique, called the "ax cut."

Few if any works from the collection of Huizong had come south with the court in retreat; the collection had only partially been taken over by the Jin and had otherwise been dispersed. News that there was an active market on the northern border for objects from the former imperial treasures led Gaozong to enlist the cooperation of art connoisseurs, some of whom he sent north to buy whatever they could of his father's collection. According to art historian Julia Murray, he also sent out an appeal "to institutions and private collectors to donate art works, documents, and ceremonial objects they owned" as patriotic gifts.[51] "Gaozong's efforts were surprisingly successful," notes Murray, "for by the end of his reign in 1162, the collection that he had built up from nothing was actually larger than that of Huizong. It was recorded that one individual contributed two thousand calligraphy scrolls."[52]

Like his father Huizong, Gaozong was a skilled calligrapher, and he made use of his calligraphy in his dynastic revival. He often donated pieces he had written to generals, high ministers, or courtiers, choosing the text to inspire better performance or loyalty and obedience.[53] He consciously wrote in a style associated with strong rule and the patronage of

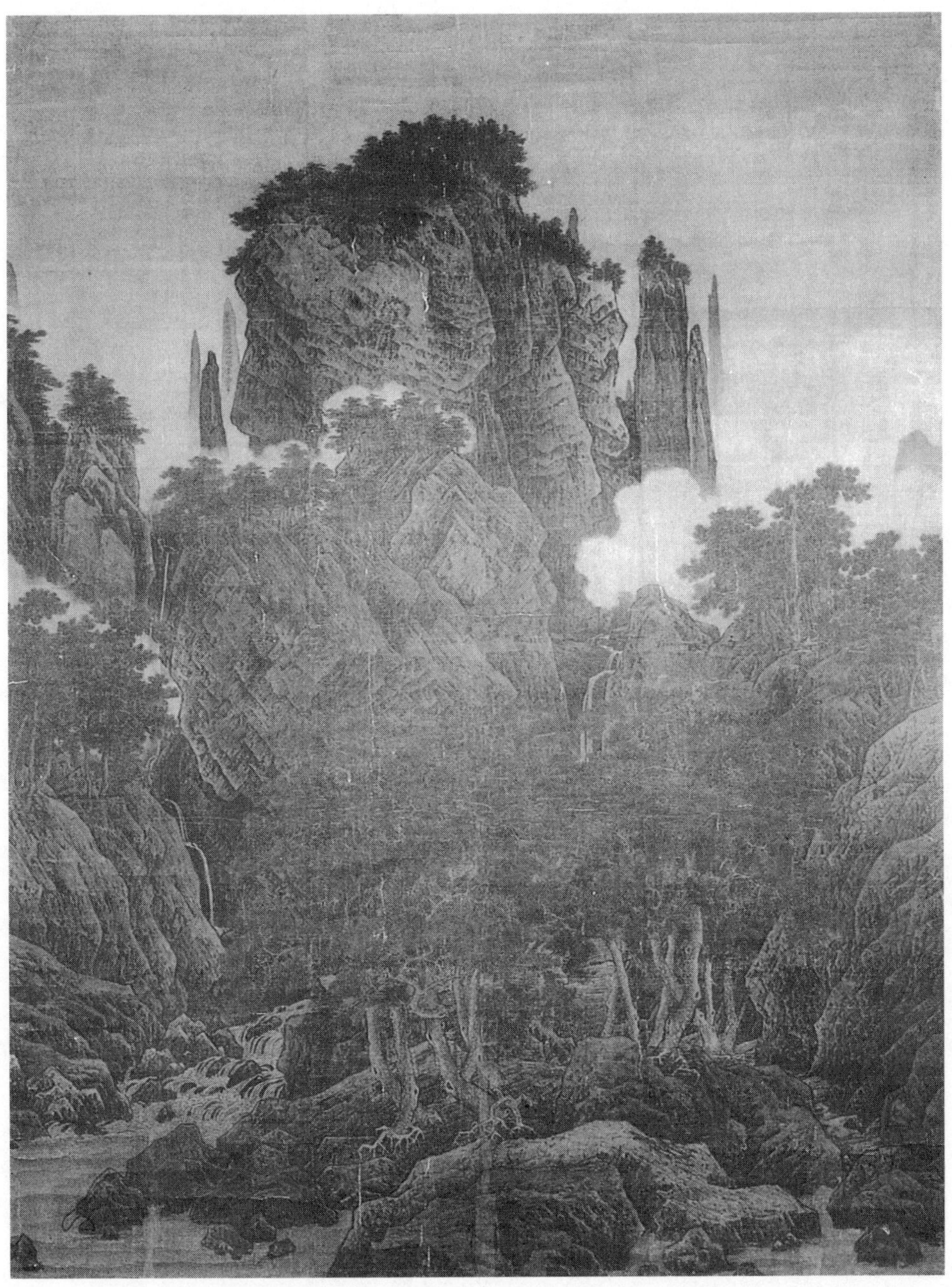

Li Tang (c. 1070s–c. 1150s), *Wind in the Pines Amid Ten Thousand Valleys.* Hanging scroll, ink and color on silk, dated 1124. National Palace Museum, Taipei.

culture—the style derived from Wang Xizhi of the fourth century. A true member of the Song dynastic family, Gaozong also made use, as had his father, of auspicious omens to fortify his right to govern under the Mandate of Heaven.

THE (MONGOL) YUAN DYNASTY

While the Southern Song court in Hangzhou (Lin'an) was vigorously promoting its legitimacy, in the north the Jin were being overwhelmed after only a century of rule by another nomad tribe, the Mongols,. Of the three nomadic dynasties that ruled northern China, the Mongols had had the least exposure to Chinese luxuries and methods of governing a settled population. These tribesmen on horseback who swept down from the northern steppes in the early twelfth century were to develop their own curious and interesting relationship to the imperial treasures.

Kublai Khan, grandson of the great Mongol conqueror Genghis Khan, became nominal chief of the Mongol empire in 1261. Kublai assumed the title of the Son of Heaven and claimed he had the Mandate of Heaven to rule over the vast domain of China. He then led the Mongols' forays into China south of the Yellow River. The Southern Song capitulated to the Mongols in 1275, and the gradual submission of southern China was completed in 1279. Kublai became the first emperor of a new dynasty in China, the Yuan (1279–1368).

Kublai Khan consistently tried to adapt to Chinese custom and precedence and was resourceful in promoting an image of himself as a Confucian emperor. In his first years in power, he established halls or temples in all parts of the eastern empire to enshrine his portrait and those of his Mongol ancestors, in conformity with Chinese-style ancestor worship. In 1278 portraits of Kublai, his father Ögödei, and his grandfather Genghis were painted by Holi-Huo-sun, of the famous Hanlin Academy of scholars. Three half portraits survive, one in the Historical Museum in Beijing, the others in Taiwan.

The Mongols continued promoting trade with Southeast Asia by land and by sea, a practice that had grown in importance during the Song. The promotion of trade was perhaps a secondary aspect of the Mongol interest in luxury goods. The merchants made use of the postal-relay system serving the overland routes between China and the Middle East, routes that had been unused since the ninth century until they were reopened by the Mongols. The postal service was remarkable for its speed, as messengers averaged two hundred miles per day. The trade carried over these routes was of extraordinary proportions, including the transport of camels, horses, carpets, medicines, spices, textiles, ceramics, and lacquer ware.[54] Corvée (or forced) labor manned the relays and provided the horses, while traveling officials, emissaries, and merchants were provided shelter and meals. The travelers all brought useful information to the emperor.

The policy of protecting and supporting artisans had been in place under the first Mongol rulers in China, and Kublai Khan had "ensur[ed] a good supply of artisans who could produce articles his people prized."[55] Kublai also took steps to make his capital, Dadu (modern-day Beijing), a center of culture.[56] In 1272 the emperor established the Mi Shu Jian (Imperial Archives), to take charge of land charts, census records, and occult texts of past dynasties.[57]

Anonymous (thirteenth century), *Kubilai Khan.* Album leaf, ink and color on silk. National Palace Museum, Taipei.

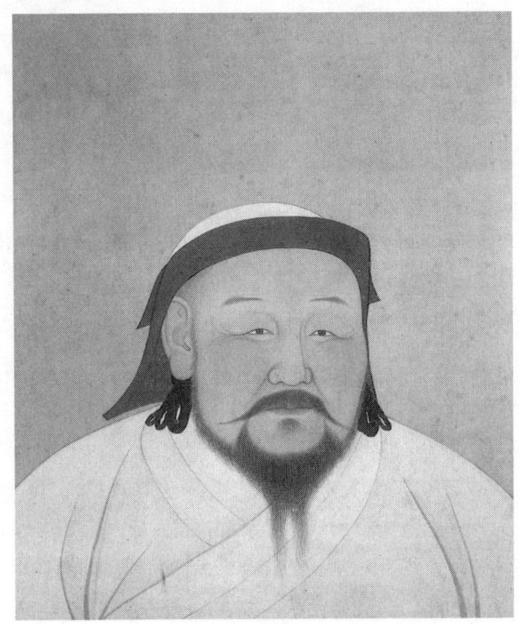

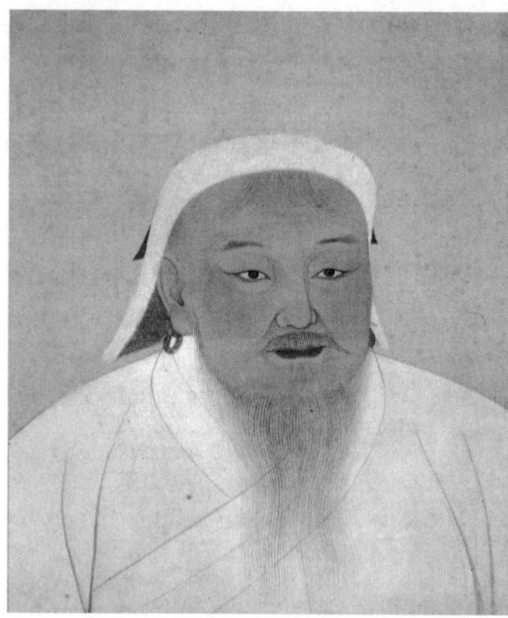

Anonymous (thirteenth century), *Genghis Khan.* Album leaf, ink and color on silk. National Palace Museum, Taipei.

Court Art of the Yuan

The Yuan imperial collection included pieces from Emperor Huizong's great collection, which had been seized by Huizong's conquerors, the Jin, before passing to the Mongols. The Mongol collection also preserved part of the huge Southern Song collection of Emperor Gaozong taken as spoils of war to the Mongol capital, Dadu. The Mongols also sponsored their own court painting, some of which was absorbed into the imperial collection. Religious art was heavily patronized in the Yuan dynasty, and the same artists worked on portraits and historical and genre subjects. Paintings of tribute bearers, modeled perhaps on those of the Tang dynasty, were commissioned for the hostelries along merchant caravan routes. Paintings on palace walls, temple walls, or in scroll form were also commissioned, including Buddhist sculpture in temples of the period.[58] All of these mediums conferred legitimacy on the new dynasty.

It is illuminating to compare the treatment of imperial art under the Song with the way Kublai Khan and his successors viewed the imperial treasures inherited from the Song and Jin. Whereas members of the Southern Song court were immersed in ancient Chinese historical precedents and were competent connoisseurs of art, the Mongols were a nomadic people, with an unbounded zest for combat. In view of the lack of any tribal tradition in collecting fine art, it is not surprising that Kublai did not at first seem interested in the Southern Song imperial collections.

In the autumn of 1275, when the final conquest of the Southern Song was imminent, Jiao Yuzhi, director of the Yuan Imperial Archives, took it upon himself to go south to seek out books and records from the Song imperial collection. All of these—books, paintings, paper, brushes, ink, and ink stones—were moved north in eleven carts to Dadu and, in 1277, were turned over to the archives.

In spite of the speed with which Jiao acted to preserve the Song imperial collection, it was not intact. During the long years that the south was under siege, the emperor had sold or given away many valuable items to reward loyal subjects and refurbish his depleted coffers.[59]

The Yuan imperial collection also included items that came following the defeat of the Jin court at Kaifeng in 1127, as well as booty from the capture of the Southern Song capital at Lin'an in 1280. The size of the Yuan painting collection can be deduced from the report that, early in 1277, the emperor ordered the repair of all damaged paintings and books; in the next month 1,009 paintings had been remounted. The maintenance of the collection continued under Kublai's successor. Five painting mounters from Hangzhou were brought to the capital in 1301 and they remounted 646 scrolls. The director of the archives invited famous personages to write the title strips on the newly remounted paintings.

After the fall of the Southern Song, many scholar-officials, blocked from government service by the termination of civil service examinations, withdrew to live reclusive lives. A few prominent scholars, however, were given honorary posts at the Mongol court. Of these, Zhao Mengfu (1252–1322)—scholar, painter, and calligrapher—was the most prominent. Sent for by Kublai Khan in 1286, he was awarded high offices by Kublai and was honored by the four Mongol successors; for this Chinese historians have labeled him a traitor. Zhao is remembered most for his classic calligraphy, which conformed with the Song royal style, although he was also a talented artist who developed his own painting style.[60]

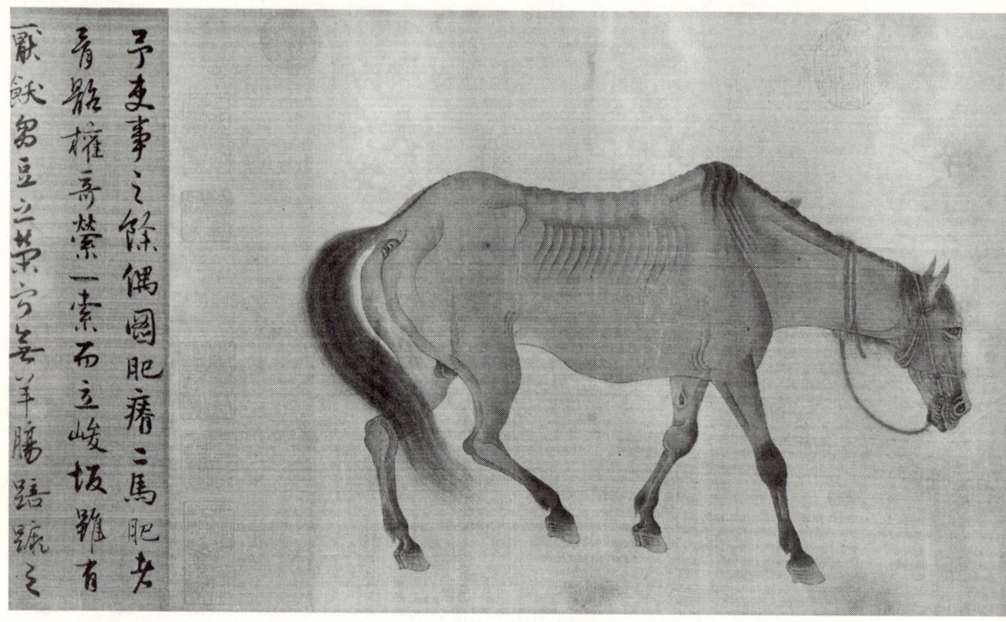

Red Renfia (1255–1328), *Lean and Fat Horses*. Handscroll, ink and color on silk. Palace Museum, Bejing.

Several other prominent painters also accepted Kublai's invitation to serve at the court, and were given honorary titles. Those who went to Kublai's court were required to paint subjects pleasing to the court, such as of portraits or scenes of Kublai hunting. To show that the Mongol horsemen understood the importance to China of bountiful crops, a sheaf of grain or mulberries and sericulture were painted to denote healthy agriculture.[61] Not surprisingly, horses were another favorite subject for these recent nomads (although horses had also been a familiar subject in Chinese painting since at least the Tang).[62]

The Mongol princess Sengge Ragi (1283–1331), sister of Emperor Ayurwabada (r. 1311–1320), had a strong influence on art at the Yuan court. Ayurwabada and the princess, both of the Mongol ruling family's third generation, had been schooled by Chinese tutors, could write in Chinese, and took pride in their calligraphy. Princess Sengge Ragi became an important collector of paintings and calligraphy, some from the Song and Southern Song collections. Her collection consisted mainly of flower and

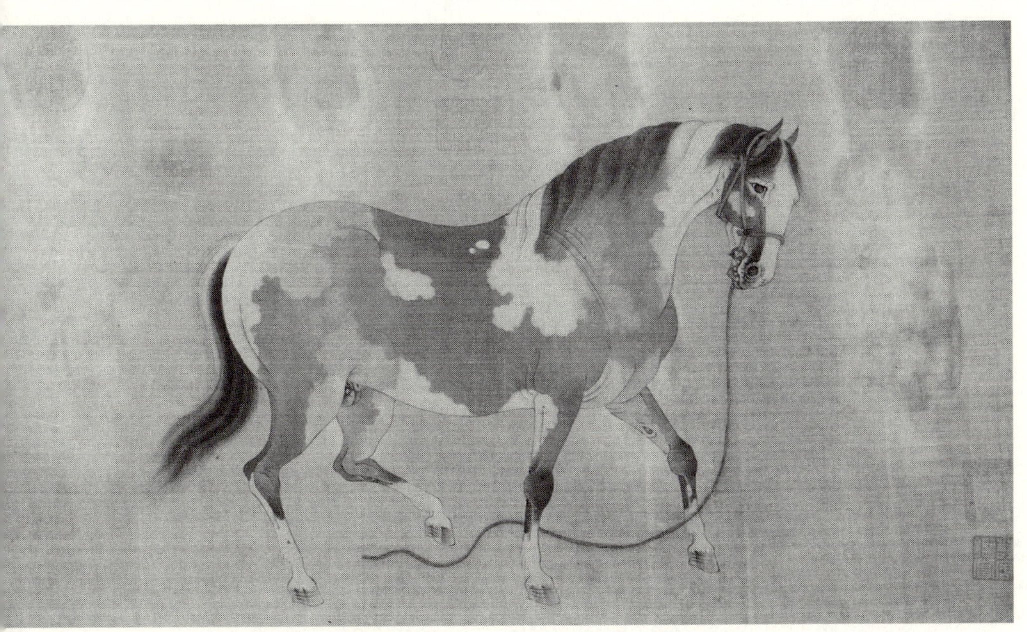

bird paintings by Song dynasty artists. Fifteen paintings and calligraphy have been identified with her seal.[63]

The princess held an historic Elegant Gathering in 1323, at which she brought out a number of scrolls from her collection and invited the distinguished guests present to add their colophons. This was a traditional way to honor guests of stature. It must have been shortly after this that the princess's nephew, Emperor Shidebala, was assassinated after a reign of only three years. Bloody successions placed Tugh Temur (r. 1329–1332), the husband of Princess Sengge's daughter, on the throne in 1329.

Tugh Temur, who reigned as Emperor Wenzong, was more devoted to Chinese culture than his predecessors. He was a serious calligrapher, often awarding his writings to his favorite courtesans. He was also said to have been a painter.[64] He is remembered for founding the Pavilion of the Star of Literature, or Kui-zhang Ge, in 1329. The artist Ke Jiusi (1290–1343), whose bamboo paintings had became a favorite of the emperor, was appointed to head the Kui-zhang Ge, which functioned as a study group for a few scholar-connoisseurs and the emperor. Their purpose was to collect classical and historical works that could instruct the emperor in the art of governance. Various paintings and calligraphies carrying the seal of the

Kui-zhang Ge or its successor group, the Xuan-wen Ge, are found in the Yuan imperial collection.

Tugh Temur's successor, Emperor Shundi (r. 1333–1367), reigned during a period of lessening Mongol control of the territory claimed under Kublai Khan. The imperial art collection still played a role in the education of the young Shundi, and many moral themes from history were presented to him in paintings. When Shundi admired a painting by Huizong, his mentor advised him that though Huizong had many skills, he lacked the skill to govern and consequently was dethroned.

Mongol rule progressively atrophied during the mid-fourteenth century. Finally, in 1368, a southern Chinese warlord named Zhu Yuanzhong sent his armies north to oust the occupiers. His forces captured modern-day Beijing, soon unified the realm by restoring lands lost to the northern invaders, and established a new dynastic capital in Nanjing.

Liu Guandao (active c. 1275–1300), *Kubilai Khan Hunting*. Hanging scroll, ink and color on silk, dated 1280. National Palace Museum, Taipei.

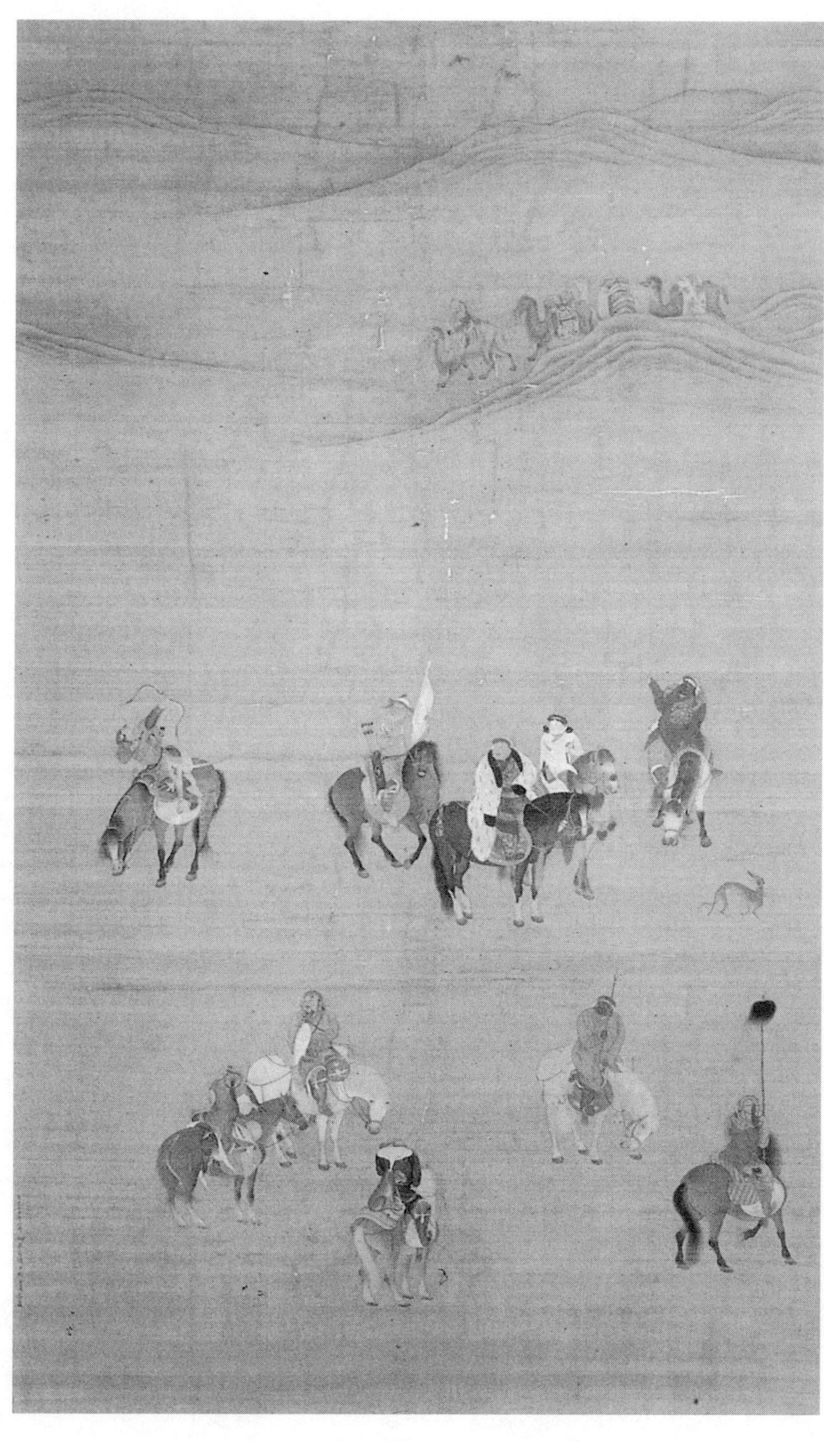

2

Imperial Treasures under the Ming and Qing Dynasties

The founder of the Ming dynasty, Zhu Yuanzhang, was a rebel who drove the Mongols from power in the mid-fourteenth century and brought an end to the Yuan dynasty, pronouncing himself the Hongwu Emperor. He ruled from 1368 to 1398 and named the dynasty he founded the Ming—or Bright and Enlightened—dynasty. The population of China increased from roughly 80 million to 160 million during the Ming dynasty (1368–1644), and the empire was generally at peace. It was to be China's last native dynasty, however, sandwiched as it was between the Mongol Yuan and the Manchu Qing dynasties. But the Ming was a period of Han unity, as well as economic and cultural prosperity.

At the beginning of Hongwu's reign, scholar-officials hoped to revive Song traditions and looked forward to regaining their traditional portion of respect within the imperial bureaucracy. But Emperor Hongwu, who had received just four years of schooling in a Buddhist monastery, had a lifelong distrust of the relatively well-educated literati and bureaucrats. He was also paranoid that people were plotting against him and he seldom delegated any power, thus undermining the role of the bureaucracy. Instead of respect, scholar-officials under Hongwu were met with suspicion and were often persecuted for allegedly plotting against the emperor. Their writings were censored, and many were imprisoned or put to death.

Hongwu created the Brocaded Uniform Guard (the *jingyiwei*) to serve as his personal spies, giving them almost unlimited authority over officials and commoners alike.[1]

IMPERIAL ART IN THE MING DYNASTY

The emperor's persecutions also extended into the realm of art and culture. When a court artist failed to please, or when the emperor suspected a work to be critical of his supreme authority, the result was frequently prison or death. Many prominent artists and literati who were called to serve the court during the first decade of the Ming dynasty met such a fate. The painter Wang Meng (c. 1309–85) and his friend the poet and painter Xu Ben (c. 1320–85) both aroused the emperor's suspicions and died together in prison. A painter named Zhao Yuan (active c. 1370–85) was decapitated when the emperor thought his painting of ancient heroes lacked appropriate veneration. Another artist was executed for painting a fairy riding a dragon, viewed as ridicule of the emperor, whose emblem was the dragon.

When the artist Zhou Wei (active late fourteenth century) was painting the walls of the palace, the emperor came by and instructed, "Paint all the rivers and mountains in the land." Zhou tactfully asked the emperor to sketch his idea, at which Hongwu grasped the brush and made a rough sketch. Zhou Wei bowed deeply and said, "Your majesty has already fixed all the rivers and mountains; I can add nothing to it." But even this clever ruse did not save him; he was later slandered and put to death.[2] The episode may have led to reports that Hongwu was himself a landscape painter and calligrapher of some skill. One artist who escaped death or imprisonment, Chen Yuan (active late fourteenth century), was commissioned to paint the emperor's portrait. This portrait survives in the National Palace Museum in Taipei and is a veritable caricature—a pock-marked face with gimlet eyes and a protruding and large square chin. Surely, the irascible Hongwu was never shown this portrait!

Hongwu and the Imperial Collection

Emperor Hongwu clearly understood the value of images in legitimizing his Ming dynasty. As had his predecessors, he ordered portraits of the meritorious officials of old as well as a full set of paintings of the now-royal Zhu clan: himself, his empress, and his ancestors. This was one of his many moves to reinforce his image as the model Confucian ruler. Unimpressed with the graduates of the civil service examination system, Hongwu suspended the exams and revived the custom of bringing worthy officials, sometimes retired and living as hermits, back into the government. Hongwu promoted paintings depicting the worthy hermit being invited to serve at court, a theme that continued in popularity during the Ming.

During the Ming, eunuchs came to be entrusted with the security and comfort of the emperor and members of the imperial family. They were also given command of the imperial palace guards and were gradually entrusted with the management of the palace workshops manned by craftsmen and painters. The numbers of workers engaged in these areas had by the end of the fifteenth and early sixteenth centuries increased to hundreds, hired or fired by the eunuch.

Significantly, the eunuchs also controlled the tribute sent to the emperor from the provinces and foreign nations, and their authority encompassed the storage of the imperial art treasures. With their control of the treasure storerooms, they could steal works of art and bestow them on others to gain valuable influence. After the mid-fifteenth century, the eunuchs gradually usurped the emperor's role in choosing the court artists. Not surprisingly some eunuchs amassed their own considerable collections.

Aware of the eunuchs' access to tribute and imperial treasures, Hongwu ordered an inventory of the imperial treasures in the fifth year of his reign, 1373. An office was created to monitor errors and illegalities of palace officials. This Office of Regulations and Investigations conducted an inventory of the former Yuan dynasty collection between the twelfth lunar month of 1373 and 1374. Each inventoried painting or calligraphy was given the distinctive Ming half-seal (*Ming siyin banyin*), in which the left half of the seal appears on the margin of the painting itself and the other (right) half presumably appears on a palace inventory document. Several dozen paintings bearing this half-seal exist. It is of great use and interest to art collectors and historians, for it identifies the scrolls captured from the Yuan imperial collection, which became the foundation of the Ming imperial collection.[3]

Court art at this time must be understood and judged largely as the art of patronage, created to satisfy an individual emperor's taste and, directly

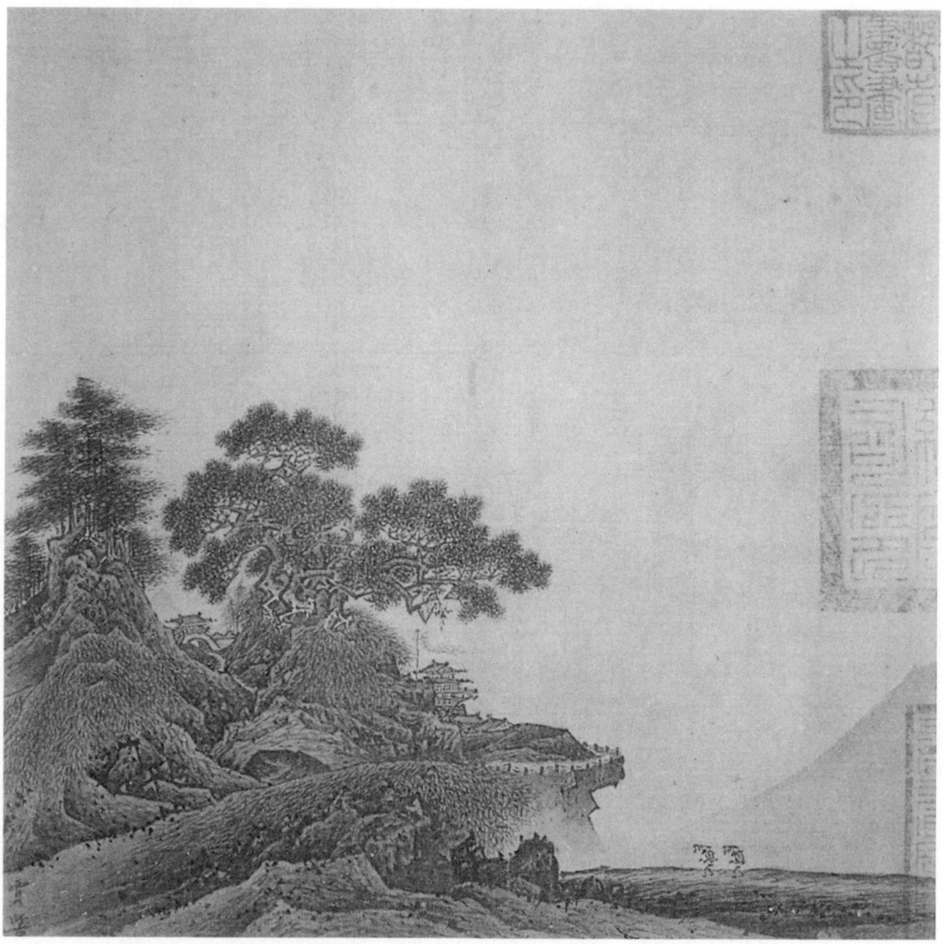

Jia Shigu (active c. 1150), *Temple by the Cliff Pass.* Album leaf, ink and color on silk. National Palace Museum, Taipei.

or by inference, to support the vision of a world at peace by virtue of the conscientious and benevolent ruler (*wangdao*). That is not to say that this era of imperial art was of lesser artistic quality and skill. On the contrary, the best artists at court could paint in different styles with a high degree of competence.

The imperial collection has been likened to an imperial gift shop, to which each emperor had unlimited access and whose treasures, as gifts, served to reinforce the dynasty's legitimacy.[4] Hongwu followed this practice, making gifts of many works from the collection to cement the loyalty of the recipients. When his son Zhu Gang (1358–98) was enthroned as the prince of Jin in 1378, the prince became entitled to a rich art collection (although he was not able to receive it until he turned twenty, when he took formal control of the fiefdom). Thirty-three important paintings are known to have the prince's seal, and no less than fifteen of these works bear the Ming half-seal. When Prince Zhu died at age forty, his collection was disbursed among collectors.[5]

Another beneficiary of Ming emperor Hongwu's gifts was an adopted son, General Mu Ying, who used the emperor's gifts to found a significant family art collection. The emperor's grandson, Mu Sheng (1368–1439), was another avid collector whose seals appear on more than one hundred fine paintings, many also bearing Song dynasty imperial seals and the Ming half-seal.

Emperor Hongwu also rebuilt the ancient capital in Nanjing, protected by a city wall with a twenty-mile circumference. Artists and artisans were actively recruited to serve at court during the rebuilding, and they came in great number. Nanjing, the first Ming capital, became "the capital district where all in the empire capable in the arts have gathered together" and where all forms of art were called upon to create appropriate symbols to "legitimize and enhance the emperor's own role and position."[6] Many skilled artists came from the Jiang'nan region surrounding the former Southern Song cities of Suzhou, Hangzhou, and Yangzhou, where the high standards of court art had survived the century of Mongol rule. The southern regions around Suzhou and Hangzhou had been centers for artists, writers, and the cultivated literati since the Southern Song.

The Great Undertakings of the Yongle Emperor

In 1402 Emperor Hongwu's eldest son, Zhu Di (1360–1424), usurped the throne from his nephew, Jianwen (r. 1368–1402), and installed himself as emperor. Zhu Di immediately executed all officers who refused to recognize him as emperor, as well as their relatives, neighbors, teachers, servants, and friends, and he chose the reign name Yongle, meaning Lasting Joy.[7] His era was notable for two significant endeavors that encouraged the arts: the creation and voyages of a merchant fleet to enlarge and reinforce the tribute system to the Ming empire, and the decision in 1407 to move the capital to Beijing. Both had an enormous impact on the life and culture of the era.

The Ming rulers saw China as the veritable Middle Kingdom, superior to other nations in culture, power, and importance. The decision to build a huge merchant fleet was premised on the Yongle Emperor's belief that China's prestige, wealth, and prosperity would increase commensurate with the number of kingdoms forced to pay tribute. Work on the fleet began in 1403, producing the largest wooden sailing ships built to that time (approximately 400 by 160 feet). This extraordinary fleet was put under the command of Yongle's friend and closest adviser, the eunuch Zheng He, and it consisted of "more warships than the Spanish Armada, carrying tons of the Middle Kingdom's finest silks, porcelains, lacquer ware and art objects."[8] It could be used to force Southeast Asian countries to bear tribute to China, but it may have served another purpose as well: protecting the China coast from the endemic piracy of the early fifteenth century.[9] China's giant treasure-laden ships helped to both protect and enforce China's interests, by persuasion or at gunpoint. Between 1405 and 1433 the fleet made seven epic voyages throughout the China Sea, the Indian Ocean, the Persian Gulf, and to Africa.[10]

Yongle was an uneasy usurper, not comfortable in Nanjing among the aristocratic bureaucracy drawn from the families of the lower Yangzi River region. He preferred his own fiefdom in the north—near the capital of the former Mongol Yuan dynasty. Thus, the second great enterprise carried out under the Yongle Emperor was the building of an entirely new capital, with new palaces and a surrounding city wall, in northern China. Here he had the loyalty of the army and eunuchs who had assisted him with his coup. This group was mostly from northern, less aristocratic families.[11]

The emperor called for a high-walled Forbidden City to be built in the north, surrounded by a three-mile-square area that included fifty supply shops producing arts and crafts. Work on the grandiose Forbidden City began in 1407 and its construction was a phenomenal feat. One million conscripts worked in Beijing and untold thousands of workers labored in the provinces to quarry stone, fell trees, and to ship materials to the capital. Sixty-two trades were listed and 232,089 craftsmen were registered to fabricate items for the palace. In all it is estimated that about 2 percent of the population of fifteenth-century China contributed to this effort.[12]

Beijing, meaning "northern capital," became the Ming capital in 1421.[13] The transfer of government offices took place gradually, aided by the restoration of the Grand Canal, which ran between Hangzhou and Beijing. The restoration took more than three decades and was completed in about 1450.

Thousands of artists were imported to embellish the new imperial setting. Typically, an artist was recommended to the court by an official and might receive a low rank in the Brocaded Uniform Guard, the same group assigned to serve and protect the emperor. But painters apparently had no guard duties and were free to pursue their art.

Many artists brought the imperial art styles of the south to the new northern capital; as a result, Ming art became as court-centered as it had been under the Song emperor and art patron Huizong. Court art of the Ming thus continued to function "as part of a sustained, systematic program of imperial art, the purpose of which was to create a symbolic visualization of a cultivated emperor's reign."[14]

An impressive variety of styles and repertoire of subjects could be produced on command by artists of the imperial court. As the Ming dynasty evolved, bird and flower paintings became more ostentatious, especially

Bian Wenjin (active c. 1354–1428), *The Hundred Birds and the Three Friends.* Hanging scroll, ink and color on silk, c. 1413. The Cleveland Museum of Art.

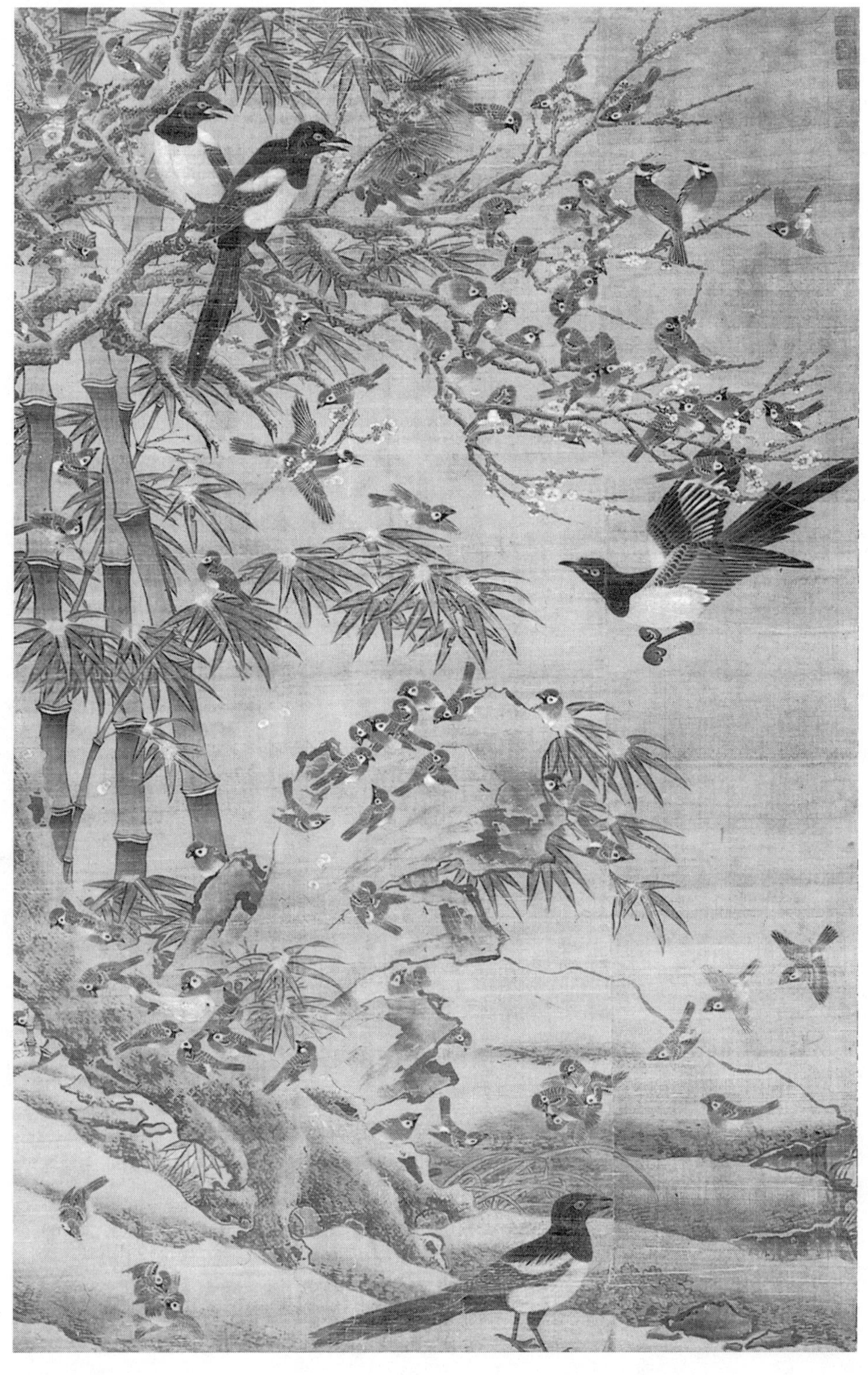

compared with the intimate fan and album paintings popular at the court of Emperor Gaozong. These Ming court painters still based their bird and flower works on keenly observed nature, often implying a eulogized message, as in *The Hundred Birds and the Three Friends* by Bian Wenjin (c. 1354–1428), or his dramatic *Two Cranes*.[15]

The popularity of styles fluctuated with each emperor's preferences. Some of the Jiang'nan region artists invited to court brought the Ma Yuan–Xia Gui tradition, a court style of the Southern Song, as filtered through the Yuan period. The Yongle Emperor apparently rejected the Ma-Xia tradition with the comment, "They are nothing more than stagnant rivers and leftover mountains of the Song refugees (from Northern Song)—what can we find there?"[16] His successor, Emperor Xuanzong (r. 1426–36), also preferred northern styles: the lofty mountains and clear air, sometimes rendered in the blue-green style, sometimes in the ink style of Li Tang and others. The blue-green landscape style, which had denoted imperial privilege since the Tang dynasty, can be seen in the work of Shi Rui, called to serve under Emperor Xuanzong.[17]

The Xuande Emperor's Patronage of the Arts

Xuanzong, also known as the Xuande Emperor, brought court artists together into a structured art academy, with offices, rank, duties, and emoluments, supervised by the emperor himself. His personal interest gave vitality and direction to the new academy. He took a hand in judging candidates for acceptance at court, disciplined and rewarded the artists, and personally awarded imperial seals and higher rank, terminating the appointments of those who displeased him.[18] The momentum of Xuanzong's academy carried forward for several generations: "through the systematized practices of the court academy, of the studio and workshop, and of the structure of apprenticeship and education in the craft of painting, the effects of a true academy were maintained for a century."[19]

An emperor's taste set the styles followed at court, and those styles that were not in favor were avoided by artists. Thus the court art of the Ming, as court art under earlier dynasties, was created in response to a patron and was not a form of individual expression. The choice of subject was key. A painting was valued for its meanings, rendered in subtle symbolic ways, but high standards of craftsmanship were also mandatory.

Chinese have a fondness for pictures with symbols that give multiple meanings. A heron, for example, is auspicious because the word for heron, *lu*, sounds like the word that means a road or the "path" of the Daoists and also like the word that means salary; therefore h tues; the crest means literary achievement, the claws a martial spirit, its fighting nature means bravery, the sharing of food means benevolence, the announcement of dawn means trustworthiness, and so forth. The phoenix is an imaginary bird, popular on bronzes of the Zhou dynasty and ever since equated with imperial status; it is a cosmic symbol of the south.

The importance of learning to interpret a court painting is illustrated by a large painting entitled *Emperor Xuanzong's Pleasures*, now in the Palace

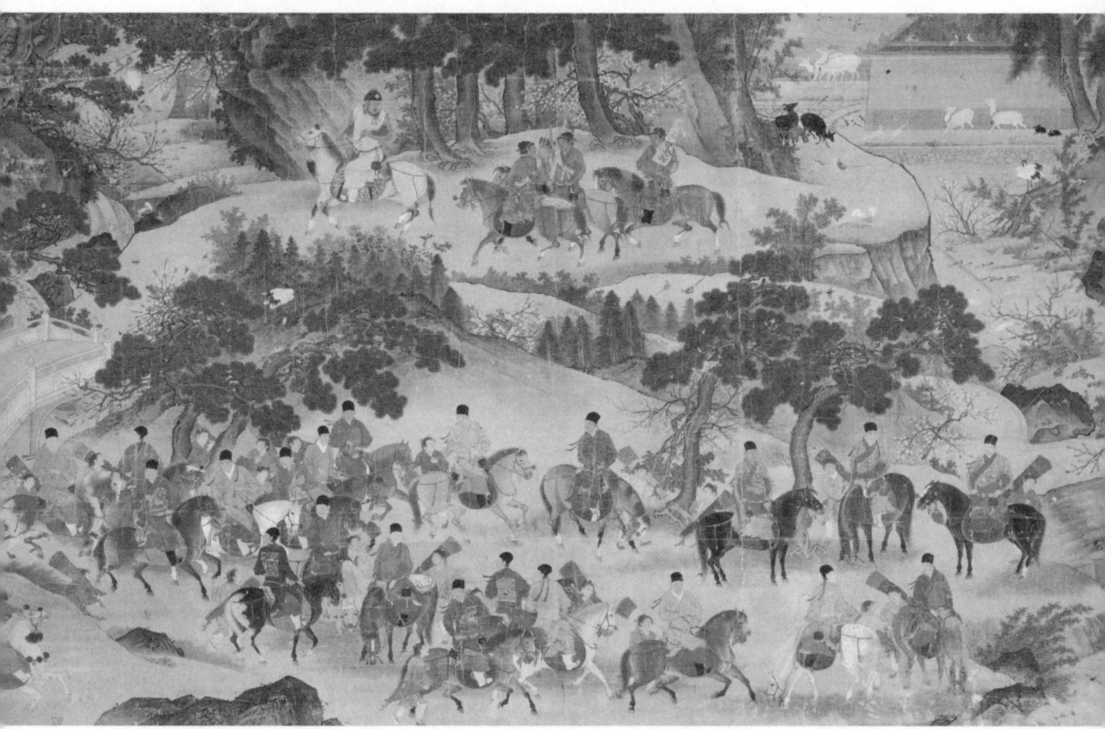

Shang Xi (active c. 1430–1440), *The Emperor Xuanzong's Pleasures*. Hanging scroll, ink and color on silk. Palace Museum, Beijing.

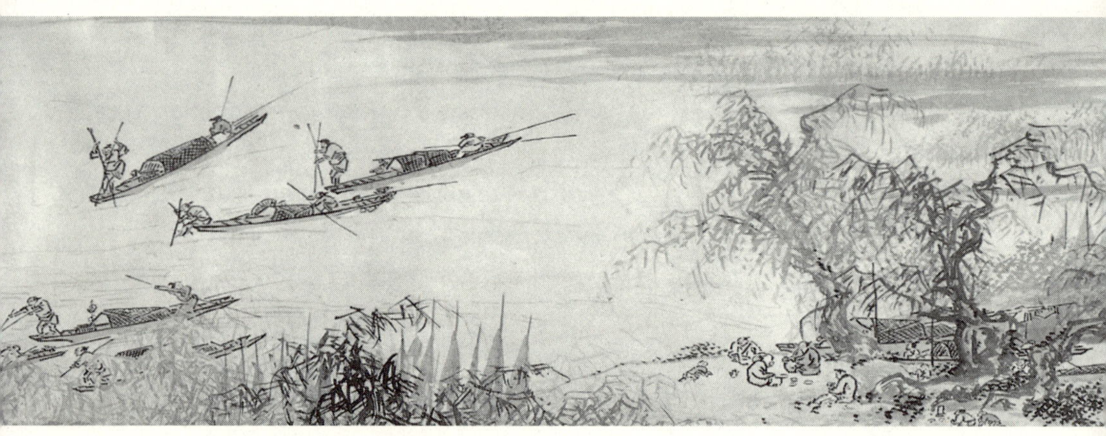

Dai Jin (1388–1462), *Fisherman on the River.* Handscroll, ink and color on paper. Freer Gallery of Art, Washington, D.C.

Museum (or Gugong) in Beijing. It is packed with imperial symbolism, designed to legitimize and enhance the emperor's role and position and to nurture the Confucian state.[20] The crowded scene features the emperor astride a white horse on a flat mesa well above and symbolically isolated from the throng of courtiers and attendants who spiral down below the bridge. His importance is indicated by the walls of a palace in the background, as well as by several favorable omens: two pair of white deer, a pair of black deer, and two black rabbits, black and white connoting auspiciousness.

As under the first Ming emperor, the misreading or misinterpretation of an artist's intention still continued to pose a threat (albeit a less deadly one) to later artists. Dai Jin (1388–1462), considered the greatest painter of the period, was recommended by a eunuch to Emperor Xuanzong, to whom he presented landscapes with figures of the four seasons, rendered in his original and forceful brush style. One painting showed a man in a red jacket fishing, and therefore Dai Jin was accused of implying that an aristocrat was declining to serve the unworthy emperor.[21] The emperor had by his side an artist who had served many years at court, whom he asked to comment on the paintings. That artist, probably threatened by Dai Jin's originality and skill, said that Dai's four paintings were critical of the emperor. So Dai never received a court appointment, although he remained a popular painter with ministers and other court officials.

Court painters were often commissioned to produce paintings intended as gifts. When a gift was commissioned and bestowed by the emperor in person, it was a singular mark of his favor. The Xuande Emperor, himself a credible artist, inscribed some of his paintings to particular officials at court, to members of his family, and to eunuchs. These gifts of his paintings enabled him to establish "potent personal bonds."[22]

Court artists were also called upon to paint for special occasions: for a birthday or for annual festivals, such as the Lantern Festival or the spring Qingming Festival, when one visited and swept the tombs of one's ancestors. The Ming court also commissioned paintings of Buddhist icons and Daoist figures for the court and temple walls as well as for imperial patrons. The Immortals, those Daoist deities whose presence was invited by emperors of old to improve one's longevity, were a popular subject considered flattering to the emperor. These figure paintings, of extremely fine quality, held to the traditional style of the great sixth century Tang dynasty painter Wu Daozi (active c. 710–760).

Horse paintings were of continuing interest in every dynasty and were painted in the Ming with total mastery. Paintings of Emperor Xuanzong, usually astride his horse, emphasized the Ming dependence, like that of their Mongol predecessors, upon a steady supply of horses. Painters of horses were given high positions in the Imperial Guard, but their paintings are usually anonymous.[23]

The Ming court in the dynasty's later years gradually gave up its powerful patronage and support of professional painters and their craft. As it did so, the bonds of hereditary training weakened. The climate for court painting had changed. The dynasty had lost the vigor of the first rulers, the fleet of Zheng He had been grounded as an economy, and the eunuchs who controlled the workshops had unlimited power to manipulate and even hire unqualified artists. The workshops became sinecures for the eunuchs' toadies. The court became a less attractive place for artists, and with few exceptions, the professional artists worked in their own regional locales.

IMPERIAL ART OF THE QING DYNASTY

The Manchus, who seized the Ming capital of Beijing in 1644, took several routes to legitimize their Qing, or Pure, dynasty. They paid traditional honors to the late Ming emperor and adopted Chinese administrative organization, which they controlled by placing a Manchu official in tandem with every highly placed Chinese official. The Manchu elite was expected to adopt Chinese classical learning wholeheartedly, a stipulation intended to win over the Chinese literati and civil bureaucracy.

The Forbidden City was damaged by fire and fighting during the chaos of the dying Ming dynasty, and there is evidence that imperial treasures may have been pilfered from the Ming palaces. Sun Chengze, a prominent Chinese official of the mid-seventeenth century, has left a written record of his personal art and calligraphy collection, known to art historians as the *Gengji Xiaoxia Ji*, or *Notes Written to While Away the Summer* (1660). Some of these works bear Ming imperial seals and may have been salvaged from the Ming imperial collections before the palaces were set on fire.[24]

The Manchu rulers had developed an appreciation of Chinese art and architecture even before their conquest of China. Nurgaci, who had led the nomadic Ruzhen tribes of northeast China, built a palace in the 1620s at his capital of Mukden (modern Shenyang) in the style of a modest Chinese palace. It was laid out on a typically Chinese central axis entered by a series of gates, the courtyards spaced to give pause before each new gate and series of reception or throne rooms, all lending dignity and importance to the ruler seated on the throne and ready to receive a properly humbled subject. Nurgaci also began to collect objets d'art, or treasures, for this palace in emulation of Chinese emperors.[25]

Art Patronage in the Early Qing Court

China's new Manchu rulers gained a deeper appreciation of the Chinese aesthetic from their Chinese retainers, former Ming civil servants who became bond servants to the Qing imperial family.[26] These bond servants were entrusted not only with administration of the imperial household but also with control of the large workshops that supplied the court with luxury products—porcelains from Jingdezhen and silks from Nanjing,

Suzhou, and Hangzhou. By 1680 there were twenty-seven workshops within the enclosure of the palace in Beijing alone.[27]

The Manchu child emperor Shunzhi (r. 1644–62) became a gifted painter in traditional style, a testament to the rapid Sinicization of the Manchu rulers.[28] Shunzhi likened himself to great imperial art patrons of the past such as Ming Xuanzong and Song Huizong, and he set a style of painting followed by many of the Manchu Bannermen.[29]

The Kangxi Emperor (r. 1662–1723) used the arts for practical ends. He was a pragmatic arts patron; artists and artisans were employed at court for specific projects and included architects and landscape designers as well as painters. Many artists worked on ceramics.

The emperor also supported important compilations of Chinese scholarly works. He followed Chinese tradition by engaging many older civil servants in the task of editing and publishing the traditional official history of the preceding dynasty. The great *Kangxi Dictionary* was also compiled during his reign, and its prescriptions influence the Chinese lexicon to

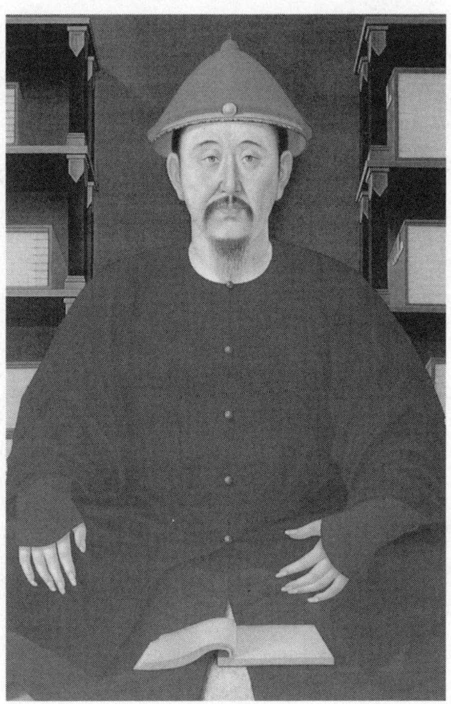

Anonymous (Qing dynasty), *Portrait of the Kangxi Emperor.* Hanging scroll, ink and color on silk. Palace Museum, Beijing.

this day. A large collection of Chinese literature was prepared along with a collection of Tang poetry. In addition, a one-hundred-volume catalogue of Chinese paintings and calligraphy was printed (*Peiwenzhai Shuhua Pu*), not confined to holdings in the imperial collection. These scholarly efforts increased the credit and acceptance of the Manchu overlords and reinforced their dynastic claims.

Kangxi collected art treasures during his six inspection tours of southern China. One modern historian has given a lively account of how this worked: "The pattern on these tours was that [at each venue] the officials offered a large variety of presents to the Emperor, who then selected a few items and returned the rest . . . When the Emperor landed near Yangzhou,

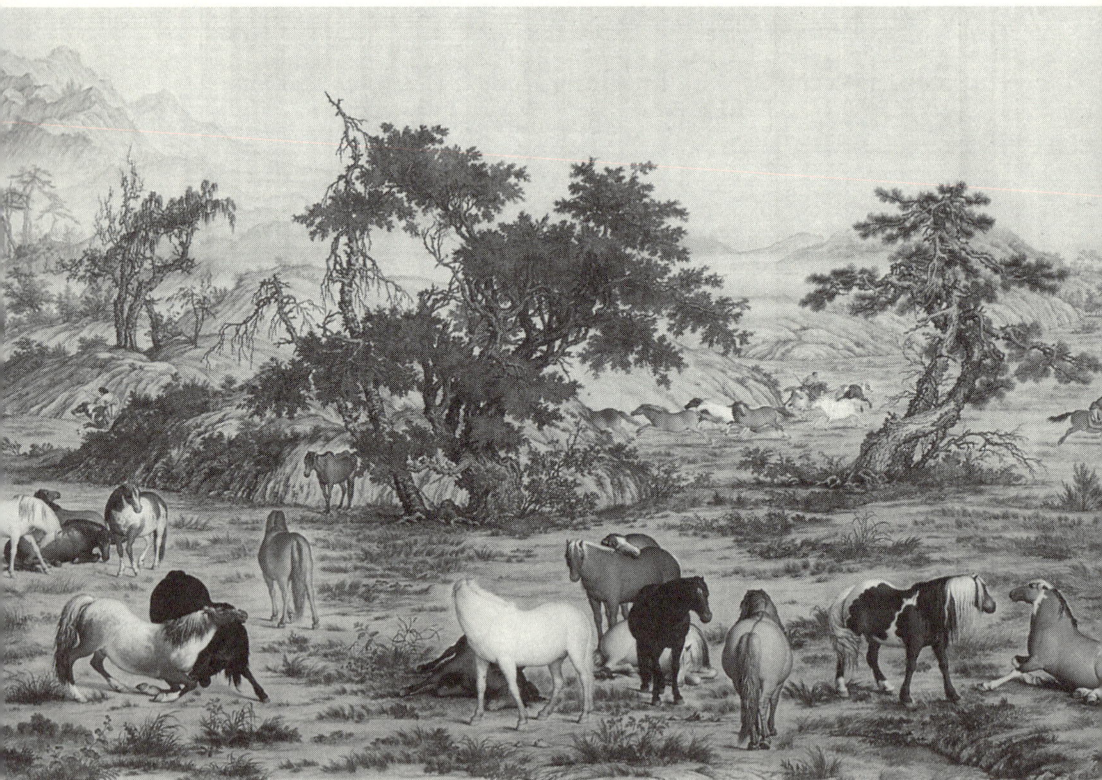

Lang Shining (Giuseppe Castiglione; 1688–1766), *One Hundred Horses.* Handscroll, ink and color on silk, dated 1728. National Palace Museum, Taipei.

he was greeted not by officials but by the local salt merchants who offered him presents of antiques, curios, books, and paintings, which the Emperor accepted."[30] Other offerings were in the form of banquets, operas, or plays, as well as gardens carefully prepared for his viewing. Sometimes the emperor gave out presents in the form of sums of money, or small gifts such as fans, bamboo, silk, and ink sticks. Occasionally he presented something he had written himself.

The Jesuit fathers who came to China in the 1600s in search of Christian converts introduced Western art techniques to the court. They were tolerated and valued by the Kangxi Emperor primarily for their practical and scientific knowledge. But Chinese court artists looked askance at Western style paintings saying, "These painters have no brush-method (*bifa*) whatsoever; although they possess skill, they are simply artisans and can consequently not be classified as painters."[31] The Jesuit artistic influence is most plainly seen in the realistic portraiture style they introduced.

Jesuit priest Giuseppe Castiglione (known in China as Lang Shining; 1688–1766) came to court in 1715, bringing a new style to the long and distinguished tradition of horse painting in China. Horses were a potent symbol of Manchu dominance and Castiglione's paintings became very popular. His artistic ability was exploited by the emperor, and he spent many years working long hours in the imperial studio.

The Legacy of Qianlong

In 1736, Emperor Qianlong (r. 1736–96) ascended the Qing throne. He was to become the most important Chinese imperial collector of all time—at least in terms of quantity. He became emperor at age twenty-five, inheriting a realm conquered, tamed, and organized by his predecessors.[32] While still dominated by his father's advisers he "seized on the art of painting for self-glorification."[33] He may have seen art as an area in which he could function independently, as opposed to statecraft where he could not—at least as long as the advisors appointed by his father were in his service.

The Jesuit Giuseppe Castiglione still held a favored position under Qianlong, who was intrigued by the three-dimensionality of the Western

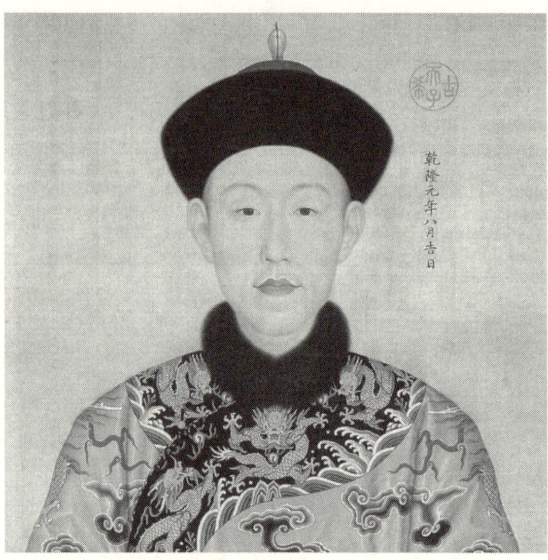

Lang Shining (Giuseppe Castiglione; 1688–1766), *Inauguration Portrait of Emperor Qianlong.* Handscroll, ink and color on silk. The Cleveland Museum of Art.

mode of painting. Qianlong did not like the strong contrasts of light and dark in this style, however, and insisted that the Jesuit painters change their technique, leading to a hybrid style combining Chinese and Western elements.[34]

While there is no evidence of a painting academy during the reign of the first three Qing emperors, the Qianlong Emperor sponsored such an academy in each place he held court during his annual migrations.[35] In the capital, some artists worked in the Forbidden City while others labored in the Old Summer Palace, or Yuanmingyuan. Some accompanied the emperor to the palaces and hunting grounds in Manchuria where hunting scenes, believed to enhance the imperial image, could be well observed. The painters in the Qianlong Academy were more highly paid than the craft workers, and salaries seemed to be linked to quality of work. The Qianlong Academy is generally considered the most important of the whole Qing period, comparable to the Imperial Painting Academy set up under Song Huizong.[36]

The relative stability within the empire allowed Qianlong to indulge his taste for collecting. Like his grandfather Kangxi, Qianlong eventually made six southern tours (*nan xun*), which gave him opportunities to secure important art works using the polite coercion of his office. According to one account, Chinese connoisseurs despised him for what they considered his pompous ignorance.[37] One local art collector, knowing the emperor's thirst for rare paintings—including those that were privately owned—had skilled copies made of his best works so that should the emperor express an interest in a work he could be gulled into taking the copy.[38]

In terms of sheer numbers of artwork, Qianlong collected more than any previous ruler.[39] An analysis of a major 1816 inventory reveals some fifteen thousand paintings and calligraphies that had graced the various imperial palaces in Beijing and the summer palace in Jehol (modern Rehe), two-thirds of which had been painted since 1644.[40] Some of the artists were members of the imperial art academy; others were simply members of the court bureaucracy who were frequently called upon by the emperor to create a painting or calligraphy with no extra remuneration. The work of these bureaucrats represents 77 percent of the Qing imperial art collection, compared with the only 12 percent produced by the salaried court academy artists. This raises the interesting issue of whether the work of the academy artists was less appreciated by the emperor than the works of amateur scholar-officials to whom he seems to have given more patronage.[41] The Qianlong Emperor himself produced 2,516 of the works in the inventory, an astonishing 27 percent of the signed works found in the imperial collection. They are cited by weight, but are generally ignored by art historians.

Qianlong was also a prodigious compiler of written material. He left another important legacy by sponsoring a huge compendium of writings from China's earlier dynasties. Known as the *Siku Quanshu* or *Complete Library in Four Branches of Literature*, this monumental work totaled thirty-six thousand volumes. Emissaries were sent throughout China to seek out every book ever written. Perhaps five thousand people were engaged in this project, which continued into the next reign, that of Emperor Jiaqing (r. 1796–1820). While some praise the enterprise for preserving texts that might otherwise have been lost, others decry the fact that it led some texts to be destroyed forever, since the emperor required the editors to remove all writings hostile to the Manchus. The aging Qianlong, seventy-six years old when he initiated the project, ordered two summaries so that he might use one for his own perusal. One of the two summarized editions is preserved at the National Palace Museum in Taipei.

Despite his massive art collection, Qianlong is not considered a gifted art connoisseur. Throughout his life Qianlong depended on written records and seals to establish the genuineness of a painting. He therefore never developed a critical eye able to distinguish the genuine from the copy or to evaluate artistic technique. His advisers were often as unschooled as the emperor. A man of no small ego, Qianlong brushed his comments in his easily recognized calligraphy on many masterworks of earlier centuries and made frequent use of the largest of all imperial seals.

Qianlong's aesthetic failings have been variously described. One scholar described Qianlong's failures as an art connoisseur as "due not to limited experience but rather to a personal disinclination—even inability—to make stylistic judgment in a studied manner."[42] Another described Qianlong as "a man of tireless energy, a voracious art collector, a niggardly and opinionated connoisseur, an unstoppable writer of inscriptions and inscriber of seals [on paintings] who was determined . . . to leave his indelible mark on China's artistic legacy. His seals almost obliterate some of the finest paintings in the imperial collection. . . . Few ancient masterpieces . . . were not gathered [by him] behind the high walls of the Forbidden City, shut away from [generations] of painters who might have studied them had they remained in private hands."[43]

Qianlong abdicated the throne in 1796, leaving a succession of six Qing emperors (Jiaqing, Daoguang, Xianfeng, Tongzhi, Guangxu, Xuantong) before the dynasty—China's last—finally crumbled, owing to a combination of external aggression and internal rebellion. During the final years of the Qing reign, the imperial collection witnessed continued growth in painting, ceramics, decorative arts, textiles, and furniture. Indeed, the impressive artistic growth—both in quality and quantity—during the nineteenth century highlights the paradox of the time: a sequestered elite isolated from the chaos consuming the country.

During the remainder of the Qing, resulting from different causes, the imperial collection gradually atrophied. Several fires in the Forbidden City destroyed a number of perishable objects, mainly rare books and paintings. The Wenshou, Shaoren, Wuying, and Yiyuan halls all burned to the ground. Just as regrettable was the pillaging by British and French forces of the Yuanmingyuan in 1860. Numerous priceless pieces became the spoils of war and to this day are to be found in the British Museum in London and Musée Guimet in Paris. The fragmentation of the collection would only continue as China entered the new century.

3

From Private to Public Treasures: The Early Republican Era, 1911–1930

When the revolution of 1911 (Xinhai Geming) broke out, province after province rose in revolt against the authority of the Manchu Qing rulers. The dynasty quickly crumbled, and China embarked into uncharted political territory with its first republican government. Many Manchus fled north to Manchuria, from whence they had come in the seventeenth century. But the Aisin-Gioro family who inherited the Qing dynasty stayed behind. The child emperor Aisin-Gioro (Pu Yi), then only five years old, was to remain under virtual house arrest in Beijing's Forbidden City for more than twelve years, subject to the terms of an abdication agreement signed with the new government on February 12, 1912.

THE SPLINTERING OF THE COLLECTION

From the very day the abdication agreement was signed, there was inherent ambiguity in the arrangements concerning the imperial household treasures. To whom did the thousands of paintings, calligraphies, and *objets d'art* of the various Manchu palaces belong—to the Manchu Aisin-Gioro family, or to the nation, which they no longer ruled but on whose soil they resided?[1]

Problems of Custody and Ownership

The abdication agreement, known as the Articles for Favorable Treatment of the Great Qing Emperor, has been described as removing a dynasty without a bloody battle.[2] In the agreement, General Yuan Shikai, who had been installed as president of the new Republic of China, took control of the imperial court's treasury, while the imperial family retained the temporary right of residence in the ancestral palaces within the Forbidden City. The Aisin-Gioro family also retained the forms and trappings of a court and its attendants. Pu Yi was supervised by the former imperial consorts (empress dowagers) and was attended by more than six hundred eunuchs and countless other servants, all managed by the Neiwu Bu—literally the Inner Household Department (hereafter referred to as the Household Department).

Article VII of the agreement stated that, after abdication, the emperor's private property would be protected by the government of the Republic of China. But it did not specify who actually owned the personal property of the Qing household. More than fifty years later, Pu Yi recalled how he had always considered the art treasures his personal property.

That view seems to have been born out by a 1914 agreement concerning a joint expedition representing the Ministry of the Interior and the Qing household to Manchuria to collect treasures from the four royal summer palaces: in Mukden (Shenyang), Rehe (Jehol or Chengde), and two in Beiping (Beijing). This agreement stated that the treasures were the private property of the imperial family and that all items brought back to Beijing—except some withheld by the imperial household for their exceptional value or rarity—were to be bought by the Republic of China for a sum named in an independent valuation.[3] Because the republic was unable to pay the purchase price at that time, the treasures were considered to be on loan from the imperial family pending a full cash settlement. There is no evidence, however, that the Qing imperial family ever received any money for the more than seventy thousand items brought back to Beijing from the Manchurian palaces.

Zhu Jiqian, a wealthy collector and antiquarian scholar serving as minister of the interior, was the government's representative on the mission to Manchuria. He was also charged by President Yuan Shikai with repairing the imperial palaces in Beijing. It is Zhu who may have first envisioned these treasures as part of a national art collection in the Forbidden City.[4]

The Public's First View of the Treasures

In 1914 the Bureau of Internal Affairs established the Exhibition Office of Ancient Artifacts. After collecting and consolidating the collections in the Shenyang Palace, the Rehe summer mountain retreat, and in the Summer Palace in Beiping, the office mounted the first public exhibition of the imperial art in 1914.[5] It was held in two small halls located in the outer court of the Forbidden City—the Wuying Dian on the western side, and the Wenhua Dian on the eastern side—then often referred to as the Antiquities Exhibition Halls.

President Yuan Shikai's interest in restoring the Forbidden City palaces and sponsoring an exhibit of Qing treasures from the imperial family's Manchurian summer domiciles was quite transparent, at least in retrospect. He not only wanted to establish a claim on the treasures of the last dynasty for the republic, but also to hold a trump card for his plan to found a new dynasty.

In December 1915, Yuan seized his opportunity. He announced that his Glorious Constitution (Hongxian) reign would begin on January 1, 1916, and he ordered imperial porcelains to be marked "Hongxian." But Yuan Shikai's attempt to establish a new dynasty was cut short—that spring the army and the country turned against him after he capitulated to Japan's "Twenty-one Demands" and he died in June 1916.[6]

A second exhibit drawn from the treasures recovered from Manchuria was held two years later in the same halls of the Forbidden City.[7] An important shift had occurred in the interim: whereas in 1914 the display had been considered a loan from the Qing household, in 1916 the government claimed that it was the Ministry of Internal Affairs that had loaned the objects and sponsored the exhibition.[8]

The Forbidden City was a magnet for visitors at that time, as it continues to be to this day. Visitors to the Antiquities Exhibition Halls in 1914 and 1916 could enter the formerly exclusive precincts for an admission price of

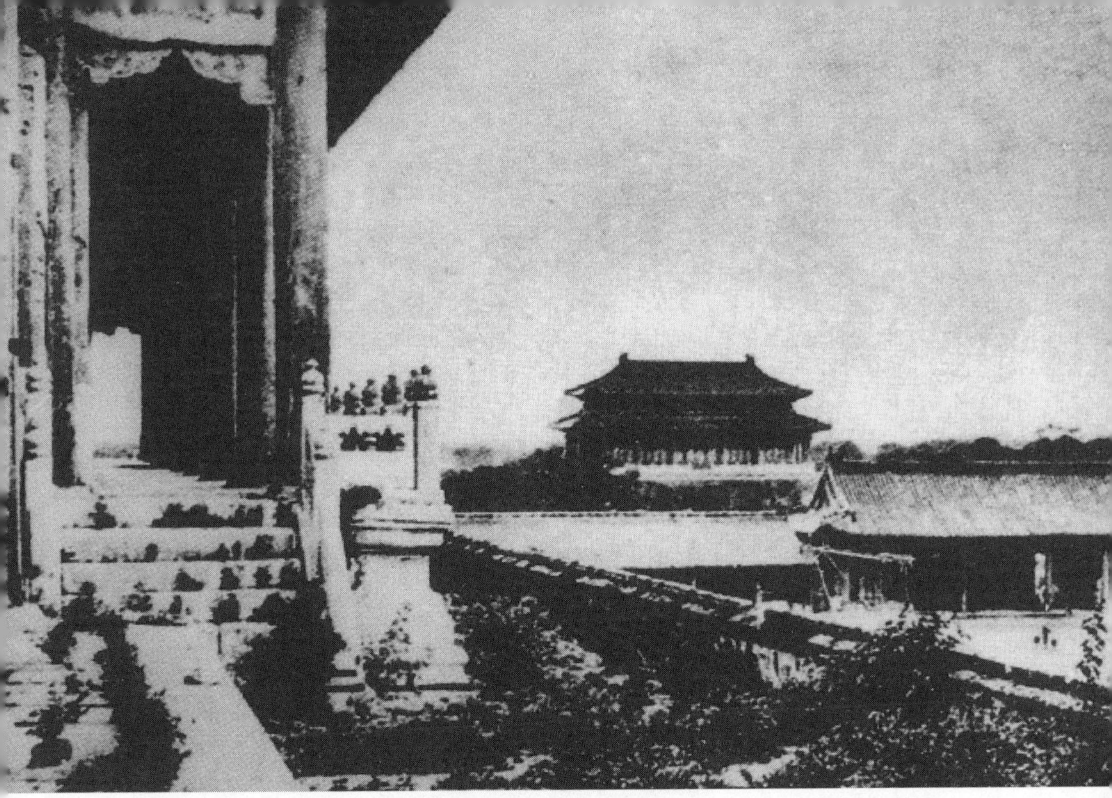

Forbidden City, c. 1900. From Liu and Xu, *Gugong zhencang*, 82.

just one yuan. Ordinary Chinese citizens could finally enjoy the formerly forbidden purlieus and glimpse some of the rare palace treasures. Some who came may have remembered that, under imperial rule, "anyone passing through any of the gates of the Purple Forbidden City (Zijincheng), incurs a hundred blows of the bamboo . . . and death by strangulation . . . to any stranger found in any of the Emperor's apartments."[9]

Reginald Johnston and the Palace Treasures

In 1919, when Pu Yi was thirteen, it was decided that his one Manchu and two Chinese tutors should be augmented by a tutor of English.[10] Reginald E. Johnston, a seasoned British diplomat and graduate of London's prestigious School of Oriental and African Studies, was engaged by the Qing court as Pu Yi's tutor. Johnston lived in a palace courtyard on the west side of the imperial garden and soon established a warm personal relationship with his young pupil. He was also to play a key role in protecting the interests of the emperor—and the imperial treasures.

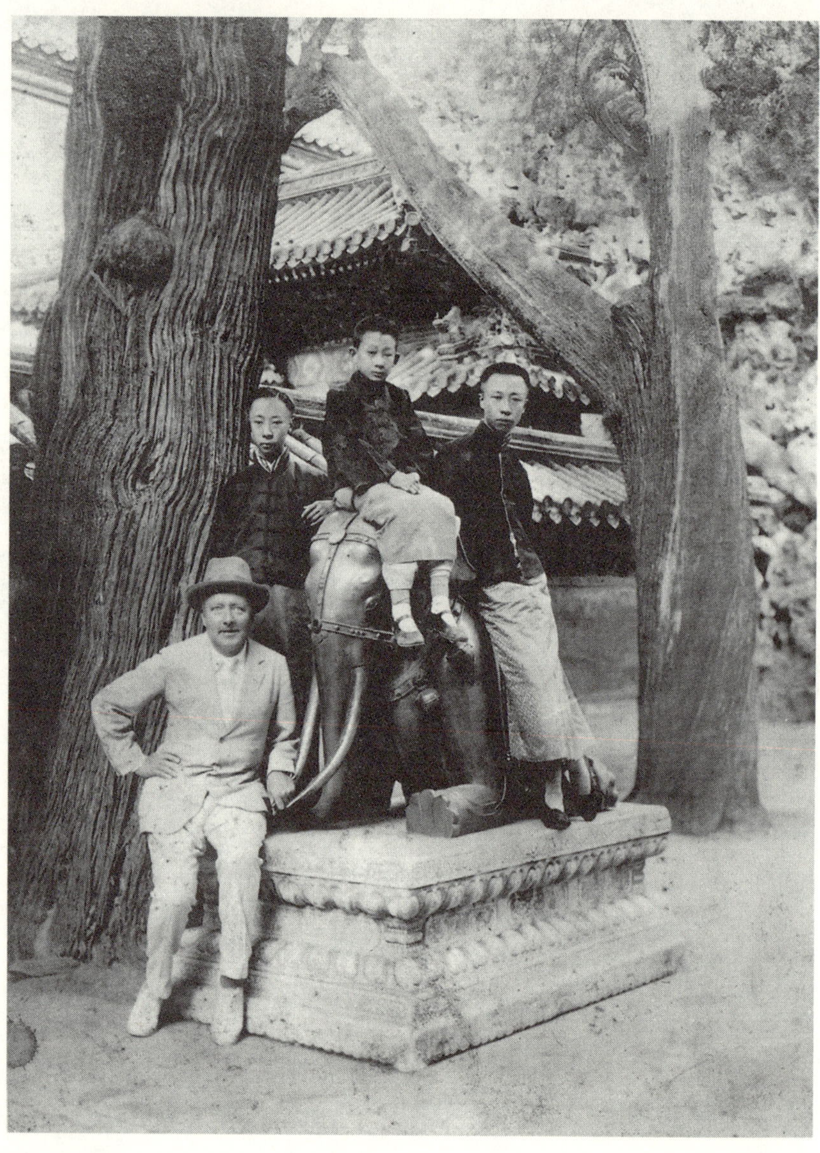

Reginald Johnston and (left to right) Pu Jie, cousin Run Qi, and Pu Yi in the Imperial Garden (date uncertain). From Liu and Xu, *Gugong zhencang*, 105.

Looking back, Johnston admitted that it took awhile for him to figure out that the traditional court and its thousand or more dependents had been allowed to continue to exist not to serve the best interests of the boy emperor, but to serve the interests of the Household Department members, whose sinecures allowed them to accumulate vast wealth. The agreement also protected the livelihood of the eight hundred to a thousand eunuchs whose only employment lay with the imperial establishment.[11]

Not the least of Johnston's accomplishments was opening the young emperor's eyes to the wastefulness and extravagance of the management of palace affairs and the losses of imperial treasures through pawning or theft. As a result, Pu Yi announced that he wanted household expenditures reduced from six million to half a million dollars per annum.[12] Pu Yi wrote in his autobiography many years later that the government's annual stipend was delivered irregularly and that the Household Department was always short of funds, so treasures were sold to make up the deficits.[13]

The imperial household's practice was to sell to a small and exclusive set of dealers, at a price far higher than would be reported in the accounts and far below the market value of the article sold. When a four-foot-high solid gold pagoda was to be sold, Pu Yi asked a eunuch how it was to be priced. By weight, was the reply. "Then you are fools," Pu Yi shouted, and quoted Johnston as having said far more could be realized on the open market. To get even with Johnston, the Household Department had the golden pagoda delivered to Johnston's house with a message, supposedly from the emperor, that Johnston should sell it. Johnston saw the trap, ordered the pagoda returned to the palace, and was thereafter even more resented by the inner palace personnel.[14]

The Household Department also reportedly took out loans of cash from several banks, leaving imperial porcelains as security. Some of these were later retrieved from the banks by British collector Percival David and became the foundation of the Sir Percival David Collection at the School of Oriental and African Studies in London.[15] In addition, private loans were made to the imperial household by an astute collector and connoisseur, Pang Yuanji, who thus acquired some very important paintings and calligraphy for his collection.[16]

Pu Yi frequently called for an antiquity to be brought for his inspection, and he ordered a full inventory of the collection. Johnston was often present and reported that an item might be in a sealed receptacle from a long-forgotten tribute bearer or a viceroy.[17] As the inventory process progressed, many items were found to be missing. In June 1923, Pu Yi announced

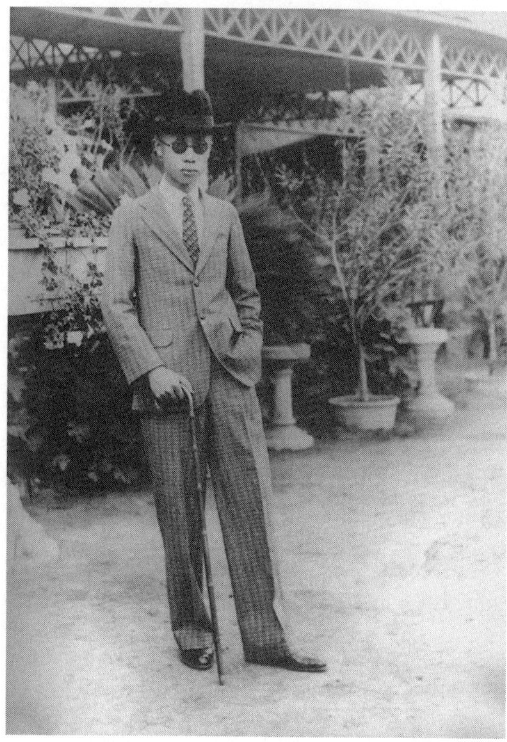

**Pu Yi in Zhang Yuan
Garden (date uncertain).**
From Liu and Xu, *Gugong
zhencang*, 153.

that he would inspect the Palace of Eternal Happiness (Qian Fugong),
or, where Emperor Qianlong's favorite treasures had been stored. The
eunuchs, frightened of having their depredations revealed, set fire to the
palace. By dawn only 387 items had been salvaged out of 6,643 originally inventoried.[18] This collection had originally included more than two
thousand gold Buddhist images, many Buddhist paintings, gold altar ornaments, porcelains, bronzes from earlier dynasties, thousands of books,
and thirty-one boxes of sables and imperial robes.[19]

Pu Yi decided it was time to move against the eunuchs. He went to stay
with his father at the Northern Mansion (Bei Fu) outside the city and said
he would not return to the Forbidden City until a thousand eunuchs were
expelled. Pu Yi arranged for a small military force provided by the republic to
be on hand as the chief of the imperial household ordered all eunuchs to assemble immediately to hear the order of dismissal. Within one hour, on July
15, 1923, nearly a thousand eunuchs had filed out of the palace—except for

175 who were retained to attend to the aging high consorts. In subsequent days the eunuchs were allowed back in small groups to gather their personal belongings and to receive their meager terminal stipends.[20]

Johnston's reports to Pu Yi that many new antique shops had opened in the Qian'men district, reportedly run by eunuchs and officials of the household, led to the idea of ordering a more formal inventory of the palace paintings. This was carried out in 1923–24 by independent Chinese art connoisseurs who could not be controlled by the Household Department. This highly qualified group included Zheng Xiaoxu, Luo Zhenyu, Wang Guowei, and Shang Yanying.

Pu Yi and his younger brother Pu Jie, who also studied with Johnston at the palace but lived outside its walls, understood the inventory procedure and developed a plan for Pu Jie to smuggle inventoried objects out of the Forbidden City. Each scroll, album, or book was marked in the inventory according to its merit, with five circles for the best in quality and one for the least. From May to December 1923, Pu Jie left for home each day after his lessons in the Forbidden City with a bundle of scrolls or books, selected from those that had been identified as being of the highest grade. According to Pu Yi's recollections, "We must have removed over a thousand handscrolls, more than two hundred hanging scrolls and pages from albums, and about two hundred rare Sung Dynasty printed books."[21] Pu Jie recollected how "difficult it was to carry the books and scrolls out of the Palace, because all the articles in the Palace were kept by the eunuchs."[22] Rare books were the first target because they were the same size as the textbooks the brothers used. Wrapped in yellow brocade in the same manner as the textbooks that the eunuchs carried for them every day, the books passed the gate without arousing the suspicion of the garrison guards. One source claims that the brothers smuggled out 1,285 handscrolls and 68 albums of paintings and calligraphy,[23] while another asserts that the "last emperor" absconded with more than 1,000 handscrolls, more than 200 album leaves and hanging scrolls, and more than 200 rare books dating to the Song dynasty.[24]

After hiding these treasures somewhere in Beijing, Pu Jie had them packed into seventy to eighty wooden boxes.[25] A permit exempting examination and taxes at the railway station was obtained and Pu Jie himself escorted these boxes of treasures to Tianjin, where they were later stored in a house purchased for Pu Yi by the Manchu prince who backed their escape plan—a chore that Pu Jie later said was a great bother.[26]

By 1922 the public had developed a sense of ownership of the imperial treasures, which was reflected in a news item of that year: "Recently some articles of great value have been sent from the palace to a foreign bank, and it is hinted the intention of the palace authorities is to sell them, in which case these priceless treasures will probably be lost to China."[27] This sense of public ownership differed substantially from the implications of the 1914 agreement, which had been that the treasures brought to Beijing from the Manchurian palaces were on loan from the imperial household.

Between 1911 and 1924 the Qing household thus assumed it retained rightful possession of all the treasures in its palaces, while the republic assumed that it had the right to define which were to become "public" possessions—the foundation of a national museum—and which were to remain in the possession of the Qing household. Moreover, the republic did not admit that it owed any debt to the imperial family for the treasures held in the public domain.

Leaving the Forbidden City

In 1924, Pu Yi and the imperial household were getting ready to move permanently to the Summer Palace (Yiheyuan) in the city's outskirts, as originally stipulated in the 1912 Articles of Favorable Treatment. This palace, on the northwest fringe of Beijing, had been the old empress dowager's favorite retreat but had not been used as a residence since her death in 1908. Reginald Johnston promoted the move because the "temporary" occupation of the Forbidden City had already been extended by eleven years, and Johnston feared the government might use this extended occupation as an excuse to cancel the state's obligations to the Qing household.[28] The planned move raised the issue of ownership of the imperial treasures left in the Forbidden City, so Johnston advised that a joint commission be appointed "with a view to allocating to the State such articles as might reasonably be regarded as *guo bao* (national treasures) [so that] the imperial family might be left in undisputed possession of all that remained."[29] The move to the Yiheyuan was never realized, however. Instead, it was forestalled by warlord General Feng Yuxiang, who captured Beijing in a coup against a rival warlord on October 22, 1924.

General Feng unceremoniously ordered Pu Yi and his household to leave their palaces in the Forbidden City on the afternoon of November 5, 1924. Did Feng Yuxiang have his sights set on controlling the vast treasures in the Forbidden City? On November 4, the day before the expulsion order, Feng and his advisors had revised Article V of the Articles of Favorable Treatment to read, "The whole of the private property of the Qing imperial family will remain in their possession, and the government of the Republic will have the duty of seeing that they are left undisturbed in the enjoyment of it. All public property will belong to the Republic. All articles in the Palace are to be checked over so as to separate the treasures and historical relics which are state property, from the articles of clothing and daily use, which are the private possession of the Qing."[30] This order

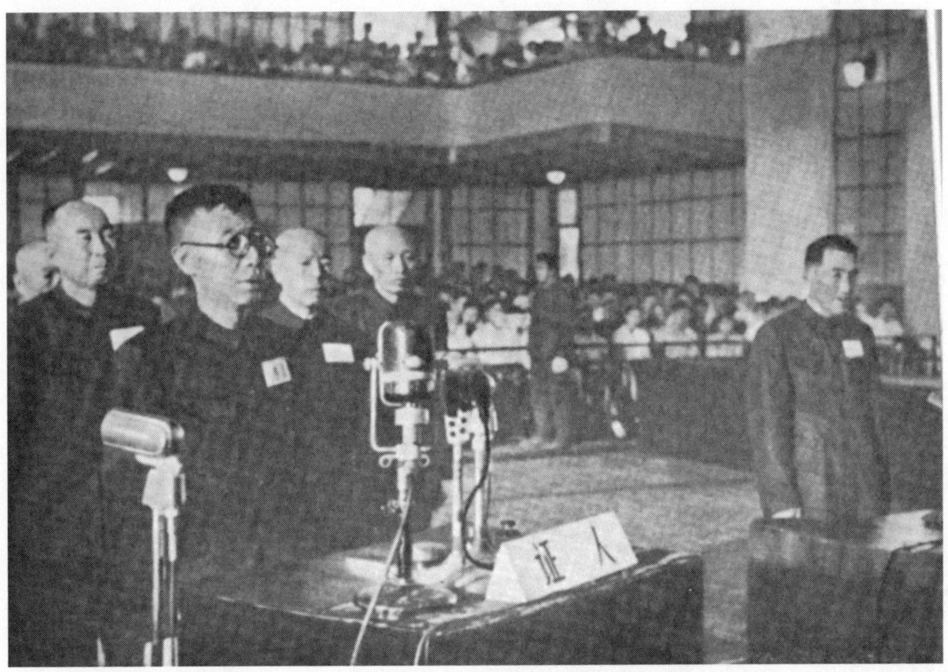

Pu Yi on trial. From Aisin-Gioro, *From Emperor to Citizen* (1986), vol. 2.

extended the ambiguous language governing the Qing household treasures from the past into the present and became the basis for counterclaims by various parties in the years ahead.

Pu Yi was eating apples with the empress when he was interrupted by Geeral Feng's ultimatum and a maid screaming, "The soldiers have come to take you!"[31] After an initial refusal, he had no recourse against the implicit threat of force, so he handed over two imperial seals and agreed to leave the palace that very day. The two aged empress dowagers were allowed to stay on briefly to complete the mourning for a recently deceased dowager-consort, accompanied by a small number of eunuchs and guards at the gates, but they departed the palace on November 21.

The Fate of Pu Yi

Pu Yi's first move was to go to the home of his father outside the Forbidden City. None of the Western legations wished to host Pu Yi, but the

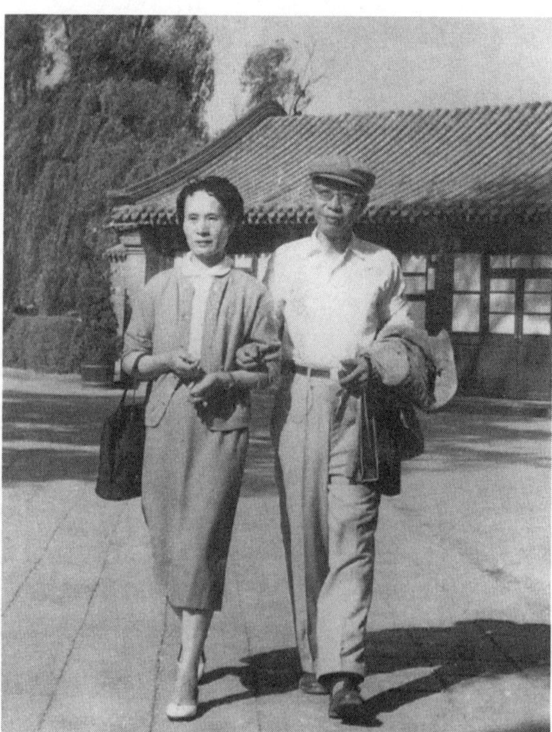

Pu Yi and his wife, Li Shuxian (1924–97), walking in Beihai Garden in their later years. From Pu Yi, *Wode Qian Bansheng.*

Japanese quickly realized that he could be useful to their designs and made overtures. Pu Yi soon escaped from his father's home and the Japanese then offered him a large house in Tianjin and the protection of the Japanese consulate, where he remained from 1925 to 1931.

Pu Yi apparently had a sense of humor and could joke about the issue of the Qing household's private versus public property. On his birthday early in 1925, celebrated at the Japanese consulate in Tianjin, Pu Yi raised his cup and said, "Does the republic find our teapot and tea cups and cooking vessels all *guo bao* (national treasures) that they have allowed us so few?"[32]

After Japan invaded Manchuria in 1931, Pu Yi moved there and eventually became the titular head of the Japanese puppet state of Manchoukuo, where he was known as Emperor Kangde. Pu Yi still had in his possession the books, paintings, and calligraphy that he and Pu Jie had smuggled out of the Forbidden City. Some items had been sold or bestowed as gifts by Pu Yi during his years in Tianjin, but most were shipped to Manchuria and stored in the "small white outbuilding" (literally, the *xiaobailou*) behind Pu Yi's "palace" (the former Salt Monopoly Building) in the city of Changchun.[33]

Pu Yi remained the puppet emperor of Manchukuo throughout World War II. On August 15, 1945, shortly after the atomic bomb was dropped on Hiroshima, Japan declared its unconditional surrender. Pu Yi was instructed by a Japanese army representative to gather up a few belongings and get ready to move to a small town near the Korean border, pending evacuation to Japan. Pu Yi prepared for his departure by choosing his most important imperial seal, Xuan Tong, fashioned from eight interlocking pieces of jade. He stuffed his attaché case with jewels and uncut gems, and left with his family and entourage. But he had to leave behind most of the art that he and his brother had smuggled out of the Forbidden City. Later, the director of the Liaoning Provincial Museum in Shenyang, Yang Renkai, traced the fate of this group of treasures, known as the "northeast goods" (Dongbeihuo) in detail, as described in chapter 5.[34]

On August 18, Pu Yi was waiting at the Shenyang airport to be flown to Japan when a Russian squadron took control of the airport. The commanding officer recognized him, extended his hand saying, "Mr. Pu Yi?" and took him into Soviet custody.[35] Pu Yi remained in the Soviet Union until 1950, when he was turned over to the new Chinese Communist government and imprisoned for a number of years. He lived out his final years working as a gardener in his former city of Beijing.

The Committee for Disposition of the Qing Imperial Household Possessions

From the moment the last Qing emperor and his empress had been unceremoniously ordered to leave their palaces in the Forbidden City on the afternoon of November 5, 1924, the imperial treasures they left behind were in jeopardy. The huge walled complex with yellow tiled roofs was left virtually unoccupied.

The government moved quickly to prevent theft. The Regency Council met the day after the expulsion, November 6, and appointed Li Yuying chairman of the Committee for Liquidation of the Qing Household. Li Yuying, a faculty member of Beijing University and a prominent government figure, had been made a member of the Central Supervisory Committee of the Kuomintang at the First National Congress in 1924. He had also helped to secure the return to China of the French portion of the Boxer Indemnity Fund.[36] He was considered a progressive educator well qualified to represent the government in determining the fate of the former imperial household.

The Committee for Liquidation took control of the Forbidden City and its contents. On November 7, Li Yuying, who understood the symbolic importance of the imperial seals, immediately ordered all twenty-five of the seals returned in their original order to the hall where they were stored, and the hall sealed and locked.[37] That same day, thirteen other members of the committee were named, eight representing the Nationalist government and five representing the Manchu imperial household.[38] The committee members were in place by November 20, and two days later the committee ordered a complete inventory of the palace contents. Committee members agreed on procedures and inventory work began on November 24, 1924, although the five representatives of the Qing household refused to attend.[39]

To share his great responsibility for the palace treasures, Li Yuying put his good friend Yi Peiji in charge of the important Antiquities Division. Yi had first made his mark as an activist in the Wuhan uprising of 1911, when the Chinese revolution had officially begun. Yi was one of many who then went abroad, to Japan, after his initial disillusionment with the revolution. After his return to China, he had a distinguished career in modernizing education. He was forced to flee from his home in Changsha, however, because he had been involved in a campaign to drive the local warlord out of Hunan. He went south and, in 1922, became an adviser to Chinese revolutionary leader Sun Yat-sen. In 1923 Sun appointed Yi his resident representative to Beijing, with orders to negotiate with foreign countries for return of the Boxer Indemnity Funds to China.[40] Several Peking University students were recruited to assist with the palace inventory in late 1924. Among them were Na Chih-liang and Chuang Yen, who both began their lifelong careers with the Palace Museum working on this initial inventory process.

Taking Stock of the Collection

The first task of the Committee for Liquidation was to distinguish between state and private property. It was initially decided that "state" referred to historical relics, and "private" to articles of daily use.[41] At least in the beginning, almost all objects were claimed by the inventory staff to have historic value.[42] As Chuang Yen remembers the inventory process, there was one clerk taking notes, one to identify each object, another to give it a number, and a fourth to attach a tag. Only the first and the last persons on the team were allowed to touch the objects. A photographer was on hand to photograph unusual items. No one could be left alone inside the palace; the halls were to be locked even during a temporary absence of the team; no one could leave the building except at certain hours; and all packages had to be inspected. These precautions were instituted after a very rare and important calligraphy was found in the bundle of a departing eunuch.[43]

A simple catalogue number system was adopted, based mainly on location. The objects were categorized according to type and period. In the end, about nine thousand paintings and calligraphy or stele rubbings were catalogued, more than ten thousand porcelains from Song to Qing, more than five thousand bronze mirrors, more than seven hundred other bronze objects, over sixteen hundred seals, and innumerable jades, as well as hundreds of objects of minor arts, tapestries, cloisonné, and the like.[44]

During the first few months of the inventory, in the winter of 1924–25, Yi Peiji was at the palace every day despite the bitter cold, which was only slightly alleviated by charcoal braziers. Ink froze in the wells, writing brushes were stiff and hard, and the workers' hands and feet were subject to frostbite. Na Chih-liang began to wear heavy socks to protect his feet. Money was needed to buy more coal for the braziers and to pay the salaries of the young students and the guards, but the unsympathetic government did not supply the promised funds.

In April 1925, however, huge storerooms were found in the palaces and Yi Peiji arranged for some of these stored items to be sold to pay for the ongoing museum work. These sales included gold dust, silver ingots, tea, silk, and clothing, all of it classified as not important for a museum collection. But the funds did little more than buy coal and pay salaries that first year.

Despite the difficult working conditions, the museum staff's daily work was filled with excitement and surprises. Chuang Yen remembered that, when he and other members of the new team first entered the inner courts of the Forbidden City, they were awed to think they were the first "common people" to see them. During an interview in 1970, Chuang recalled how unbelievable it was, as a young student, to be permitted to walk through the gates, over the now grass-grown courtyard, and to anticipate entering the formerly forbidden inner palaces.[45]

Late in 1924 the staff was delighted by the discovery in the Kunming Palace of a round bronze two-handled vessel with inscriptions cast on its sides that helped identify it as the famous grain measure cast in the reign of Wang Mang (AD 9–23).[46] Another memorable moment came in 1925 with the discovery of a set of wooden cases containing more than one thousand paintings and calligraphy, apparently ready for shipment. There also was great excitement in 1925 when lists were found of all the articles that had been stealthily removed from the Forbidden City by Pu Jie during 1924. These lists proved very useful in later attempts to recover these unique artistic masterpieces.[47]

The inventory work was not without controversy. Even though the Commttee for Liquidation had been created promptly, with reliable men in key positions, the palace treasures were as vulnerable to China's political vicissitudes as they had been under monarchical rule. The first set of problems arose when pro-monarchists in Beijing began to call for a restoration of the emperor, which they saw as preferable to the chaos of rival warlords. These pro-monarchists were suspicious of the Committee for Liquidation, since Li Yuying and Yi Peiji were both clearly anti-monarchic and pro-republic. The term "liquidation" in the committee's name also raised the hackles of Qing sympathizers because it created doubt about what the committee might actually do with the fabled imperial treasures.

The Committee for Liquidation proceeded with their work in an orderly and efficient way designed to forestall any irregularities or criticism. They also hoped to allay the suspicions of the Qing household by allowing them to send additional observers of the inventory process. In return for this gesture, the Ministry of Finance promised funds for the committee's work.[48]

FOUNDING OF THE PALACE MUSEUM

Plans were made to open a new museum to display the imperial treasures to the public. It opened on October 10, 1925 (National Day of the Republic of China), less than a year after the seizure of the palaces and their contents, and was proclaimed the Palace Museum. Yi Peiji was aware of the great public interest in this museum. He promoted publication of photographic reproductions of paintings, manuscripts, and calligraphy as well as bulletins on interesting treasures as they were identified. He hoped by so doing to involve the public, instill confidence that the treasures were indeed being saved for the people, and to promote financial assistance for everything from maintenance of the physical plant to salaries.

Some of the early restoration work on the palace buildings was funded by gifts from Chinese and foreign philanthropists even before the founding of the museum.[49] John C. Ferguson (1866–1945), an American who went to China as a Christian missionary and became the wealthy founder and publisher of Shanghai's *Shen Bao* and Hong Kong's *South China Morning Post*, devoted himself after about 1915 to connoisseurship of Chinese art and culture. He arranged for Joy Morton, a banker from Chicago, to visit the Forbidden City in 1917 and to provide funds for the restoration of a hall to display bronzes.[50]

Later, work to repair, renovate, and alter the neglected buildings in the Forbidden City for museum purposes was made possible by private gifts from foreign and Chinese philanthropists.[51] In 1931 a second Chicagoan, Robert Allerton, gave fifteen hundred dollars to restore a hall in the eastern section, while British collector Sir Percival David (1892–1964) contributed to restoring a hall for the display of ceramics from the Song, Yuan, and Ming dynasties.

The opening ceremony took place at the great Qian'men, literally the front gate of the Forbidden City. The invited guests, many of them important political figures, were joined by perhaps twenty thousand people who purchased entrance tickets for one yuan, eager to see the treasures of the palace. Everything was displayed in its original location, just as Pu Yi had left it. The speech made by Huang Fu (the Regency Council premier and associate of warlord Feng Yuxiang) captured the moment: "This is the first day of the Palace Museum, as well as the Double Tenth. From now on, this day will be a double anniversary, both National Day and Palace Museum Day. Any sabotage of the Palace Museum will be regarded as sabotage to this great day of the Republic."[52]

Plans for the museum, however, would not be implemented until after the end of the Japanese occupation of Beijing in 1945, long after Yi Peiji's death in September 1937.[53] Encroaching war with Japan and revolution within China were to throw the museum and its collections into chaos for much of the next two decades.

4

The Treasures through Times of War, 1931–1947

As China entered a long and intense period of fighting, with Japanese aggression and world war followed by civil war, the fate of the imperial treasures was more than ever tied to political events. On September 18, 1931, Japan's army captured Mukden (Shenyang), the capital of Manchuria. As the Japanese army overran Manchuria, many Chinese feared that the next move would be a strike below the Great Wall. In response, Palace Museum director Yi Peiji made the prompt but bold decision to move the best of the collection south in order to protect them. Thus began a new stage in the odyssey of the collection. It would be many moves and many years before the imperial treasures again found permanent homes.

RELOCATION TO THE SOUTH

The governing board of the Palace Museum agreed to move the treasures south in September 1932. As in the past, the museum held a sale of articles from the palace storerooms to finance the undertaking, and the complicated process of packing the treasures began.

During violent dynastic turnovers, China's imperial treasures had often been captured and treated as spoils of war. This time, however, great care was taken in preparing the treasures for the move. Curator Chuang Yen described, for example, the painstaking process of preparing the ancient Stone Drums for transport.[1] This group of ten dome-shaped stones, redis-covered in the early Tang dynasty, displayed a script older than the small seal script created before 221 BC. Under custody of the Palace Museum, they were included in the great removals of palace treasures to the south in 1933. First, layers of wet paper were wrapped around each stone until it was half again as large as itself. The stones were then bound tightly with hemp cording. Over this was added a thick layer of quilted cotton. Finally, each stone was sealed in a wooden crate containing rice straw and cotton wadding. The Palace Museum curators selected the finest objects, divided them into categories (bronzes, jades, porcelains, paintings, calligraphy, rare books, and other objects), and packed them into twenty thousand crates.[2] The objects were transported to the train station and loaded onto boxcars for a journey that would eventually cover seventy-five thousand kilometers over a span of fourteen years, from 1933 to 1947.[3]

The heroic effort to pack up the treasures was completed by January 1933. From his childhood, Nelson Wu remembers hearing the sound of carts transporting the crates at night:

> Many a night in the early spring of 1933, sections of the dimly lit streets of Peking would be cleared of all traffic. Under curfew, the southern gate of the Forbidden City would then swing open and wooden carts laden with securely nailed heavy crates would move out on the quiet street and travel south. Outside the great city gate, Qian'men, the carts would turn right and enter the Western Railway Terminal. Heavily guarded throughout the trip by policemen and soldiers, the caravan's cargo was then transferred to a waiting train under the armed protection. Taking a zigzag inland route, the train would first travel in a southwesterly direction, then swing back eastward, and south to Shanghai, where the crates would be kept in storage for four years. From February to May the operation cautiously continued, and some 19,557 cases of art objects, rare books, and historical documents . . . were thus moved out of war-threatened Peking and away from the exposed and uneasy northeastern coast. No one knew how the Japanese invasion would develop or how long the treasures would stay in exile."[4]

The stealth was not only for security, but because it was thought that the city residents might interpret the crates being moved as a signal that the government was abandoning Beiping (Beijing). To calm the public, Yi Peiji asked the Ministry of Internal Affairs to guarantee that the treasures would return to their ancestral home when the political situation was stabilized. Foreign Sinologists, who sought access for research, were also eager to have the treasures returned to Beiping because the collection had not been fully inventoried or studied. Few saw the long-term Japanese threat with any clarity. Instead, most worried about "the Palace Museum standing empty except for the mediocre residue left behind to make some sort of display for the benefit of lamentably occasional tourists."[5]

The Ouster of Yi Peiji

As the treasures were being readied for their journey southward, another drama was unfolding within the Palace Museum. Zhang Ji, a member of the museum's board since 1929, had become jealous and suspicious of Director Yi Peiji. Zhang claimed he had been promised the position of deputy museum director. He also apparently thought that Yi and his son-in-law

Yi Peiji (1880–1937). From *Gugong Zhoukan*, no. 3 (October 26, 1929).

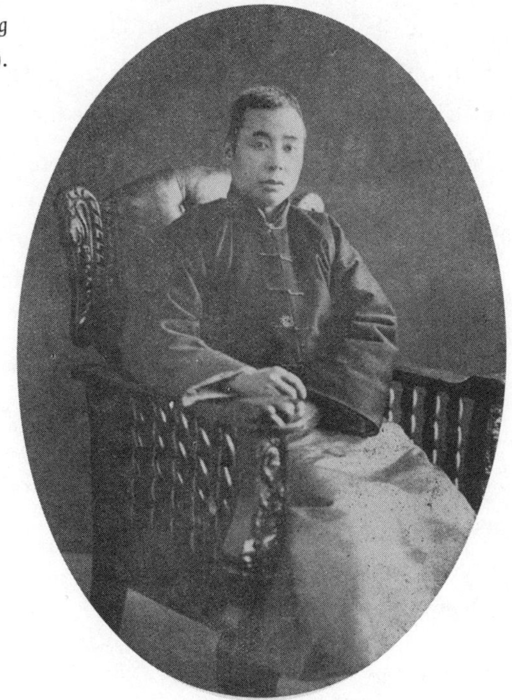

were profiting from the sales of items from the palace storerooms and from the decision to move the treasures away from Beiping. At the same time, Zhang's wife, Cui Zhenghua, a wealthy woman notorious for her bad temper, held a special grudge against the museum leaders because she had failed to obtain a fur coat and other items she craved during sales of the museum's stores in 1932.

Zhang and his wife made their first overt move against Yi in January 1933, alleging an illegality in the museum's handling of the 1932 sale of gold wares from the palace storerooms. A court dismissed the charge, but the two made a second accusation in April, this time of inadequate accounting for sales of silk. The court procurator found that some bills had indeed been tampered with. Yi submitted his resignation in June, "for the sake of the honor of the museum and the country," thus ending his five-year service as museum director.[6]

But Yi's resignation did not stop the vendetta against him. In October 1933, a formal indictment was brought against Yi, his son-in-law Li Zhongdong (the museum's secretary-general), and seven others in the Palace Museum. They were accused of "malpractice, forgery, perfidy, jeopardizing government functions, and injuring reputations."[7] Yi and his son-in-law were accused of misappropriating the jewelry collection bit by bit; thousands of items were cited. The court sent inspectors and an appraiser to examine all the jewels in the palace as well as those sent to Shanghai; many fakes were found.[8]

The accusations described at length the illegality of Yi and Li's handling of treasures during the 1923–1924 inventory: they had taken an object without registering it in a log; they had failed to have a supervisor always present when moving an object. In sum, they were accused of violating the rules formulated in November 1924 to prevent thefts during the inventory work. Yi quickly published a defense in the newspapers, titled "Describing the Facts in the Palace Case."[9] However, on the last day of December 1933, the court ordered both Yi Peiji and Li Zhongdong arrested. For the third time in his official career, Yi went into hiding in the foreign concessions.[10]

New indictments were brought against Yi and Li in October 1934, charging massive theft from the Palace Museum. The court ordered the investigation and examination of bronzes, paintings, and calligraphies from among the museum antiquities already stored in Shanghai. No questions were raised concerning articles outside of Yi's authority. Huang Binhong, a painting connoisseur and himself a renowned painter, was appointed to rule on the genuineness of the articles in question.

Curator Na Chih-liang has pointed out that, while it is easy to distinguish between fake and genuine jewels, it is not so easy to do so with paintings and calligraphy. Experts differed in their judgments during the inventory, since the imperial collections were not free of fakes. Many items from the Manchu collection had been incorrectly judged by the Qing dynasty's Emperor Qianlong, and these mistaken judgments were still accepted in the twentieth century.

Another source of error was in the naming of articles during the early stages of the inventory done by the Committee for Liquidation of the Qing Household. The committee staff members were mostly laymen without antiquities expertise. The fact that their descriptions did not always exactly match the object in question (they mistakenly described a long hollow carved jade ceremonial *cong* from an ancient tomb as a vase, for instance), was taken by Yi's accusers as proof that he had deliberately substituted one article for another. Na Chih-liang saw how ridiculous it was to claim counterfeit substitutions. The issue, for him, was whether or not there had been embezzlement.

Huang Binhong has been criticized for making many new mistakes in judgment during his examination in 1935–1936. Huang doubted the authenticity of 594 paintings and calligraphies, 218 bronze vessels, 101 gilded bronze Buddhas, and a lone jade Buddha. These second court examinations started in December 1935 and continued sporadically throughout 1936. A final indictment against Yi and his son-in-law was entered in September 1937 with two volumes of evidence.[11] Huang Binhong's sole judgment was accepted by the court, although he doubtless made mistakes.

Ma Heng, who took over management of the museum after Yi Peiji's resignation, was not active in Yi's defense during the period of these various accusations and court proceedings from 1933 to 1937, perhaps because he had his own problems during these years. However, in 1949, after the Communists came to power, Ma Heng wrote to Dong Biwu, vice premier of the State Administrative Council, asserting that the court had been mistaken to assume that the only fakes in the imperial collections had been inserted by Yi and his son-in-law for their own benefit. "I disagreed with such an assumption, though I found it inappropriate for me to make any comments at that time. An article I wrote for the Commercial Press made that point and elaborated on the difficulties in authentication."[12] Generalissimo Chiang Kai-shek, president of the Republic of China (ROC), was somewhat more supportive of Yi during his trials. He is said to have remarked that the case should be handled with discretion. But Chiang Kai-shek left the affair to be settled by the government departments concerned.

After the formal indictment was handed down against Yi, he and his son-in-law fled again, this time to the Japanese concession at Tianjin. Yi lived disguised in the foreign concessions of Shanghai, Tianjin, Hong Kong, and Dalian until his death of tuberculosis and diabetes in Shanghai in September 1937. Some said that this gentle looking but determined reformer had been hounded to an early death. His accuser, Zhang Ji, died in 1943. Only then did the Supreme Court announce that it would not hear the Yi Peiji case.[13]

Ma Heng Takes Over

After Yi Peiji's resignation in June 1933, the work of the Palace Museum was carried on under Ma Heng (1881–1955), first in his role as acting director in the summer of 1933, and then as full director in the fall. Ma would remain in charge of the museum until he retired in 1954.

Ma's association with the imperial treasures had begun in 1924, when his friend Yi Peiji had asked him to become involved with the inventory project being carried out by the Committee for Liquidation of the Qing Household. In 1928, when Yi was appointed director of the Palace Museum, Ma had gone to Beiping to accept the post for his ailing friend. He then became the museum's vice-director of antiquities.

Ma Heng had been a member of the faculty of the Peking University

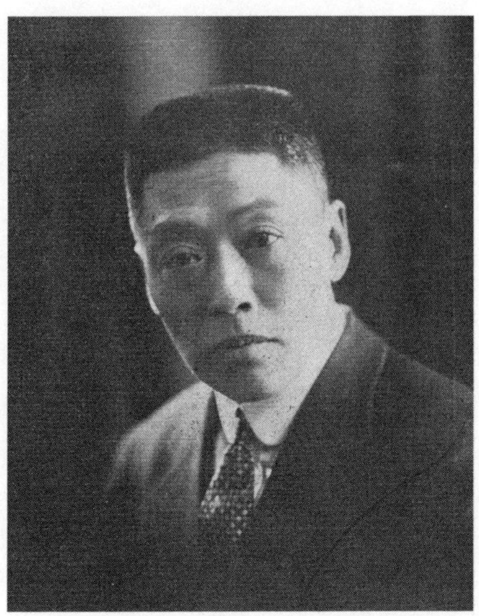

Ma Heng (1881–1955). From *Gugong Zhoukan*, no. 28 (April 19,1930).

Research Institute since 1922. He was a well-regarded member of the academic community when he began his association with the Palace Museum collection. His expertise in epigraphy and archaeological art history were particularly valuable to the museum staff. He brought a new dimension to epigraphical studies by comparing excavated materials with written records and is therefore considered an innovator in methodology.[14]

In 1924, for example, Ma's knowledge of bronze ceremonial vessels helped him to recognize a curious bronze vessel found in the Kunming Palace, Yunnan province. Its unusual and archaic calligraphy led him to conclude that this two-handled round vessel was indeed the very grain vessel cast by Liu Xin for Emperor Wang Mang (r. AD 9–23).[15] Previously known only from written records, this vessel is considered the progenitor of all grain measures used in China. Known as a *jia liang*,[16] this national treasure is also a reminder that Emperor Wang Mang, a usurper, was fulfilling one of an emperor's important legitimizing duties: establishing standard units of measure for the empire and, in so doing, fulfilling the Mandate of Heaven.[17]

When Ma became acting director of the Palace Museum in October 1933, it was on the heels of the formal indictments against Yi Peiji and his son-in-law and in the midst of the complicated transfer of the imperial collection to south China. Ma thus inherited a very complex situation and a veritable minefield of problems.

A New Home in Nanjing

Ma Heng's first challenge was to determine where in southern China to store the museum treasures. When the shipments had gone south by rail in February and March 1933, their final destination had still not been determined.[18] Temporarily, it was decided to send the cases containing paintings and calligraphy to Shanghai to await more permanent storage in Nanjing. In Shanghai they were stored in two warehouses in the relative safety of the Shanghai foreign concessions—one in the French zone and one in the British, each guarded by its French or British police assisted by plainclothesmen from the Chinese police. The boxes of official books and documents from three museums in Beiping—the National Central, the Historical, and the Palace Museum—went directly to the capital of the Nationalist government in Nanjing.[19]

Ma's efforts to find long-term storage in Nanjing were complicated by the demands of the court proceedings against Yi Peiji, which required opening many cases of treasures for investigation. Cases also were opened on occasion to photograph relics for the museum's weekly and monthly publications (the *Gugong Zhoukan* and the *Gugong Yuekan*). The many photos published in these journals helped acquaint the public with the contents of this hitherto unknown collection.

In November 1934, Ma began a complete inventory of the cases in Shanghai. This made it easier to comply with government requests related to the Yi Peiji trial. It may have also been designed to help clear the record regarding Ma's own tenure. Eventually, every box sent to Shanghai was given a new inventory designation and a more accurate description. Ma Heng also suggested applying a seal denoting "Examined by the Ministry of Education" to each object as it was checked. This seal was applied only to articles in Shanghai; those left behind in Beiping were considered of lesser importance.[20]

It took several years to find suitable long-term storage in Nanjing for all the treasures. Finally, in July 1935, the museum acquired the Zhao Dian

Palace property. Construction of storage areas began in March 1936 and was completed in December. At that time, the treasures that had been stored in Shanghai since 1933 were also shipped to the Zhao Dian in Nanjing. On January 1, 1937, the Nanjing branch of the Palace Museum was established.

The first task for the Nanjing museum staff was to mount an exhibition. In May 1937 the Second National Art Exhibition from the Qin to the Qing Dynasty opened in the National Assembly Hall.[21] The significance of the 1937 exhibition must be remembered in the context of the Nationalist government's need for political legitimacy. The Ministry of Education, the museum's government sponsor, promoted the exhibition as a public affirmation of the legitimacy of the Nationalist government in its capital city of Nanjing. The grand display also served to reassure the public that the imperial collection had survived its move to the south.

Besides securing storage for the crated palace collection and taking inventory in Shanghai, Ma Heng also initiated modern museum preservation and exhibition methods, and made important reforms. In May 1935, he announced revisions of the regulations for the specialized committees that were to provide competent examiners in each specialty: painting and calligraphy, ceramics, bronze vessels, works of art, historical documents, musical instruments, religious scriptures, portraits, and architectural maintenance and design. All committee members were to be appointed by the director of the Palace Museum, and were to serve without salaries, although they could be reimbursed for expenses.[22]

FIRST OVERSEAS EXHIBITIONS

During the last months of 1932, when the Palace Museum curators were preoccupied with moving the treasures south, a group of English collectors began planning a comprehensive exhibition of Chinese art in London. They decided to invite fine examples from collectors and collections all over the world and to hold the exhibit at the Royal Academy of Arts in Burlington House. The organizers, familiar with the recently founded Palace Museum in Beiping, saw the loan of China's imperial art treasures as the jewel in the crown of their vision. This was to become the first of several great international loans of China's imperial art treasures to the West.

In 1934, China's Ministry of Education agreed to the proposal and a Chinese Selection Committee was established to decide which works of art would be sent to London. The Chinese committee included Ma Heng, Chuang Yen, and Na Chih-liang, as well as collectors who were not on the museum staff. John C. Ferguson, the knowledgeable American connoisseur of Chinese painting, was an advisor. He wrote that the Chinese Selection Committee spent many hours choosing the best works, removing from consideration only those that were unique to an artist or too fragile to travel.[23] A small catalogue was prepared of the works selected and was sent in 1935 to the British Selection Committee for review. In the autumn of 1935, a small party of delegates from the British Selection Committee landed in China to consult with the Chinese Selection Committee on works for the London exhibition. The group was led by Sir Percival David. One of the initiators of the exhibition, David had developed an interest in Chinese porcelain a decade earlier while serving as British consul in Hangzhou.

It had been David's understanding that the selections would be made by consultation between the committees of both countries. British collectors were traditionally interested primarily in porcelains, and more recently in mortuary jades and bronze vessels. The English collectors and specialists in Chinese antiquities had seen very few Chinese paintings. There were no Chinese paintings of significance in England, with the notable exception of the famous *Admonitions* handscroll in the British Museum, mentioned in chapter 1 (attributed to Gu Kaizhi of the fourth century AD, which been carried to England as loot by a member of the British expeditionary force that vandalized the Qing palaces in 1900).[24]

After the British delegation arrived in Shanghai in October 1935, they were taken to a small exhibition hall to view the selected paintings. After some pleasantries were exchanged, the official catalogue suggests that selections were expeditiously made.[25] But Basil Gray, former Keeper of Oriental Antiquities at the British Museum, presented a different view:

Having failed to persuade the Chinese side to allow the joint Sino-British Committee to make the selection, the London Committee assessed the gaps from the brochure sent [by the Chinese] and set about to fill [in] the gaps, visiting Europe, the United States, and China. After having assessed the Chinese loans in Shanghai, and having failed to persuade the officials to modify their selection by addition or subtraction, they proceeded to Japan.[26]

The British had a certain sense of their weakness in painting and calligraphy and had invited the famous French Sinologist and Chinese art historian Paul Pelliot to Shanghai to advise them. His input to the selection remains uncertain, but the paintings finally selected were assessed as highly unusual. C. C. Wang (1907–2003), an internationally renowned collector and connoisseur, argued that only 13 of the total 175 paintings were deemed to be copies or of poor quality, although other experts maintain that the number was considerably higher.

After the treasures arrived in London, the British changed the labels to conform with their own ideas about the dating of porcelains and their doubt about certain works being genuine. Ferguson was dismayed that any divergence of opinion had not already been aired during the meetings in Shanghai—where, had the Chinese known, they would not have include the controversial works. Ferguson later wrote, "The final description furnished [by the Chinese Selection Committee] . . . *may be considered the official view of the Chinese Government* . . . it was a rash act on the part of the London Executive Committee to set itself in opposition to this official opinion and it amounted to a challenge to Chinese experts to show cause why a small group of British experts was not qualified to teach them how to label their own national treasures."[27]

The importance of the London exhibition is not to be measured by this controversy. In general the exhibit got rave reviews, and it fulfilled the goal of the organizers to present a unique showing of the best of Chinese art over the centuries. Even Ferguson said it was a grand success and that it daily attracted such large crowds from many countries that it was difficult to see the exhibits. Art historian Laurence Sickman believed that the great effort put into this exhibition, more than any other event, inaugurated the modern era of Chinese art historical studies.[28]

Many recognized the political significance of the event. An official of the British Museum noted that the "official participation of the Chinese government invests the event with political significance and, from the cultural point of view, cultural relations are now recognized as having profound significance."[29] A Chinese resident of London reminisced on the importance of the event: "Politically it had a great impact; people have a greater understanding of Chinese culture, thus influencing them to have sympathy for China at war with Japan."[30]

What did the Republic of China gain from their willingness to ship such valuable objects on the high seas? As one historian observed, "The show provided a stimulus for the study of Chinese art . . . and for China it was an almost unimaginable public relations success."[31]

Other International Loans and Requests

The London exhibition of Chinese treasures, the first major exhibit of these works abroad, triggered tangible ripples in other countries. H. E. Winlock, director of the Metropolitan Museum of Art in New York, suggested that the treasures go directly from London to the United States for a second exhibit before returning to China. He noted that an exhibit in New York at this time would be an excellent way for China to boost the ROC's image in the United States. The Chinese were amenable, but asked for official support from the American government. The State Department's assistant secretary for Far Eastern affairs, Stanley Hornbeck, turned down the request, however, because he did not want to give the anti-American and pro-Communist forces in China an excuse to force the United States into a confrontation with Japan. So the treasures were shipped from London directly back to Shanghai.[32]

The return trip included one worrisome episode, when the HMS *Suffolk*, the British naval transport for the treasures, ran aground off Gibraltar. It was raised without any damage to the cargo and returned to Shanghai on April 8, 1936—one year to the day from its departure.[33]

Because of the high profile loan to London, China received a request from the Soviet Union for what might be called "equal access" to the imperial treasures. The Soviet Union had recently established a rapprochement with China, and as part of their growing exchanges, the Russians requested a loan exhibition. The exhibit was small, just one hundred objects of secondary importance.[34] These items left from a storage depot at Anshun, Sichuan province, on July 18, 1939, and traveled overland via Gansu and Xinjiang, arriving in Moscow in early September. They were exhibited in Moscow from January to August 1940 and in Leningrad from March to June 1942, before returning to Chongqing (then China's capital city) in September 1942.

THE TREASURES MOVE WEST

The eighty cases of imperial treasures returned from London to a China in the midst of unfolding catastrophe. The widening of the war with Japan would soon force the treasures to be relocated again.

At the end of 1936 the palace treasures had only just moved into their new home at the Zhao Dian Palace in the capital of Nanjing, where they were presumed to be relatively safe. This sense of security was reflected in the decision to mount the Second National Art Exhibition from the Qin to the Qing Dynasty, which opened in May 1937 in the National Assembly Hall in Nanjing. That sense of security vanished with the rapid advance of the Japanese army. On July 7, 1937, the Marco Polo Bridge Incident occurred on the outskirts of Beiping, thus triggering the Sino-Japanese War. The Japanese soon occupied Beiping and rapidly swept south. Less than three months later, on August 13, Shanghai was attacked by land and air. The fearsome massacre of Nanjing's population just weeks later was a disaster beyond the imagination of Palace Museum officials, the Chinese government, and the world at large.

Palace Museum authorities had no time to lose in planning to protect the palace treasures. The Administrative Council of the Palace Museum approved a plan to send groups of cases containing treasures westward along three routes, to relocate (along with the Nationalist government) to Chongqing. On August 14, 1937, the eighty steel cases loaned to the

London exhibit were among the first treasures to leave Nanjing, just before the infamous Rape of Nanjing, barely escaping destruction.[35] This first group went by ship along the Yangzi River to Hankou (near Wuhan), and then by rail to Changsha. Within months, Changsha was no longer safe, so the crates were sent on via Guangxi to Guizhou—and none too soon, as the library where they had been kept in Changsha was leveled by a bomb. After a year, they were moved to a safe cave near the city of Anshun in Sichuan, where they remained from 1938 until 1947.[36]

Meanwhile, in early November, the second batch of treasures was being prepared for travel. Museum staff worked day and night to pack, load, and carry 9,369 trunks to the docks. This huge shipment left Nanjing during the last days of the city's defense, between November 20 and December 8. Na Chih-liang's diary entries for those days convey the sense of fearful urgency: "November 4th, speedily move all from Nanjing by land and by water. December 8th, speedy shipment halted. December 10th, 9,369 cases to Hankou via Yangzi steamships. The Confucian temple in Hankou [where the cases were housed] was destroyed the day after the trunks had been moved on, in March, to Yichang."[37]

In Yichang the cases had to wait months for the river to rise. In the autumn, they resumed their journey through the treacherous Yangzi River gorges to Chongqing, which had by then become the wartime capital of Chiang Kai-shek and his battered Nationalist government. It took nearly a year for the cases to travel from Nanjing to Chongqing. Chongqing, in turn, became too dangerous, so in the spring of 1939 the cases were again loaded onto small wooden vessels, some of which were pulled up the rapids by trackers.[38] In one memorable incident, a rope broke, the helmsman lost control, and the vessel was swept downstream carrying many trunks and the men escorting them. Fortunately no serious losses or damage occurred. On the final stretch the trunks were carried on the backs of porters to Leshan in western Sichuan.[39]

The third shipment, sent from Nanjing to Shaanxi and then to Sichuan, was the most difficult. It left Nanjing on December 10, 1937, just days before the Japanese captured the capital. The 7,286 cases were taken overland by train to Xuzhou, and then moved by three hundred trucks to

Hanzhong between February and May 1938. The route followed primitive roads over the Qin mountains, roads that were sometimes muddy and subject to landslides. A heavy snow marooned the caravan without food and shelter. Rescue supplies reached them and they arrived in Sichuan on April 10, after forty-eight days en route.

Only a month and a half later, the government ordered the curators to find a safer place. The Hanzhong shelter, a Confucian temple, was destroyed by Japanese planes soon after the cases had been evacuated. The route to Chengdu, capital of Sichuan province, involved many ferry crossings, and boats were pulled upstream by manpower. After the cases had arrived in Chengdu the order came to move them another 150 kilometers to Mount Emei, where the trunks remained in two temples until the end of hostilities with Japan.

The sudden exodus of the palace treasures from Nanjing was costly. Hang Liwu, a member of the board of the Palace Museum and executive secretary of the former Boxer Indemnity Fund, arranged for money to be made available in November and December 1937. (Since 1925, the English share of the Boxer indemnity funds had been renamed the British Educational and Cultural Foundation.) Generalissimo Chiang Kai-shek's personal vehicles were also enlisted to aid the "frantic speedy loading" of treasures from Nanjing westward.[40]

As director of the Palace Museum, Ma Heng was ultimately responsible for managing all these precarious travels, which he evidently did from the wartime capital of Chongqing. The curators traveling with the trunks received orders to move again and again. Their record is utterly admirable; moreover, not a single trunk was lost during the ten years from 1937 to 1947.

Once the cases of treasures arrived at a safe haven, their contents needed to be unpacked, for it was essential that the curators give the paintings and calligraphies semiannual, or at least annual, airings in order to protect them from dampness and insects.

Despite the danger of bombing and hardships of life during the war with Japan, some of the Palace Museum art treasures were actually exhibited in western China during this time, proving a welcome diversion for the population. In December 1943, a small exhibition of calligraphy and painting opened in three display rooms of the Central Library of Chongqing. A second small exhibition was mounted in 1944 in the Provincial Art Gallery in Guiyang, Guizhou province. In 1947, a final small exhibit was mounted in the Central Library in Chongqing to bid farewell to the treasures after the Japanese defeat. Wang Shixiang, a protégé of Director Ma Heng's, was the curator of these exhibits and would play an important role in the later history of the treasures.

WAR WITH JAPAN AND ITS AFTERMATH

Little is known about events at the Palace Museum in Beiping during the city's eight years under Japanese occupation. When the Japanese captured the city in September 1937, the museum's director, Ma Heng, had already gone west with some of the treasures. The museum staff, sensibly, sent a petition to the Nationalist government in Nanjing requesting guidance. After waiting more than a month in occupied Beiping, they received this reply in November: "Your petition has been received. We are aware that the situation confronting the staff remaining in the Beiping Museum is difficult and precarious . . . We hope you will do your best to maintain the museum."[41] In other words, from a safe distance the orders were: You are on your own; stay at your posts and carry on!

In the absence of Ma Heng, day-to-day supervision of the Palace Museum after 1937 was handled by Zhang Tingji, head of the General Affairs Department. The museum staff refused to follow a Japanese order to accept a Japanese director or adviser and did not allow any Japanese to enter the museum without a letter of introduction.

There were several incidents of destruction. On June 15, 1938, less than a year after the occupation began, some Japanese officers seized hundreds of volumes of books from the Ancestral Temple (Tai Miao) and reportedly burned many of them.[42] Six years later, when the Japanese were desperate for metal to supply their arms industry, they plundered the Palace Museum of 54 bronze vats, 4 bronze cannons, and 91 bronze lampstands. In July 1945 they again tried to take bronze vats, this time from the Tai Miao, but were prevented by museum personnel. When the Japanese admitted defeat in August, all the bronze lamp stands and cannons were returned. Although some vats were smashed, in the end 4,460 kilograms of metal were recovered thanks to Wang Shixiang and others.[43]

In June 1942, the Japanese puppet government appointed Zhu Shuyuan provisional acting curator of the Palace Museum.[44] Zhu's appointment discouraged monarchic adherents from laying claim to museum holdings—a sign that some members of the Qing Aisin-Gioro family might have been trying again to claim palace property.[45]

The year of Zhu's appointment, Coal Hill (Jinshan) north of the Forbidden City and the Tai Miao within the Forbidden City were opened to visitors.[46] Admission fees were reinstated and staff salaries (albeit very low) resumed. When Yang Boda (who later became senior research curator) visited the Palace Museum in 1945, near the end of the Japanese occupation, he found a few elderly curators, including Shen Shiyuan, who had been at the museum since its founding.[47]

In 1943 the staff were ordered to consolidate the Antiquities Exhibition Halls and the Historical Museum into one administrative unit under the Palace Museum. This consolidation had been suggested for efficiency's sake many years earlier, when Yi Peiji was director. The move was finalized in 1947, after Ma Heng had returned to Beiping.[48]

Consolidation after Japan's Defeat

After the defeat of Japan in August 1945, the first task of the museum staff was to bring the treasures that had been sent westward back to Nanjing. It took several months after the war's end before any transport could be spared from the job of moving the government itself back to Nanjing. Finally, in December 1946, all three shipments of treasures were ready to return to Nanjing by whatever primitive means of transport could be obtained, including porters, wooden boats, and old trucks. The Stone Drums, for instance, were brought back safely to Nanjing in 1947.[49] A year later, all the treasures sent westward had been reassembled in Nanjing.

Once the treasures were back from the west, attention turned to retrieving those treasures that had been lost, looted, or otherwise removed from the Palace Museum during the war years. Museum Director Ma Heng returned to Beiping at the end of 1946. One of his first tasks was to bring back to Beiping those articles impounded as fakes after the Huang Binhong inspections, which had been left untended in the south after the termination of the Yi Peiji trials in 1937. These impounded boxes had been sealed for ten years, with no measures taken to prevent them from being eaten by moths. "It didn't matter [now]," Na Chih-liang wrote, "if they were all fake. Unfortunately, some were genuine and [all] were poorly treated."[50] In 1947, these "wronged spirits," some of them rare and important paintings and calligraphies, emerged to be cared for again.

TRACKING DOWN THE TREASURES

Wang Shixiang, who had helped to care for the treasures in Chongqing during the war, was to play a key role in tracing stolen and missing relics. In 1944, Ma appointed him to the newly created Committee for Handling Wartime Losses of Relics, which was charged with finding treasures that had been removed by the Japanese or otherwise dispersed since 1924.

One major category of missing art was the hundreds of rare books, jewels, calligraphies, and paintings taken to Manchuria by the former Qing emperor (and later Japanese puppet emperor) Pu Yi. This group of important relics from the imperial collection had been stored in a small white building behind Pu Yi's Manchurian palace. After Pu Yi was captured by the Soviet army in 1945, his palace and storage were looted by his former soldiers.

After Japan's defeat, important relics from Pu Yi's former collection began to appear in Beiping and Tianjin curio shops.[51] Wang promised rewards to antique dealers whose leads proved fruitful and, in early 1947, the Nationalist government allocated 250 million yuan to help purchase back these national treasures. In one lucky find, an American colonel quartered in Pu Yi's former Tianjin residence sent word to the Palace Museum of an unopened safe in the house. Wang Shixiang journeyed to Tianjin to see the safe, which had to be forced open. Inside were more than one thousand small ancient jade pieces and four painting scrolls. The jades were later identified as having been taken from brocade-lined cases designed for them in the museum, to which they were eventually returned.[52] Wang made a promising start in the late 1940s tracking down the Northeastern Treasures (Dongbeihuo), a process that lasted well into the 1960s and is described further in chapter 6.

Wang helped retrieve many other important treasures. A German businessman, Werner Jannings, had acquired an important collection of precious bronze vessels unearthed in north China during the Japanese occupation. Acting on a tip in November 1945, Wang went to Jannings's office in Tianjin, where he noticed the secretary typing up a list of Chinese bronze vessels.[53] Herr Jannings admitted having such a collection but said it was under seal at his house, which was being used as a military headquarters. Wang journeyed to Tianjin three times, only to be turned back by the military, despite his official credentials. Wang then appealed for help to T. V. Soong, chairman of the Nationalist Executive Yuan and brother-in-law of Chiang Kai-shek. In January 1946, the Beiping Bureau of Enemy and Personal Property Control took over Jannings's collection, and the whole collection was inventoried by the Palace Museum with witnesses for both parties. A small party was given to celebrate Herr Jannings's "donation," and the collection went on view in two rooms at the museum from October 30 to November 11, 1946.

The collection of John Ferguson, the scholar of Chinese art and adviser to the Palace Museum in the 1930s who had since returned to the United States, was taken into custody by the museum in 1948 and stored in the Antiquities Exhibition Hall. Ferguson bequeathed his collection to Nanjing University, although some of it was displayed at the Palace Museum in Beiping in the 1940s.

The years 1945–1947 were characterized by efforts to reclaim the treasures for the nation after the long war with Japan. Gradually, curatorial work resumed at the museum's sites in both Nanjing and Beiping. Both cities mounted exhibitions in May-June 1948 to celebrate the defeat of Japan.

But the treasures were not yet at rest. The nation was in the midst of a civil war that was to prove the most devastating threat of the century to the

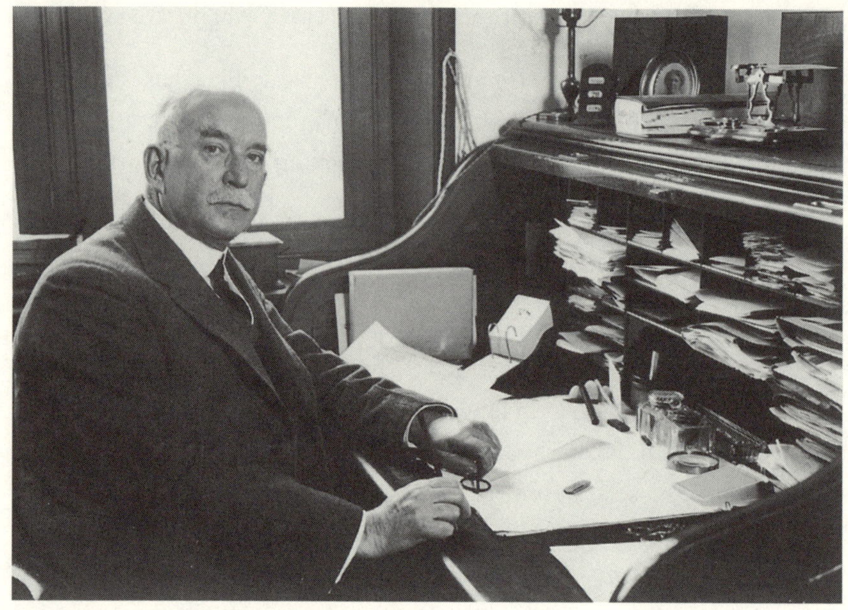

Dr. John C. Ferguson (1837–1916). Freer Gallery Archive, Washington, D.C.

integrity of the imperial treasures. It would lead to the complete breakup of the palace collection and the establishment of two separate, rival museums: one in Beijing, the People's Republic of China, and one in Taipei, the Republic of China.

5

Relocating and Rebuilding
the Palace Museum on Taiwan

By 1948 China was engulfed in a bitter civil war between the Nationalists and the Communists. The process of retrieving and consolidating the
imperial treasures in Nanjing and Beiping, which had been the museum
staff's focus from 1945 through 1947, came to a halt. It was replaced by
competition between the opposing sides over who would lay claim to the
treasures. Both Beiping and Nanjing were directly threatened by Communist military forces. When the city of Xuzhou (in northwestern Jiangsu
province) fell to the Communists in November, so did the last major obstacle protecting the Nationalist capital of Nanjing.

In the autumn of 1948 the Executive Yuan (the executive branch of government) in Nanjing sent an urgent message to Palace Museum director
Ma Heng, requesting that he compile a list and description of valuable
relics still in the Beiping Palace Museum and arrange for them to be sent
in batches by plane to Nanjing. The Nationalist government was making
contingency plans to retreat to the island of Taiwan off the east China
coast, and senior officials wanted the treasures consolidated in Nanjing
so that, if necessary, they could be taken to safety on Taiwan.

In December, Hang Liwu, secretary to the board of the Palace Museum,
as well as director of the National Central Museum and Library, summoned
Ma Heng to an important meeting in Nanjing to decide how to protect the

palace treasures and prevent their possible capture by the Communists. Ma replied by telegram that he was too ill to attend the meeting. In his absence, it was decided that the treasures should be moved to Taiwan as soon as possible, and Hang Liwu was appointed to manage the transport.

Although Ma asked his staff to prepare the requested list of important relics in Beiping, he did not seem to be in any rush to pack the articles.[1] When the Executive Yuan telegraphed Ma pressing for the shipment, Ma replied that the shipment was not ready, that the weather would not permit packing, and, in any event, that the airport was not safe enough to store or ship out the objects.

These apparent delaying tactics, coupled with Ma's disapproval of a colleague who left for Taiwan without permission, indicate that Ma may have deliberately obstructed orders to ship the treasures. A member of Ma's staff later asked, "Mr. Ma, was it your intention not to ship those relics by plane?" Lighting his cigar, Ma smiled and replied, "Was that not [also] your intention?"[2] Ma did not change his determination to stay in Beiping even at the urging of his old friend and colleague Chuang Yen, who eventually went to Taiwan with the Nationalist government and continued his work with the treasures that were taken there.[3]

THE TRANSFER OF THE TREASURES TO TAIWAN

Hang Liwu failed to secure Ma Heng's cooperation and the Nationalists had to leave behind many of the imperial treasures still in the Forbidden City when they left for Taiwan. They were able to take almost 20 percent of the treasures that were in Nanjing with them to the island retreat. These included the eighty crates from the London exhibit of 1935–1936 and almost four thousand of the twenty thousand cases that had recently come back from their hideouts in western China.

All transport was controlled by the Nationalist military. Generalissimo Chiang Kai-shek personally approved the decision to send the treasures to Taiwan, allocating a sum of eight million yuan to cover the costs of the move. Curator Na Chih-liang's meticulous records have preserved the details of that epic transfer. Five shipments were planned, but only three actually took place.[4] Altogether, nearly four thousand crates of precious objects were shipped to Taiwan.[5] Chuang Yen was assigned to accompany the first shipment, which included all the cases from the London exhibit.

Chuang described the chaos as he and the museum curators sent cases to the dock from a storage area without knowing how much space had been allotted for them on board ship. The dock workers, probably instructed by the Communists, staged a work slowdown; if a case needed two men, they put on three, and then four, until loading almost came to a standstill. On December 22, 1948, Chuang Yen sailed with the first shipment on the freighter *Zhongding*, from Shanghai to the northern Taiwanese port of Keelung. He later recalled a dreadful five-day passage on very rough seas, as the cases of treasures shifted alarmingly from bulwark to bulwark, each shift accompanied by the howls of a dog.[6]

Na Chih-liang accompanied the second batch, consisting of rare books from the National Central Museum and Library. Hang Liwu had recovered many cases of precious books and art from Japan after the war, and these were among the items sent to Taiwan.[7] Na departed Shanghai on January 9, 1949, on a commercial carrier of the Zhao Shan Steamship Corporation.

The third shipment was carried on the steamer *Kunlun*, which left port on January 29, 1949, but did not make port in Keelung until February 22, a period of great anxiety for the waiting curators. Chuang Yen said most of the books that had been moved south from Beiping in 1933 were shipped, except for sixty trunks left on the wharf as the *Kunlun* sailed. In the final chaotic moments, the families of Kuomintang officers—terrified of the Communist retribution—were given precedence over the books.

Before a fourth shipment could get underway, Chiang Kai-shek resigned as president of the Republic of China and Li Zongren, his successor, ordered all further shipments halted. No American ships were involved in this operation, an erroneous idea once current in the United States.[8]

In all, 3,824 crates were shipped to Taiwan. This figure represents only about one-fifth of the original cases moved south from Beiping in 1933, but these crates included many of the best works.[9] Most of the large unique hanging paintings by early painters from the Tang to the Song dynasties went to Taiwan. But the Palace Museum in Beiping retained some of the most important calligraphies and small handscroll paintings of early dynasties.[10] One important reason for these differences in the two collections had to do with the fact that when Pu Yi and Pu Jie fled the Forbidden City and absconded with some of the imperial collection, they naturally took items that were easiest to carry—particularly handscrolls and album leaves—thus leaving most of the large hanging scrolls, which were taken by the Kuomintang government and eventually wound up in the National Palace Museum on Taiwan.[11]

According to Na Chih-liang, many cases had to be left behind. The famous ancient Stone Drums, for example, had to be left on the docks, still in their elaborate wrappings.[12] Almost ten years later, the leaders of the People's Republic of China ordered the drums placed on display again at the Palace Museum in Beijing (upon taking power, the Communists changed the name of the capital from Beiping to Beijing, or "northern capital").[13] Also left behind were the many cases of treasures impounded in Shanghai for the trial of Yi Peiji.

The Nationalists made some dramatic retrievals at the penultimate moment. For example, on December 9, 1948, as Hang Liwu and others were leaving for Taiwan on the last plane from Chengdu, the artist Zhang Daqian made an urgent request. According to Hang Liwu,

> Zhang Daqian came hurriedly and told me he wanted taken along to Taiwan about seventy of the paintings he had copied in the 1940s for the government, of the Buddhist frescoes at Dunhuang in western China. The pilot would not allow anyincrease in weight. So I gave up three of my suitcases for these paintings on one condition: that Zhang Daqian would donate them to the government. Zhang hastily wrote his assent on a visiting card, and all sixty-two of his paintings are in the National Palace Museum [on Taiwan], where they have been displayed.[14]

In fact, these paintings were given to the National Historical Museum on Taiwan.

Taken together, the three shipments would make up the reconstituted collection on Taiwan. In time, it would grow to become one of the great art museums of the world, containing the richest collection of bronzes, calligraphies, handscrolls, and rare books anywhere on earth. This collection would lend, and be claimed to give, legitimacy to the Nationalist government as it sought to maintain its identity as the representative government of all of China and the inheritor of China's imperial cultural traditions.

THE NATIONAL PALACE MUSEUM OF THE REPUBLIC OF CHINA

It was to be many years before the collection would have a permanent home to rival that of the Forbidden City palaces. As it became clear that the Nationalists' retreat to Taiwan was to be more than short-lived, the authorities on the island began to think about longer-term options for the collection. At first, storage for the museum treasures was found in the central highlands of Taiwan near Taichung, in two warehouses of the Taichung Sugar Company. By April 1949, three new storerooms were completed. Almost immediately, a complete inventory and "Handlist of Palace Museum Objects Moved to Taiwan" were completed. The curators soon resumed the practice of opening and airing all the scrolls, a routine that had been followed every six months during the ten years when the scrolls were stored in caves and temples of western China.

In 1953, some caves near the storerooms were carved out for displaying the treasures. A more permanent home for the treasures was badly needed, however, especially since the caves were too damp to store the imperial treasures. Henry Luce, the wealthy American publisher of *Time* and *Life* magazines and an ardent supporter of Chiang Kai-shek and the Kuomintang cause, made a visit to the collection in February 1954. He was able to influence the new U.S. government (and CIA) funded Asia Foundation to provide funds to build a small museum, which opened in March 1957 in Beigou (Peikou), a suburb of Taichung in central Taiwan.

In November 1955, this museum was combined with the National Central Museum and the Central Library into one joint administrative department and became known as the National Palace Museum.[15] Shortly thereafter, the Ministry of Education decided to publish a volume showing the best painting, porcelain, tapestries, and embroideries in the collection.

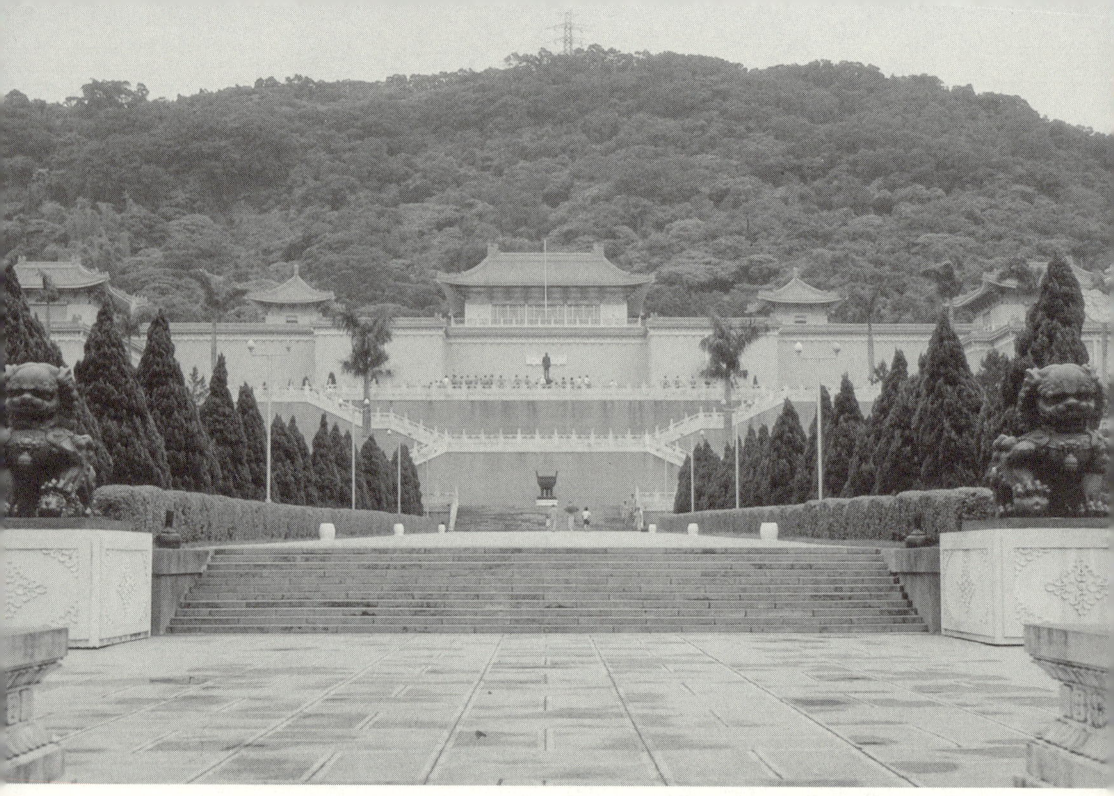

National Palace Museum in Taiwan. The National Palace Museum, Taipei.

A committee composed mainly of National Palace Museum officials frequently went up to Beigou to select works for these volumes. The members of this committee were Wang Shih-chieh, Luo Jialun, Jiang Gusun, and George K. C. Yeh. Knowledgeable curators such as Chuang Yen and Na Chih-liang acted as advisors.

The list they compiled became known as the Main List, or the Zheng Mu, from which three volumes were published in 1956, known as the *Gugong Shuhua Lu*. The description of each painting or calligraphy was often taken directly from the eighteenth-century Qianlong catalogues. Although these catalogues were of great historical value, by the 1950s art-history scholars—some on the National Palace Museum staff, some foreign—had revised their opinions on the attributions and dating of some items. But when new research was not in agreement with the Qianlong attributions, no change was made in the text of this 1956 publication.

The National Palace Museum on Taiwan extended this policy of adhering to Qianlong attributions to the gallery labels as well. Differences of opinion between National Palace Museum officials and some Chinese and Western scholars of Chinese art over these attributions would erupt in a few years, when items were loaned for international exhibitions.

A second list of items from the Taiwan holdings (those not included in the Main List) was compiled and became known as the Simple List (Jian Mu). In 1972, Na Chih-liang explained that the Simple List works were neither fake nor of poor quality; they were simply not chosen by the committee for the first publication. James Cahill, then a young scholar of Chinese painting on the staff of the Smithsonian's Freer Gallery of Art in Washington DC, learned of the two lists during a visit to Taiwan in 1955. Art historians were extremely interested in learning more about the Simple List paintings. In 1959 Cahill signed a contract to write a book on Chinese painting and was determined to locate and photograph the best examples from every source.[16]

In search of the most important works, Cahill had spent a month in Japan before arriving in Taiwan accompanied by C. C. Wang (Wang Jiqian), the noted Chinese art connoisseur and collector from New York. Wang had become familiar with some of the imperial paintings in 1934, when he was an observer of the Shanghai selection process for the 1935–1936 loan of palace treasures to London. After selecting and photographing paintings from the published Main List, Wang and Cahill were able to review some of the paintings on the Simple List and confirm that it included some first-rate works. Cahill went away inspired with the ambition to someday make high-quality photographs of the entire collection in Taiwan.

The First Exhibit in America

Many Americans had long hoped to bring the imperial treasures to the United States for an exhibition. This idea had first been raised in 1935, immediately following the London exhibit (see chapter 4), and again in 1948, but had not yet come to pass.

Publisher Henry Luce revived the idea of exhibiting the National Palace Museum treasures in the United States during his visits to Taichung in the 1950s, but at first nothing came of it. The idea was kept alive by prominent American curators and scholars of Asian art who urged officials in

Taipei to consider the loan. They included Aschwin Lippe of the Metropolitan Museum of Art in New York, John Pope of the Freer Gallery of Art in Washington DC, and Richard Edwards of the University of Michigan. Two leading Taiwan diplomats also helped keep the idea current—Wang Shih-chieh (who had worked with the palace collection in the 1930s and 1940s and was now an elder statesman of the Taiwan government) and Yeh Gung-chao (George Yeh), a former minister of foreign affairs who had become the Republic of China's ambassador to Washington.

Henry Luce had known Wang Shih-chieh since the days of the 1935–1936 Chinese exhibition in London, and they became reacquainted during Luce's visits to Taiwan in the 1950s. Luce finally persuaded Wang that it would be useful for the Republic of China to allow a major exhibition of Chinese art in the United States. Luce's opinion was fortified by the fact that, beginning in 1948, a series of Japanese art exhibitions in the United States had helped soften American feelings about Japan despite bitterness after World War II.[17] Luce pointed out how such exhibitions of Japanese culture influenced American public opinion about Japan. Wang, a member of the board of the National Palace Museum, then helped to persuade the Executive Yuan in Taiwan to support the idea of a loan to the United States. It was finally agreed in 1960 that a major overseas loan from the collection would travel from Taiwan to several U.S. cities in 1961–1962.

Five American museums sponsored the exhibition of National Palace Museum treasures: the National Gallery of Art in Washington DC, the Metropolitan Museum of Art in New York, the Museum of Fine Arts in Boston, the Art Institute of Chicago, and the M. H. De Young Memorial Museum in San Francisco. There was also a promise of financial support from the Luce Foundation. To give it the proper cachet, the exhibition was organized to honor both nation's presidents: Chiang Kai-shek and John F. Kennedy.

A prime interest of the sponsoring museums was to participate in the selection of the paintings.[18] Curator Li Lin-ts'an, who kept a diary throughout the planning process and the exhibit, noted that Chinese painting scholars of both countries were to make the selections for the loan.[19] The Chinese Selection Committee consisted of research curators of the museum, art connoisseurs, and several prominent political figures. It included two of the same connoisseurs that had been involved in the 1935 loan to London, Jiang Gusun and Luo Jialun, and two of the same curators, Na Chih-liang and Chuang Yen (both of whom had joined the museum staff in 1924). Chuang had now become the director of the National Palace Museum on Taiwan. The main responsibility for selections, however, was in the hands of Wang Shih-chieh and Wang Yun-wu, both of whom represented the conservative school that generally supported adherence to Qing dynasty attributions and labels. Negotiating on behalf of the American museums were John Pope of the Freer Gallery of Art; Aschwin Lippe, curator of Far Eastern Art at the Metropolitan Museum of Art; and Tseng Hsien-chi, curator at Boston's Museum of Fine Arts. They spent many weeks in Taipei and came away with a promised list of more than one hundred "masterpieces" of painting and calligraphy and more than one hundred porcelains, bronzes, and woven tapestries.

Writing the catalogue was the responsibility of Aschwin Lippe and John Pope, with assistance from James Cahill. When the text of the catalogue was sent to Taipei for corrections and comments, however, a controversy erupted. The American scholars who wrote the catalogue had given each item an attribution and a date or period conforming to the latest Western scholarship and research, even though this information was sometimes at variance with the traditional labels taken from the eighteenth-century palace catalogues compiled under the Qianlong Emperor. Cahill and other American scholars saw the matter of the corrected labels as an issue of professional integrity; Cahill pointed out that this catalogue would be used as a teaching tool for decades.

As in the case of the 1935–1936 loan to London, the Chinese side disagreed with many of the newly assigned labels, dates, and attributions. At the National Palace Museum on Taiwan, the traditional labels and attributions were used even when a work was tacitly understood to be at variance. For the Americans to presume to change an attribution or date was considered, as it had been in 1936, an affront to the Chinese. The message that came back from Taiwan was essentially, restore the traditional labels or the loan exhibition will be cancelled.

Fortunately the Republic of China's ambassador to the United States, George Yeh, understood the delicacy of the situation and immediately called a conference at the embassy in Washington. John Walker, director of the National Gallery, the first venue for the planned exhibition, said it was the policy of the National Gallery always to use whatever attribution was claimed by the lender of a work of art. Cahill objected. Yeh then resolved the deadlock by asking the Republic of China's consular official in charge of cultural affairs to work out a compromise with Cahill. This they achieved. An example of the compromise can be seen in the attribution of the first item in the catalogue. This handscroll, Foreign Envoy with Tribute Bearers, traditionally attributed to Yen Liben of the seventh century, is not accepted as such by modern scholarship, Chinese or Western. It does, however, carry a very old label, written in the calligraphy of Emperor Song Huizong of the twelfth century. The catalogue's compromise was to give the traditional attribution to the seventh century artist and then to add in the notes: "One body of opinion declines to support this attribution and assigns the painting to a later date."[20] Thus face-saving and intellectual honesty were both served.

The political ramifications of the art loan were not overlooked in the catalogue. In the catalogue introduction, Wang Shih-chieh wrote, "In these troubled times . . . a fuller understanding of Chinese art and culture by the American people, on whose shoulders largely rests the future of the free world, assumes a new significance. This exhibition may also serve as a reminder that the free Chinese are fighting to save their cultural heritage as much as to recover lost territories."[21] The foreword for the American catalogue focused on the educational benefits of the exhibit. It optimistically asserted that because "the American public has become accustomed to the best in every phase of Chinese art . . . the Republic of China has [therefore] generously agreed to exhibit in our museums a selected group of masterpieces." The foreword also asserted that the exhibition would "sharpen the standards of scholars."[22]

Once the labeling controversy was resolved, the American exhibition of Chinese Art Treasures was a great success. Although only half as many paintings were lent to the United States in 1961–1962 as had been to London in 1935–1936, the selections were of the highest quality and were presented in an austere fashion with no distracting concessions to popular taste (such as using embroidered hanging scrolls as decorative background panels for porcelains). Li Lin-ts'an, the curator who traveled with the treasures, gave the following attendance figures in his diary: 144,358 in Washington from May through August 1961; 105,061 in New York from September into November 1961; 47,896 in Boston from December 1961 into January 1962; 59,637 in Chicago from February into April 1962; and 108,254 in San Francisco from May through June 1962.

The exhibit contributed a great deal to American understanding of Chinese art traditions. The landscape paintings were greatly admired on the tour, even by those who did not know how to fully appreciate their brushstroke artistry, although the works of some of the later scholar-painters of the Yuan dynasty were less well understood. According to a detailed American review of the exhibit, "The huge gulf that separates Chinese art, in its more sophisticated manifestations, from the average educated Western 'gallery-goer' will never change until Chinese and Indian art are part of art education from its beginnings."[23] In part to bridge this gulf, lecture series were arranged in conjunction with the exhibition in each city, and a gratifying number of people attended, including many prominent citizens invited to the openings and special events. Li Lin-ts'an wrote in his diary that he found the most knowledgeable public in Boston, which had had the best collection of Chinese painting in the United States since before World War I. In New York a scholarly symposium on the exhibition was held at the Asia Society.

Li also wrote about his many worries concerning transportation en route: trucks were less safe than trains, and at one point train dispatchers temporarily lost the freight car carrying the entire exhibition—although it was found within 24 hours.[24] All treasures were returned safely to Taiwan after their year and a half in the United States. They were then displayed at home, as had been done in 1936 when the treasures returned from London, in part to reassure the Taiwan public that these national treasures had been returned intact.

Several other important developments resulted from the 1961–1962 loan exhibit. Before it opened, the National Palace Museum had sent some objects to be exhibited at the National Gallery and, by previous agreement, two of the paintings were taken to the Freer Gallery for repair and remounting. These were Emperor Song Huizong's *Two Birds on a Branch* and an anonymous painting *The Emperor Minghuang's Flight to Shu*.[25]

Another important benefit of the exhibition in Washington was the ability to make a more complete photographic record of the treasures from Taiwan. James Cahill, who had taken excellent photos of paintings while in Taiwan for his book, *Chinese Painting*, was able to photograph more of these works in Washington before the exhibition opened. Color slide sets were made available at cost to the participating museums as well as to other museums and to most major educational institutions where Chinese art history was taught. These high-quality color slides inaugurated a new era in Chinese painting studies, freeing teachers and scholars from their prior dependence upon poor reproductions.

Cahill then went back to Taiwan to complete his goal of photographing all of the art collection of the National Palace Museum. The project was accomplished expeditiously between November 13, 1963, and April 23, 1964. All the famous paintings were photographed, as well as a selection of other objects in the museum collections, altogether approximately six thousand black and white and two thousand color negatives.

In return for allowing Cahill to photograph works from both the Main List and the Simple List, which amounted to virtually all the paintings in the museum, the museum asked for photographic negatives of objects of Chinese art in foreign museums and private collections. Cahill agreed to provide prints of as many as he could assemble from Western collections.

A NEW HOME IN TAIPEI

Undoubtedly the most important development that grew out of the loan exhibit to the United States was that it helped to make American funds available for a much larger museum to house the imperial treasures in Taipei.[26] In 1960, the United States Agency for International Development (USAID) awarded a grant of $888,000 (NT$32 million—New Taiwan dollars) for a national museum on Taiwan. This grant was nearly matched by a contribution from the Republic of China government totaling NT$30 million. In the fall of 1960 the Executive Yuan began to develop plans for a permanent museum. Completed in 1965, it was formally christened in honor of the centenary of Sun Yat-sen's birth. Located on the northern outskirts of Taipei, the new National Palace Museum made it possible, for the first time since 1932, for the general public to view a wide selection of the imperial treasures that had been removed to Taiwan.

Since its official opening in 1965, the National Palace Museum has been enlarged and improved many times. For many years the museum holdings were static, but Director Chin Hsiao-yi inaugurated an active acquisition policy. Despite the richness of the old Qing palace collection, it was not a systematic collection typical of a national museum. Qing emperors had little interest in, and hence had not collected, such items as Neolithic pottery, ancient stone inscriptions, export porcelains, and bronze Buddhist statuary from all dynasties. Burial objects were not included in the imperial collection because they were considered inauspicious, as were rubbings from tombstones. Weaponry of any kind was banned from the confines of the imperial palace. The imperial collection also lacked any paintings by the Four Monks of the late Ming period, who were considered political dissidents under Qing rule. And in the nineteenth century, when China's economy and political power were declining, the habit of collecting by the court gradually lapsed. Thus there were important gaps in the collection of nineteenth-century painters and calligraphers, although patronage of the minor arts, cloisonné, jade carving, weaving, and embroidery was continuous.

The National Palace Museum has made up for some of these deficiencies through donations, loans, and purchases. Gifts and loans were first accepted in 1967, but not until 1985 did the museum have an acquisitions budget of US$2 million per year. One notable purchase, in 1986, was a famous calligraphy by the Song dynasty artist, calligrapher, and poet Su Shi (1037–1101). Titled *Poems Written at Hangzhou on the Cold Meal Festival*, it had been lost to the imperial collection since 1860, when the Anglo-French Expeditionary Force destroyed the Emperor Qianlong's Yuanmingyuan

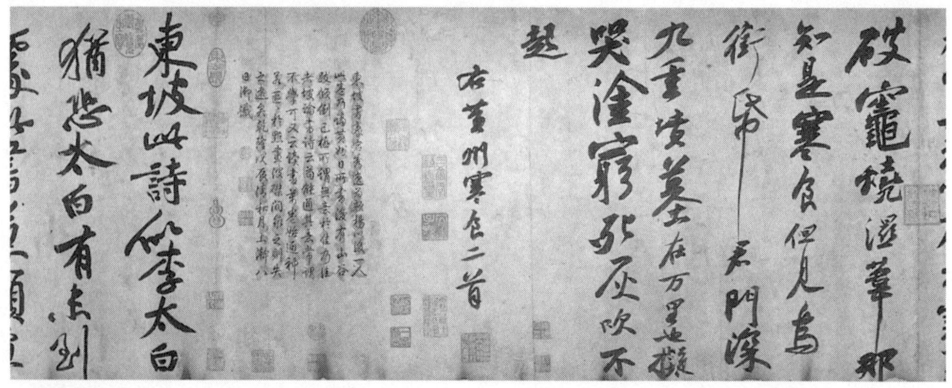

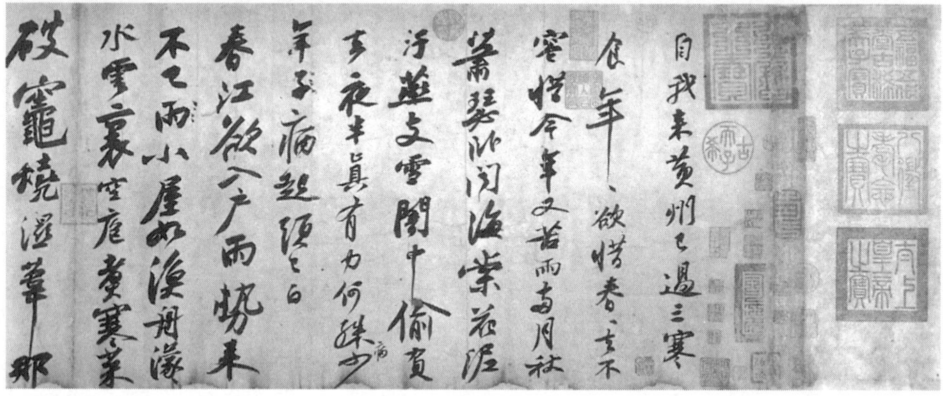

Su Shi (1037–1101), *Poems Written at Huangzhou on the Cold Meal Festival.* Handscroll, ink on paper, datable to 1082. National Palace Museum, Taipei.

palace complex. It had then been owned in Japan and survived both the Kanto earthquake of 1923 and the Allied bombings.

The museum has become an educational center for the local population as well as an important resource for students of Chinese art history from other countries. In 1986 the museum added a Contemporary Art Gallery, which displays the works of Chinese modern masters of painting and calligraphy, and in 1995, to mark the seventieth anniversary of the founding of the Palace Museum on the mainland, a documents and library building was added to house rare books and imperial archives. This major group of palace treasures had seldom been exhibited before the addition. The museum also invites loan exhibitions from Western collections. In

1995, for example, a selection of landscape paintings from the Louvre was exhibited in the new documents building.

In 1996, the National Palace Museum again became embroiled in controversy—and, again, the source of the controversy had to do with an international exhibition to the United States. Everything about the exhibit became problematic and controversial—from the funding and sponsorship for the exhibition; to the selection, preparation, and shipping of the art; to the name of the exhibition. This was, after all, the first time that an exhibition from Taiwan's National Palace Museum collection had been considered for the United States since 1979, when the U.S. government ceased recognizing the Republic of China (ROC) government in Taipei in favor of the People's Republic of China (PRC) government in Beijing.

Politics were involved in the exhibition from the start. For one thing, there was the very real issue of whether the PRC government would attempt to lay legal claim to the exhibited objects. This issue was finessed by Washington's assurance to the governments in both Beijing and Taipei that such claims would not be heard in U.S. courts.[27] Then there was the question of the name of the exhibition. The National Palace Museum (on behalf of the ROC government) fought hard to include the term "Republic of China" in the exhibition name. This battle was eventually lost, and the ROC government acquiesced to "Splendors of Imperial China: Treasures from the National Palace Museum in Taipei." Politics also affected the financing and sponsorship of the exhibition. Cognizant of their growing financial interests in mainland China, Citibank and Mobil withdrew as corporate sponsors. Even Acer America, the U.S. subsidiary of Taiwan's major computer manufacturer (with rapidly growing manufacturing facilities on the mainland), pulled out.[28]

The exhibition opened at the Metropolitan Museum of Art in New York, and then traveled to the Art Institute in Chicago, the Asian Art Museum in San Francisco, and the National Gallery of Art in Washington DC. The tour had been carefully negotiated over the course of several years by Chin Hsiao-yi, director of the National Palace Museum, and Wen Fong, curator of Chinese art at the Metropolian Museum. Contracts for the exhibition were signed in 1994. Wen Fong had all of the sponsors and backers lined up—before they got cold feet when several U.S. corporations withdrew sponsorship in 1995. It is unclear if Beijing actually brought pressure—explicit or subtle—on these potential sponsors, or whether they voluntarily concluded that such a high-profile affiliation with Taiwan may not accrue to their best commercial interests on the Chinese mainland. Once this occurred, the ROC parliament (Legislative Yuan) stepped into the lurch and earmarked NT$3.1 million to help underwrite the exhibition.[29]

Then there was the all-important issue of which paintings and objects were to be selected for the exhibition. Altogether 475 works of art were selected, including 27 works on the so-called Restricted List (early paintings dating from the seventh to the fourteenth centuries). These prize paintings are rarely displayed—usually only for forty days every three years.[30] When it became known on Taiwan that these precious treasures were slated for inclusion in the exhibition to be sent to America, a firestorm erupted on the island. Public protests took place outside the museum and the legislature mandated an inquiry. Just as the earmarked art was about to be crated and shipped to New York, the Legislative Yuan banned the 27 restricted items for "export." A major imbroglio ensued over a two-week period before a government committee offered a compromise ruling: 23 of the 27 restricted items would be withdrawn from the exhibition, 4 could be included, and 19 other important works were restricted to only forty days of exhibiting. The Met took 6 of these works, and distributed the rest among the other museums on the tour.[31] In the end, the Splendors of Imperial China tour was a success, although the political and logistical complications involved were a stark reminder of the diplomatic sensitivities surrounding the collection and the continuing struggle between the governments on both sides of the Taiwan Strait to use their respective collections to bolster their political legitimacy domestically and internationally.

The National Palace Museum today remains a wonderful repository of China's imperial art and one of the great museums of the world. The maintenance and display of the collection is of an international standard. The collection has also grown since coming to the island in 1948. Originally comprised largely of Ming and Qing painting, with a number of ancient bronzes, the museum has managed to expand its collection by acquiring early pottery, Neolithic jades, more bronzes, Buddhist sculpture from the Six Dynasties period, and calligraphy.[32]

Since the spring of 2000, under the government of the Democratic Progressive Party and President Chen Shui-bian, the National Palace Museum has been directed by Tu Cheng-sheng, with Shih Shou-ch'ien and Lin Po-ting serving as deputy directors. Consistent with the emphasis of the Chen government's concerted efforts to play up Taiwan's indigenous history and cultural distinctiveness while playing down the island's historical and cultural links to the mainland, the National Palace Museum's stated goals for the twenty-first century include incorporating native Taiwanese culture and art into the collections and programs. According to Director Tu, "In the new century, the museum will step down from its imperial throne and into the life of the local community, absorbing the rich vigor of Taiwan and introducing another dimension of culture to the people of this precious island."[33]

Whether the National Palace Museum collection will ever again be merged with the rest of the imperial collection in the Palace Museum in Beijing remains as elusive a question as whether Taiwan will itself ever reach an accommodation with the mainland. With the independence-minded Democratic Progressive Party in power, this is looking increasingly doubtful. According to Director Tu, this will never occur: "Its [the National Palace Museum] home is clearly understood, and it will remain here for all time, united with the new Taiwan."[34] Thus, it is clear that politics and art remain as inextricably intertwined for the future of the imperial collection as they have for almost three thousand years.

6

The Gugong in Beijing:
National Treasure and Political Object

By December 1948, Palace Museum director Ma Heng had apparently made his decision not to join the exodus to Taiwan. As director of the Palace Museum (Gugong), he saw it as his responsibility to protect the imperial collections in the Forbidden City during this period of great uncertainty. In a letter he wrote to Hang Liwu at this time, he questioned whether taking the best of the imperial collections to Taiwan was the optimum way to protect and preserve them.

On December 14, 1948, with Beiping under siege by the Communist forces, Ma Heng ordered the four main gates of the Forbidden City closed. This signaled an interregnum for the museum between the Nationalists' withdrawal and the advance of the Communists. It underscored Ma's decision not to ship treasures for the Nationalist government and made clear that he would remain at his post. For those of the staff who had chosen not to join the exodus to Taiwan in the fall of 1948 or who stayed on at the Gugong because they had no other choice, Ma Heng's decision was an important boost for morale.

THE GUGONG DURING THE PEOPLE'S REPUBLIC OF CHINA

The Communists entered the capital on January 31, 1949, and Zhu De, the commander of the People's Liberation Army, immediately established military occupation of the Forbidden City and the Palace Museum. The Communists' first task was to clean up the capital city. According to one witness, "Between 1949 and 1951, piles of trash and tons of garbage and stinking scum littering the streets and byways . . . were carted away."[1] Physical conditions within the Forbidden City itself were no less shocking. According to one account, "When the museum committee came back to the Palace early in 1949, soon after Beijing was liberated, they found it piled with rubbish and overgrown with weeds. Parts were half buried with windblown sand. Some 250,000 tons of it were hauled away in 83,000 truckloads."[2] Another source describes the situation this way: "The entire area of 72,000 square cubic meters of the Forbidden City were overgrown with trees and grass that had taken root, and there were large piles of trash, slag, and cinder. Some of the ancient trees were hollow and their branches were broken. Some were stricken with insects and others were

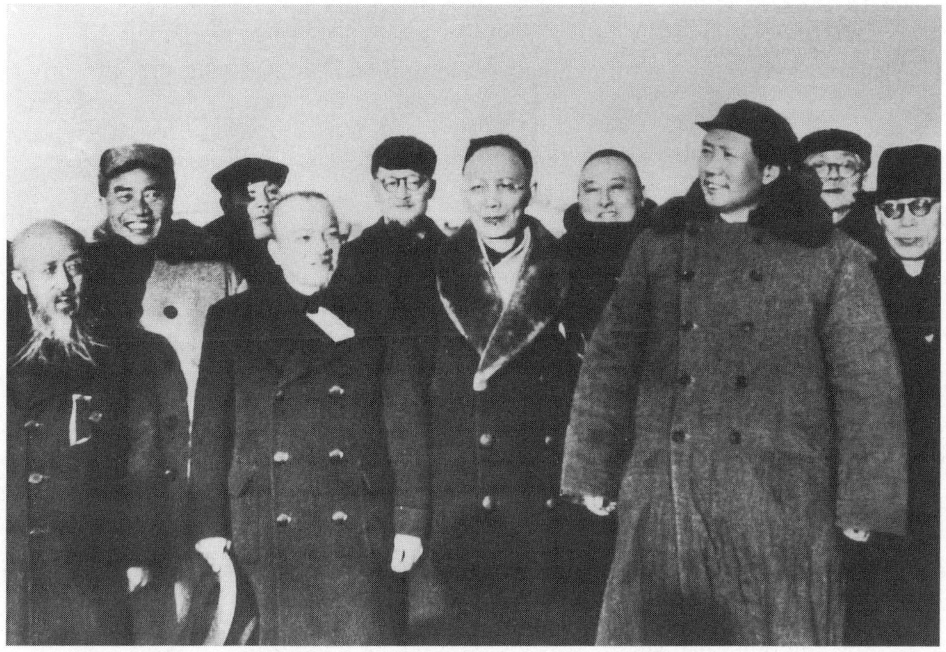

Zhu De (second from left) and Mao Zedong (third from right) on eve of entering Beiping, 1948. Xinhua News Agency Photo Archive, Beijing.

withered. The halls and pavilions were worn down due to lack of repair for years."[3] Within three years, construction workers had repaired and renovated 80,000 square meters of land and buildings, and by 1957 the entire Forbidden City had been restored.[4]

Administratively, the Gugong was immediately placed under the control of the transitional government established by the Communist Party.[5] On February 19, 1949, the Beiping Municipal Military Control Commission established a Cultural Takeover Committee, which dispatched a three-person team (Qian Junrui, Yin Da, Wang Yeqiu) to the Gugong to inspect the premises and establish a "handling and takeover group" (*banli anguan shizu*). On March 6 this group convened a large meeting in the Hall of Supreme Harmony (Taihe Dian) in the Forbidden City. All Gugong staff members were required to attend and hear a report by Yin Da, the director of the Department of Historical Relics of the Cultural Takeover Committee. Yin formally declared that the Cultural Takeover Committee was taking (temporary) control of the Gugong (ending Ma Heng's tenure). In June 1949 the Beiping Military Control Commission was dissolved, and along with it the Cultural Takeover Committee. The Gugong was then placed under the administration of the North China Higher Education Committee (Huabei Gaodeng Jiaoyu Weiyuanhui). But, this too, was to be temporary.

When the People's Republic of China (PRC) was established on October 1, 1949, the Gugong was immediately placed under the jurisdiction of the new Ministry of Culture (although for practical purposes the museum was administered by this ministry's Bureau of Cultural Relics). Except for a brief period during 1958–60, when it reverted to being administered by Beijing Municipality, the Gugong has been under the authority of the Bureau of Cultural Relics until 2002, when its supervision was placed directly with the Ministry of Culture. When the name of the city was changed from Beiping (northern peace) to Beijing (northern capital) in February 1950, the Gugong was renamed the National Beijing Palace Museum (Guoli Beijing Gugong Bowuyuan). This was shortened in June 1951 to simply the Palace Museum (Gugong Bowuyuan).[6]

Within months of taking power, China's new leaders initiated efforts to make retrievals and purchases for the Gugong. Chinese Communist Party chairman Mao Zedong and State Council premier Zhou Enlai paid personal attention to the museum and to recovering and expanding its collection. This was a clear demonstration that China's former imperial palaces and cultural treasures were still viewed as an important symbol of political legitimacy, even under the new Communist regime.

Early Acquisitions

The early efforts of the People's Republic to recover the imperial treasures were remarkably far-reaching, especially since the new nation lacked the financial wherewithal to buy back those objects that had made their way to Hong Kong and foreign countries. The recovery effort involved institutions and individuals, gifts and purchases, and work both inside and outside of China.

In the early 1950s, most of the imperial treasures were shipped back to the Gugong from Nanjing, except for 2,211 crates that were sealed and stored. Because Nanjing had been the capital during wartime, and because the Central Museum there had housed the imperial collection, the museum was given the special designation *bowuyuan*, an honorific term reserved for the museums in Beijing, Nanjing, and Taiwan. In 1999, when the Gugong requested that the Nanjing Museum (formerly called the Central Museum) return the remaining crates, the Nanjing authorities politely declined to do so, noting that they had patiently stored them for more than half a century and, at any rate, the Gugong had a surfeit of material. At the end of 2003, records indicate that 834 crates with several thousand objects, primarily ceramics and decorative arts, still reside in Nanjing. Also, according to several connoisseurs, the installation of imperial porcelains in the Nanjing Museum today indicates that the last boxes did not all remain sealed.

The newly established Bureau of Cultural Relics of the Ministry of Culture (Wenhua Bu Wenwu Ju) played an active role in the recovery effort. Headed by Vice Minister Zheng Zhenduo, the bureau recruited Zhang Heng (Zhang Congyu), a noted Shanghai connoisseur of painting and calligraphy, who in turn recruited Xu Bangda.[7] Xu would go on to play an instrumental role in the life of the Gugong during the PRC, particularly in his efforts to recover and return the lost imperial treasures to the museum.

The Gugong established a Cultural Relics Collection Group (Wenwu Zhengji Zu) to evaluate the authenticity of the recovered objects. The museum in general and this group in particular began an intensive drive to recruit trained art historians and experienced staff. The Collection Group included a number of noteworthy experts and was divided into five subgroups to evaluate incoming objects and to begin rebuilding the museum collection: jade articles (Qiao Yousheng), ceramics (Sun Yingzhou and Geng Baochang), bronzes (Wang Wenchang), painting and calligraphy (Wang Yikun and Liu Jiu'an), and stone rubbings (Ma Ziyun).[8] Palace Museum director Wu Zhongchao oversaw the recruitment of new staff. In about 1953, military veterans returning from the Korean War were assigned to the security and maintenance staff—many were later promoted to administrative positions in the museum. Thus began a tendency, which continued through the 1990s, to staff the Gugong administration with People's Liberation Army (PLA) veterans. This tendency is certainly not one made on aesthetic grounds, but probably reflects the government's view of the museum as an object of national security. During the Cultural Revolution (1966–1976), only two institutions were physically and politically protected from the rampaging Red Guards by executive order of the Central Committee and State Council: the nuclear weapons complex at Lop Nur in Qinghai province and the Gugong in Beijing.

Various methods were used to recover the Gugong's art and artifacts. The central government sometimes lent assistance, while other efforts required the ingenuity of those involved in the reclamation.

The first method of recovery was by government order. All government, military, and Communist Party organs, as well as all public institutions and citizens organizations, were instructed to inventory their holdings and to ascertain if any artwork was present. Any art objects discovered were to be submitted to the Gugong's Cultural Relics Collection Group for evaluation. In all, this effort netted 165,061 objects from a wide range of government and nongovernmental organs.[9]

Xu Bangda and the Bureau of Cultural Relics were given the job of receiving, authenticating, and inventorying the objects. This laborious process normally took place at a special site in the Circular City (Tuan Cheng) in Beihai Park in central Beijing.[10] In a 1992 interview, Xu recalled several ways that the museum acquired artworks in the early days of the People's Republic.[11] In a tiny unheated room over one of the main gates in the Forbidden City, Xu and Zhang Congyu reviewed an amazingly rich hoard of paintings and calligraphies brought in by people who were ready to exchange their art for sorely needed cash. Each day from morning until noon, and from afternoon until evening, Xu selected the best from what he saw and negotiated the price down before seeking final approval from his superiors. As many well-known collectors lived outside Beijing, Xu's work occasionally took him to other cities. In Shanghai, Xu was able to obtain some famous old collections. Wu Hufan, a renowned collector in Shanghai, was allowed to keep his collection until his death, after which it was confiscated and listed as "donated" to the Shanghai Museum. The widow of Pang Yuanji, a great Shanghai collector, had to sell his collection to the Shanghai and Palace museums.

A second method was to purchase objects from work units (danwei), cultural relics shops, auction companies, and individuals. Xu Bangda formed a team of specialists (including Tang Lan, Chen Wanli, and Zhu Jiajin) who fanned out across the country to locate and buy back objects. They concentrated their efforts in Changchun, Dalian, Shenyang, Tianjin, Shanghai, Suzhou, and Hong Kong. The antique stores and curio shops in the Liulichang district of Beijing provided an additional trove of treasures. Such purchases within China yielded an additional 53,951 objects, most of which were acquired during the 1950s.[12]

Purchasing art objects in Hong Kong presented an obstacle, given that it was administered as a colony by Britain and the price of such items was considerably higher in the territory than in the PRC. Many of the more valuable objects from the Gugong found their way to Hong Kong and were being put up for auction at the major British houses. When Premier Zhou learned of this development, on November 5, 1951, he ordered the Bureau of Cultural Relics to form a special team of experts to go to Hong

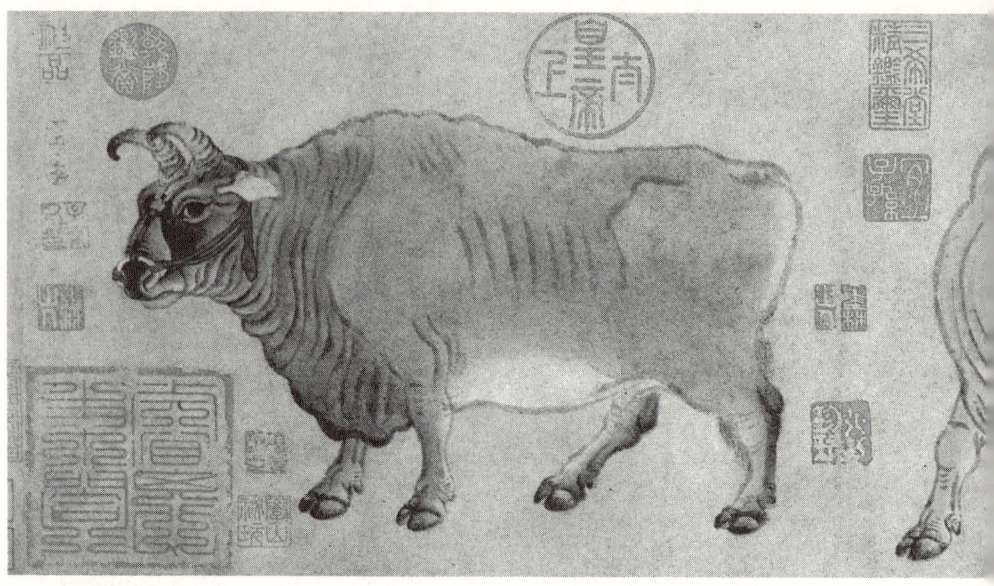

Attributed to Han Huang, *Five Oxen*. Handscroll, ink and color on paper. Palace Museum, Beijing.

Kong, with a large amount of money allocated by the central government, for the express purpose of buying back a number of the most famous artworks from the imperial collection.

The team went to Hong Kong in December 1951 and was successful in purchasing two famous Eastern Jin dynasty calligraphies, Wang Xianzhi's *Zhongqiu Tie* (*Mid-Autumn Letter*) and Wang Xun's *Boyuan Tie* (*Letter to Boyuan*). Both had been taken from the Gugong by Pu Yi, who had left them with the Yanye Bank (the former Salt Industry Bank) in Beiping as collateral.[13] They had been purchased by a Hong Kong connoisseur who, in turn, had left them as collateral with a British bank in the colony.[14] Both of these calligraphies bore the seals and original inscription of Song Emperor Huizong and had subsequently been in the personal collection of the Qianlong Emperor, who had kept them in a study attached to his residence within the palace—the Hall for Cultivating the Mind (Yang Xin Dian).

In addition to securing these two invaluable pieces, the purchasing team was also able to acquire the *Wu Niu Tu* (*Five Oxen*), attributed to Han Huang of the Tang dynasty, and *Han Xizai Yeyan Tu* (*Night Revels of Han*

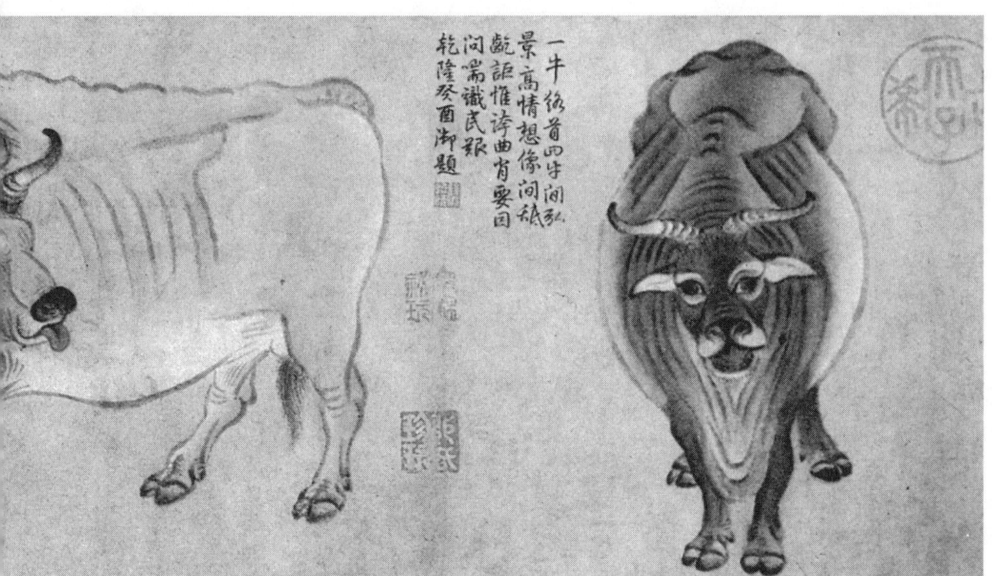

Xizai), attributed to Gu Hongzhang of the Five Dynasties.[15] These two paintings were purchased for the equivalent of 50,000 renminbi (approximately US$6,000 at today's exchange rate but worth many times that at 1950 prices).[16]

A third way in which artworks were recovered was by donation; many families voluntarily donated items in their possession. For example, the collection of Zhu Wenjun, who had worked in the Palace Museum for a decade from 1926 to 1936, included substantial collections of furniture, books, rubbings, paintings, bronzes, and jades. In 1953, Zhu Jiajin and his brothers, at the urging of their mother, gave their father's collection of seven hundred rubbings to the Gugong.[17]

A fourth source of valuable imperial art came from China's new Communist leaders. Chairman Mao fancied and collected ancient calligraphy in particular, although he also had a hankering for classical painting. He donated a number of pieces to the Gugong during the 1950s, including the famous Tang dynasty calligraphy by the poet Li Bai, *Shangyang Tai Tie* (*Writing on the Terrace*) and Qian Dongbi's *Lanting Shisanba* (Thirteen Colophons to the Orchid Pavilion). Later, as Mao became enamored with reading imperial histories, he would borrow ancient texts from the Gugong—but was reportedly careful to record each one removed (forty-six volumes

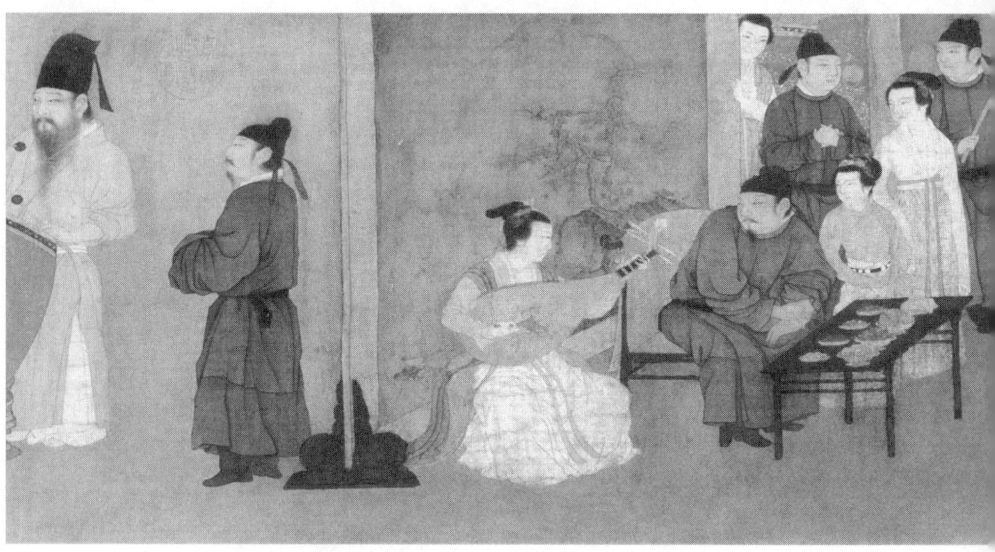

Gu Hongzhong (Five Dynasties period, 907–960), *Night Revels of Han Xizai.* Handscroll, ink and color on silk. Palace Museum, Beijing.

between 1959 and 1963).[18] This may account for many of the ancient texts and tablets that littered Mao's study in the Zhongnanhai, where he received foreign visitors.

Chairman Mao and Premier Zhou played instrumental roles supporting the Gugong's efforts to reclaim its collection and to reconstitute itself as the national museum of imperial treasures. They may have been proletarian Marxist-Leninists in other respects, but they were also staunch nationalists. For them, the Gugong was a national institution—one that, like the rest of China, had been subjected to foreign imperialism and plunder. An important element in restoring China's dignity as a nation was to protect and restore its heritage as a civilization. There may have been no greater such symbol than the Gugong. As such, both leaders attached particular importance to the restoration of the Gugong as a symbol of China's cultural greatness and past. Mao and Zhou visited the Gugong on several occasions in the early 1950s (Mao in 1951, 1952, and three times in 1954; Zhou visited four times in 1950 and twice again in 1951).[19]

A fifth method of acquiring the lost art of the Gugong was to appeal to patriotic overseas Chinese. Two individuals, Han Huaizhun and Yang Lingfu, are illustrative.

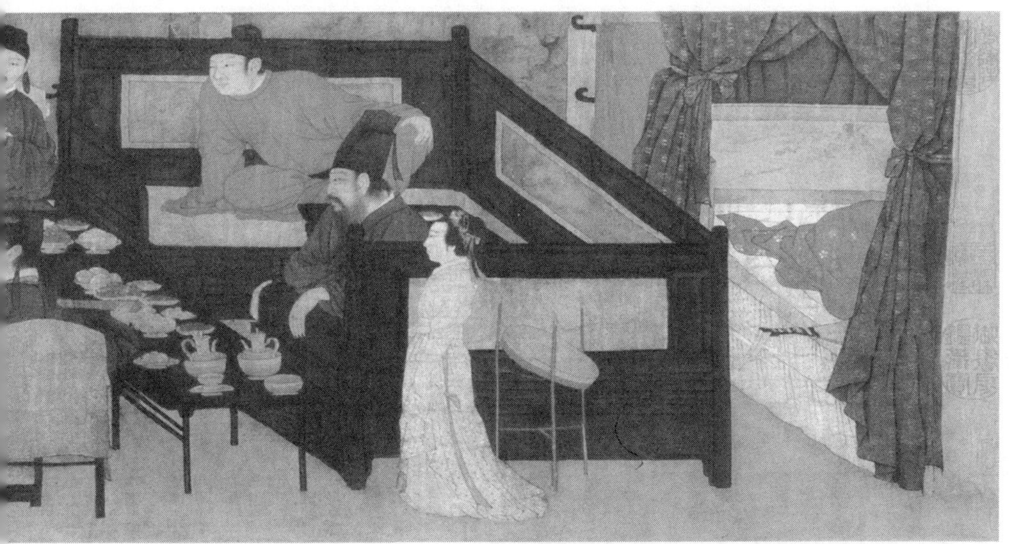

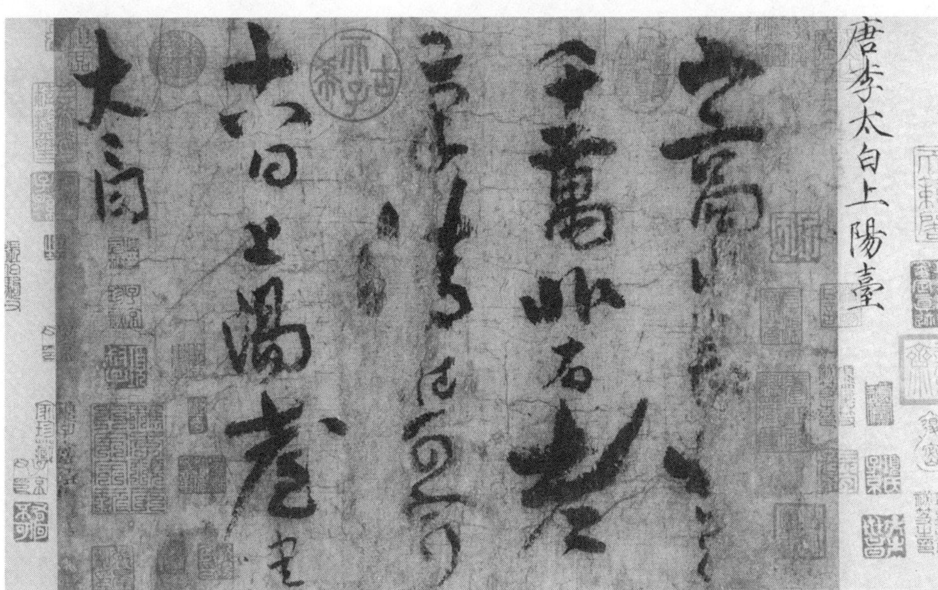

Li Bai (701–762), ***Writing on the Terrace.*** Handscroll, ink on paper. Palace Museum, Beijing.

Han Huaizhun was a businessman and well-known connoisseur of pottery and porcelain who lived in Singapore. He often lamented the loss of Chinese ancient art treasures to foreign countries (including those that were well-preserved and displayed in museums). Han sold many of his

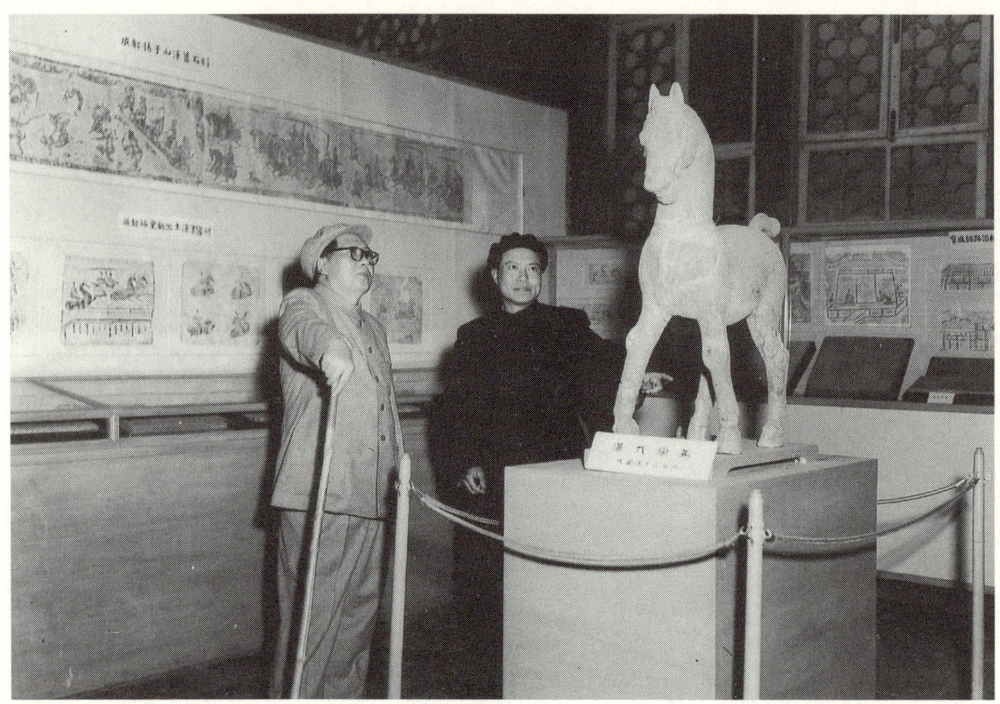

Chairman Mao Zedong viewing a Han dynasty horse in the Palace Museum (1954).
Xinhua News Agency Photo Archive.

commercial holdings in order to purchase imperial art at auctions in Southeast Asia, Hong Kong, and Europe. In the early 1960s, Han returned and settled in the People's Republic and brought with him more than 2,000 objects he had acquired—all of which he donated to the Gugong. These were mainly ceramics from the Song, Yuan, Ming, and Qing dynasties.[20]

Madame Yang Lingfu was Chinese American and a collector of Chinese art. She was a devout patriot who corresponded with Madame Song Qingling (Sun Yat-sen's widow and sister of Chiang Kai-shek's wife Song Mei-ling). Song Qingling opted to stay on the mainland after 1949, much to the consternation of the Kuomintang regime that fled to Taiwan, and she played an important symbolic role in attracting overseas Chinese to return to the PRC. In the early 1970s, Yang Lingfu made up her mind to return and wrote to Premier Zhou to this effect (presumably Yang intended to bring her art collection with her). Unfortunately, her health declined rapidly and she died in the United States before being able to realize her ambition. Her final will stipulated, however, that her collection be returned to China. A decade later her nephew and his wife, Yang Tongyi and Rong Shuren, visited the United States from China for the purpose of collecting and shipping Yang Lingfu's collection back to Beijing. With the help of the Chinese ambassador in Washington, former Minister of Culture Huang Zhen, they succeeded in retrieving hundreds of Madame Yang's paintings and jade articles.[21]

These two examples are not isolated cases. Many patriotic Chinese overseas sent their art objects back to China, including well-known Hong Kong and Macao collectors like Ye Yi, Luo Guixiang, Yang Yongde, He Xian, and others; and much of what came from overseas found its way into the Gugong collection.

There were other sources for recovering the Gugong's dispersed art treasures, such as confiscation of cultural relics seized by foreign entities inside China. For example, in the late 1940s, after the end of World War II, Chinese (Nationalist) Customs confiscated thirty-one crates containing 1,136 items that had been held by the German Mobile Bank and the Germany-China Bank and nineteen containers consisting of 21,749 items from the American Chinese School. These items were stored in the Palace Museum and formally became part of the collection in 1974.[22] Altogether, according to a definitive 1999 study of the Gugong's collection, individual contributors overseas and in China contributed 21,875 items to the museum.[23]

These combined methods for tracking down and reclaiming lost art from the Gugong collection achieved impressive results. Since 1949, and by the sixtieth anniversary of the founding of the Palace Museum in 1985, the museum's collection had grown to nearly one million items.[24] As of 2000, 240,000 objects had been reclaimed.[25] As of 2004, of the approximately one million items in the museum's inventory, Director Zheng Xinmiao estimates that 250,000 are in need of repair (mainly manuscripts).[26] Of this total, clearly the most important and valuable art that has been recouped was that taken from the palace by Pu Yi and his entourage when they vacated the Forbidden City in 1924.

TRACKING DOWN PU YI'S TREASURES

Tracking down and returning the thousands of precious objects taken from the Gugong by the "last emperor" Pu Yi and his brother Pu Jie was, of course, a critical part of restoring the collection and the museum. The Pu brothers had made off with some of the most valuable artworks and jewelry, which were easiest to carry and had the greatest value.

As noted in chapter 4, many valuable objects in the collection were pilfered by Pu Yi's assistants and were sold to antique dealers and curio shops in northern cities (particularly Tianjin). After Pu Yi was captured by Soviet forces, who occupied Manchuria at the end of the war in 1945, much of the Dongbeihuo collection was discovered in trunks at his Changchun palace. He kept some of the most valuable jewelry in a false-bottom suitcase, which he had with him when he was apprehended.[27] Pu Yi was held as a prisoner of war (POW) and the materials were confiscated and held by the POW warders at Fushun. When Chinese Communist forces took control of the region and the Fushun Prison in late 1947, they also took control of Pu Yi and the remnant collection. In 1949, after the founding of the PRC, Pu Yi was subjected to a show trial and sentenced to life in prison for "crimes against the people." He continued to be detained at the Fushun Prison, a period portrayed in Bertolucci's film, *The Last Emperor*. For some time Pu Yi was recalcitrant and refused to succumb to the interrogation and brainwashing techniques of his jailers. Ultimately, they prevailed and the former royal relented and repudiated his past through extended written and verbal "self-criticisms." Having adopted a new persona, and agreeing to "serve the people" for the remainder of his life, Pu Yi's sentence was commuted in December 1959 by executive order of Premier Zhou.[28]

While Pu Yi returned to the capital to live out his life in obscurity, the treasures remained in Fushun. It was not until 1964, on another executive order of Premier Zhou, that these objects (245 in all) were shipped back to the Gugong in Beijing. They included a gold inlaid pendent used by Emperor Qianlong, a Six Dynasties stone screen, and valuable jewelry of Empresses Long Yu and Ci Xi (including diamond and sapphire rings,

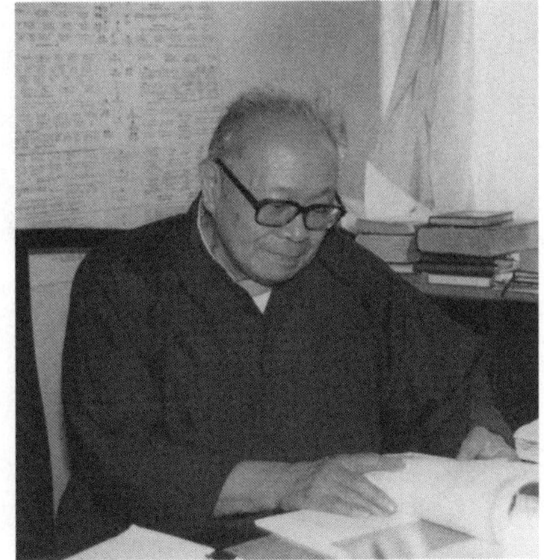

Liaoning Provincial Museum director Yang Renkai (date unknown). From Ancient Chinese Calligraphy and Painting Authentication Group, *Masterpieces of Chinese Calligraphy and Painting*, vol. 1, 2.

coral and jade necklaces, and various ornaments made of gold, diamonds, and emeralds).[29]

Yang Renkai, curator of painting and calligraphy at the Liaoning Provincial Museum in Shenyang (formerly part of Manchuria), deserves credit for recovering many of the treasures taken by Pu Yi to Tianjin and later to Manchuria. His book *Record of the Vicissitudes of National Treasures: Investigation of the Dispersed and Lost Calligraphy and Paintings of the Former Palace Museum* is also a treasure trove of adventures, covering two decades tracing every single artwork known to have come from Pu Yi's collection.[30]

The work of tracing Pu Yi's treasures had begun in the 1940s under the direction of Wang Shixiang. Yang Renkai's retrieval methods were similar to Wang's: he alerted the curio shops and informed the public that purchases of sequestered Dongbeihuo loot would be made confidentially and at a fair price. Some paintings were still held by the families of soldiers in Manchuria, who were offered rewards with no threat of persecution when items were brought forth.

Sometimes miraculous things happened. For example, in April 1963 a young man from Harbin, Heilongjiang province, came into the sales department of a famous old art shop in Beijing's Liulichang district, hoping to sell a packet of "junk" paintings and calligraphy for two thousand yuan. The clerk recognized some imperial seals of the inner court and went to find the manager. Yang Renkai, who frequented the shop, was napping

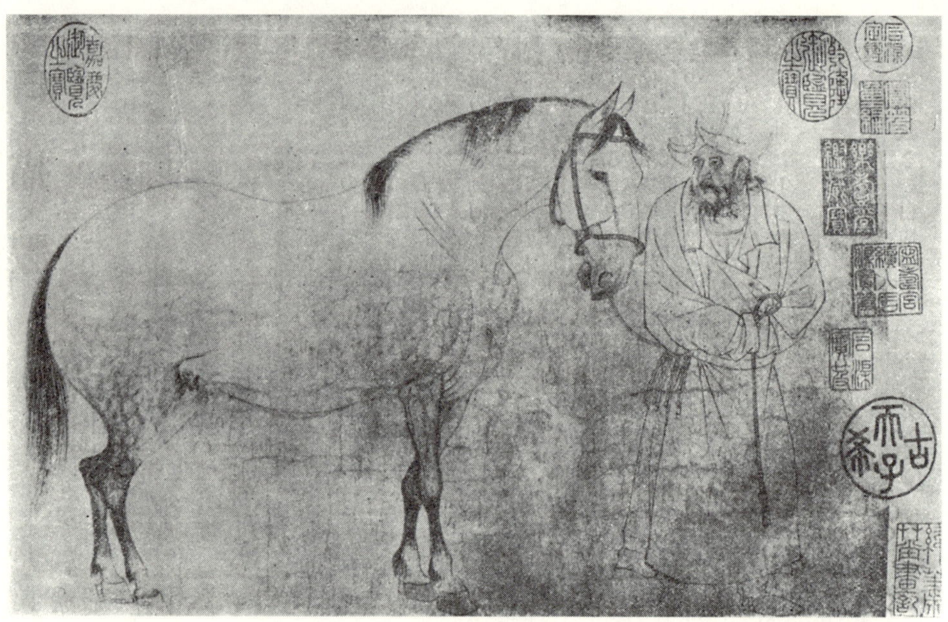

Li Gonglin (c. 1041–1106), *Five Tribute Horses.* Section of a handscroll, ink on paper (a similar example of the artist's horse painting). Collection unknown; from *Kokka*, no. 380 (January 1922).

in the office. Overhearing the word Dongbeihuo, he came out immediately, patiently unfolded the young man's pack, and sorted the scraps. From thirty-seven pieces, Yang claims that he was able to reconstitute two-thirds of the famous Li Gonglin handscroll *Three Horses*, a painting of such significance that its survival even in scraps would be important. Yang recommended that the young man be given the paltry sum he requested for having taken good care of those scraps.[31]

THE GUGONG AND THE POLITICS OF CONTEMPORARY CHINA

During the Maoist era (1949–1976) politics—or more precisely political campaigns—affected all of society. As Julia Andrews's definitive study illustrates, the artistic community was no different.[32] Because of Mao's bias against intellectuals and his belief that art should "serve the people" (*wei renmin fuwu*), artists were subjected to unending harassment and were forced to conform to communist and "practical" themes in their work. Socialist realism permeated the profession and dominated all mediums.

Art that was not "for the masses" (*dazhonghua*) was rejected and criticized as bourgeois. Printmakers, in particular, were forced into this political medium—creating images of sweating steelworkers, laboring peasants, harmonious minorities, enthusiastic revolutionaries, militant children, radical Red Guards, and so on. Even the venerable tradition of landscape painting (*guohua*) was forced to adopt revolutionary themes. However, like other intellectuals, painters and artists found ways to express their individuality within the confines imposed by the state. As Andrews's study shows, some painters (notably those working in watercolors) were particularly adept at using aesthetic techniques within broader political formats. Drawing on Soviet traditions, oil painters were also able to display more individualism of subject and style.

Given this atmosphere affecting the artistic profession writ large, one would expect that the Gugong would have been similarly affected by the Communist cause, proletarian emphasis, and Maoist campaigns that paralyzed the nation for a quarter century. One would expect this, moreover, given the Communist Party's iconoclastic approach to all things traditional in Chinese culture. After all, New China had been born. The new People's Republic drew its legitimacy in large part by attacking foreign imperialism and traditional (i.e., neo-Confucian) ways of doing things. The New China needed to stand tall in the world, attain "wealth and power" (*fu-qiang*), and it could only do so by discarding tradition—and particularly the imperial tradition.

The attacks on tradition peaked, of course, during the Great Proletarian Cultural Revolution (1966–1976), when society was mobilized to "attack the Four Olds" (old ideology, old thought, old habits, and old customs). Rampaging Red Guards fanned out across the country destroying historical sites, knocking heads off of Buddhist statues and figures, and causing incalculable damage to traditional art and artifacts nationwide. But, long before the Cultural Revolution and Four Olds campaign, the Communists had targeted the traditions and institutions of the imperial era as "decadent" and in need of "reformation" (*gaizao*).

Given this general atmosphere, one would assume that the Gugong would have been a primary target for the Communist clergy. This was not

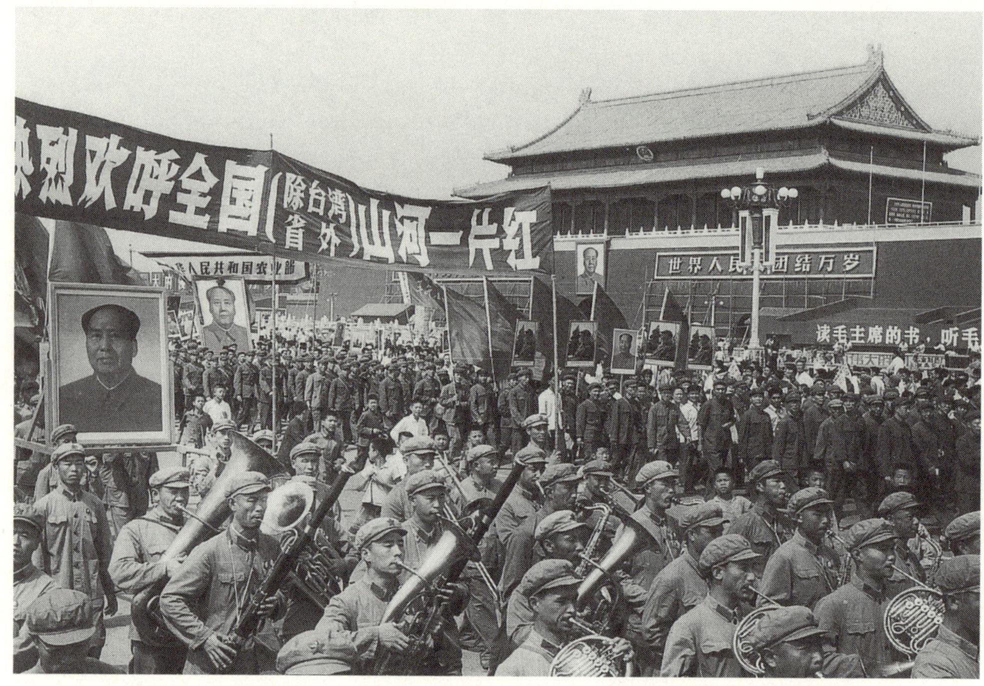

Red Guards marching outside of the Forbidden City during the Great Proletarian Cultural Revolution, 1967. Xinhua News Agency Photo Archive, Beijing.

the case. While the Gugong and its staff *did* feel the effects of various political campaigns, the museum was spared the worst—and, in fact, weathered much of the proletarian madness without great effect. The reason for this relative insulation was primarily because Chairman Mao, Premier Zhou, and other top leaders of the Chinese Communist Party (CCP)— including Zhu De and Guo Moruo—provided their personal protection and approval for the Gugong. As noted above, Mao and Zhou perceived the Gugong as a *national* institution that embodied China's tradition as a civilization—and, to this extent, by embracing the Gugong, these leaders (and the CCP) established a continuity with the nation's past. The decision to locate the leadership compound adjacent to the Forbidden City and the Gugong, in the Zhongnanhai, was a similar symbolic statement. For the Communist leadership, the Gugong represented China's *greatness* as a civilization—a greatness that began to erode seriously during the Qing dynasty but that would be rebuilt under the guidance of the CCP.

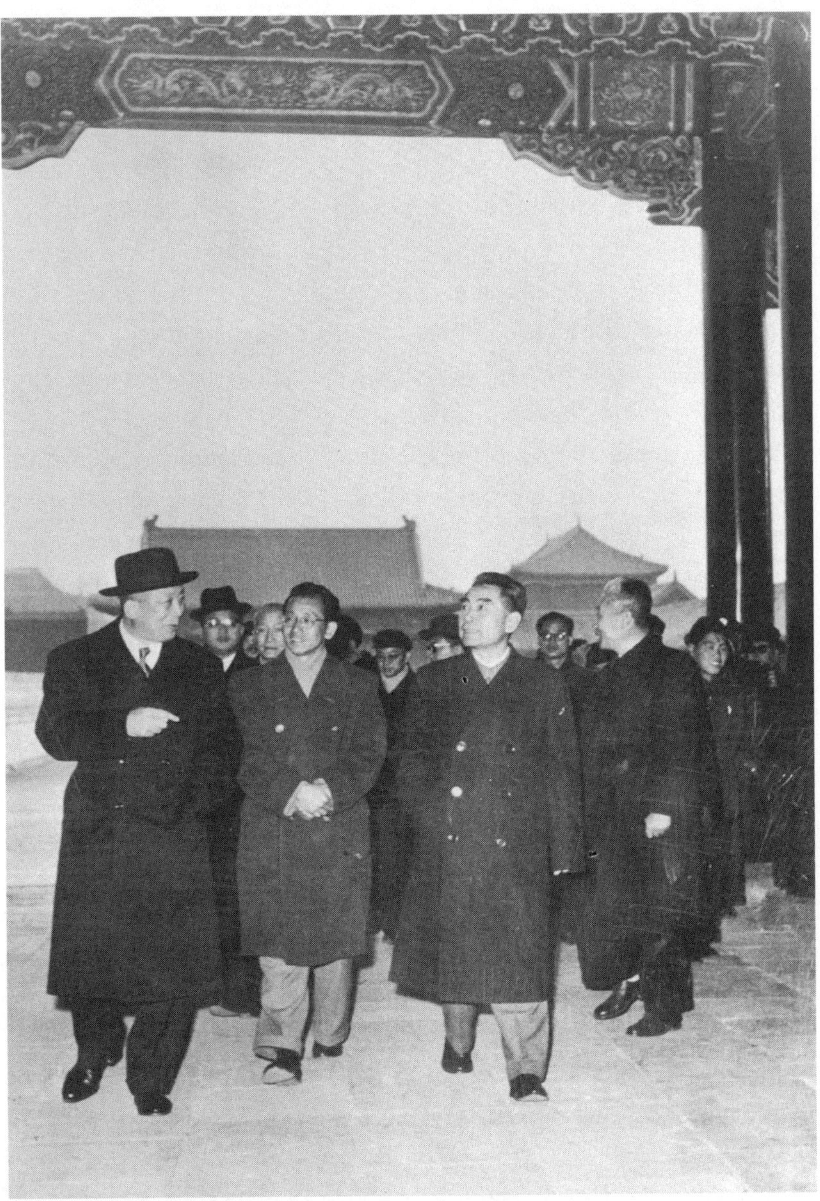

Palace Museum director Wu Zhongchao (left), honorary vice-director Guo Moruo (second from left), and Premier Zhou Enlai touring the Palace Museum, September 21, 1957. Xinhua News Agency Photo Archive, Beijing.

The symbolism of this tie to the past was not lost on China's citizenry, even as they were being subjected to campaign after campaign of political persecution.

While Mao and Zhou saw to it that the Gugong was rebuilt, its collection reconstituted, and that it enjoyed special stature, financing, and physical protection, the museum and its staff nonetheless were not completely insulated and isolated from the politics of the time and what went on outside the high crimson walls of the Forbidden City. Different campaigns affected the Gugong in different ways.

In 1952, for example, in the midst of the Three Antis campaign (anti-corruption, anti-waste, and anti-bureaucracy), the Gugong was criticized for exemplifying government wastefulness. The staff was also accused of extravagant practices, and several individuals were severely reprimanded. The museum's purchases of cultural relics were also criticized as having been made on the subjective judgment of one person without consultation. The Criticize Hu Feng campaign in 1955 had no apparent impact on the museum, although the 1957 Anti-Rightist campaign did: one former Gugong employee recalled that "several" (*jige*) staff members were "capped" (*dai maozi*) as rightists, relieved of their positions, and sent to the countryside for "reform through labor" (*laodong gaizao*).[33] The Great Leap Forward (1958–1960) did adversely affect the Gugong as it did society at large. Around the country old coins and ancient bronze vessels were melted down for reuse as industrial metal in response to the call for the nation to produce steel in backyard furnaces. There are no estimates of how many ancient bronzes were lost or melted down in these years, and it is unclear if any objects in the Gugong were contributed to the smelting effort.[34]

During the Great Leap, central-level organs (*zhongyang jiguan*), of which the Gugong was one, were ordered to downsize their staffs to make available more manpower for forced industrialization in the countryside. As a result, a large number of Gugong staff were temporarily "sent down" (*xiafang*) to the countryside.[35] Many of these individuals had been recruited as guides and general workers during the 1950s and were not professional museum staff.[36] Most of the professional staff who were "sent down" returned to work in 1959.[37] Also during the Great Leap, as part of the museum's efforts to "serve the people," the Gugong's Mass Work Department sent photo exhibitions to cities around the country and dispatched teams armed with slide projectors to communes, factories, mines, and military units in order to popularize and educate the masses about the Gugong and its art.

The largest political campaign of the Maoist era was the Cultural Revolution, which erupted in June 1966 with Mao's order to the masses to "Bombard the Headquarters!" Thus began a frontal assault on party and government institutions. As noted above, a key element of the Cultural Revolution was the attack on Chinese traditional culture—particularly via the effort to "attack the Four Olds." During the Four Olds movement, the Gugong was criticized as being a "bastion of feudalism" (*fengjianzhuyi de laozai*).[38] So the Gugong staff had reason to worry—not only about the themes of the mass movement, but because the Red Guards were gathering by the tens and hundreds of thousands daily just outside the Forbidden City in Tiananmen Square.

At the outset of the Cultural Revolution in June 1966, a group of Red Guards broke into the Gugong, and occupied the Imperial Archives (Dang'an Guan) for three days. As they decamped, they defaced the Gugong walls with big-character slogans such as "Smash the Four Olds! Smash the Forbidden City!"[39] In late June a "work team" (*gongzuohui*) was dispatched to the Gugong by the Cultural Revolution Group (which was headed by Mao's radical wife Jiang Qing and several other ideological zealots). The work team's task was to assess the "redness" of the museum's leading staff. Not surprisingly, the staff members were found to be lacking in appropriate proletarian consciousness.

At this early yet critical juncture, on August 18, 1966, Premier Zhou intervened:

(1) He issued an order (*mingling*) on behalf of the State Council to the Ministry of Culture to close the museum to the public;[40]

(2) he instructed the Central Guards Bureau of the People's Liberation Army (PLA) to seal the Forbidden City's perimeter

and occupy the grounds of the Gugong—a regiment (*ying dui*) was subsequently bivouacked inside the Gugong;[41]

(3) and he issued the directive, "The Gugong belongs to the nation, to the people, and must be protected!"[42]

Four or five days after Zhou's edicts, Red Guards again attempted to enter the Gugong, but were rebuffed by PLA troops who then sealed the compound.[43] During these years, the elite guard that protected Mao and other state leaders, the 8341 Unit, was also garrisoned inside the Gugong, just adjacent to the Zhongnanhai leadership compound.[44]

For the next five years the Gugong was closed and did not formally reopen until 1971. While the closure protected the museum and its art from the worst chaos taking place outside its walls and in the adjacent Zhongnanhai, it did not insulate Gugong staff from persecution. Initially, they were divided into two groups and told to continue their work, but were also subjected to daily political "study sessions."[45] In December 1968, as the Cultural Revolution peaked and Mao and Zhou sought to restore some order across the country, a "propaganda team" (*xuanchuan dui*) was dispatched to the Gugong to establish a Revolutionary Committee (Geming Weiyuanhui) as the new management of the museum. In August 1969, many of the senior staff were sent to the Ministry of Culture's May 7th Cadre School (Wu Qi Gan Xiao) near Xianning in Hebei province, leaving only approximately two hundred personnel living and working in the entire Forbidden City (housing was provided within the grounds for most of the Gugong staff until the 1990s).[46] One of them was Xu Bangda, who recalled spending three years sweeping the museum grounds.[47]

On May 8, 1970, Premier Zhou ordered that every month half of the regiment of PLA troops that had been guarding and occupying the Gugong should be rotated. On May 14, Zhou again issued strict instructions to the troops to carefully protect the "valuable treasures" in the Gugong. The new military units dispatched to the Gugong were not only to guard the premises, but were to begin the cleanup and restoration of the compound. Laborers were dispatched to clean up the mess that had accumulated inside the Forbidden City, engineers to reconstruct dilapidated buildings, and historical specialists to put archives and library materials in order.[48] On September 17, 1970, Zhou visited the museum in the middle of the night and proclaimed to the assembled staff that the museum would have to be ready to reopen within a year.[49] Almost a year later, in June 1971, Zhou returned to inspect the premises. Finding them fit and presentable, he instructed the museum staff to prepare to reopen.

The Gugong formally reopened on July 5, 1971. Its professional staff were recalled from the Hebei countryside and immediately sent back to work to ready the exhibition halls and display cases. But Zhou knew something that the staff did not, which prompted his sense of urgency: a secret visitor from afar was about to arrive in Beijing, and Zhou wanted him to have a tour of the imperial palace. That visitor was American special emissary Henry Kissinger, who arrived days later via Pakistan on his secret mission to begin the restoration of U.S.-China relations. Seven months later, President Nixon would arrive and also be given a grand tour of the Gugong.[50]

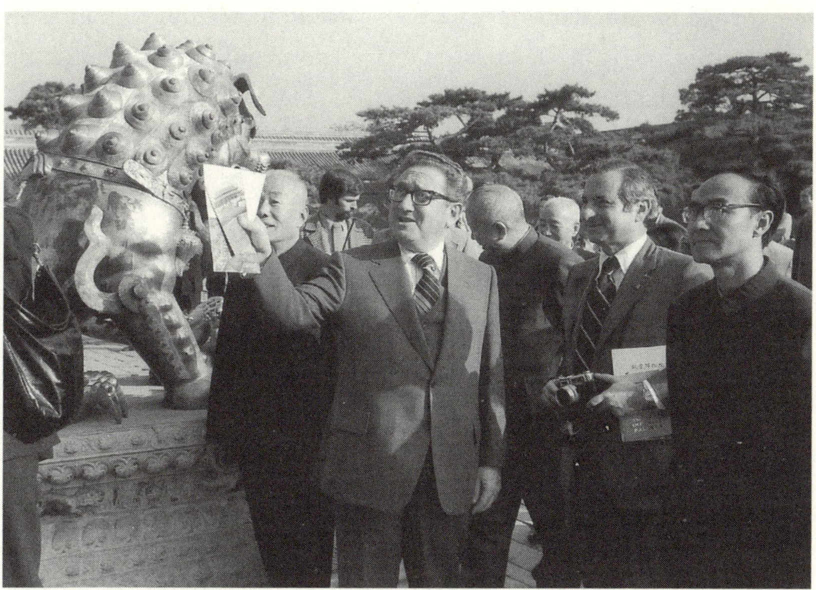

U.S. national security advisor Henry Kissinger touring the Palace Museum and the Forbidden City, c. 1971. *Xinhua News Agency Photo Archive, Beijing.*

Although the Gugong reopened, and former director Wu Zhongchao was politically "rehabilitated" and restored to his position, the museum remained under the administration of the Revolutionary Committee. This situation continued until January 1973, when the pre–Cultural Revolution administrative structure was restored.

ADMINISTRATION OF THE GUGONG

As might be expected in an institution as large as the Gugong and given the tumult in the PRC, the museum has undergone multiple structural reorganizations since 1949. Formal reorganizations took place in 1952, 1957, 1958, 1960, 1963, 1965, 1966, 1972, 1978, 1984, and 1988.[51]

In 1989, in the aftermath of the military crackdown in Beijing and Tiananmen Square, just outside the Gugong, a significant staff shakeup occurred. During May 1989, virtually the entire museum staff joined the massive demonstrations in Tiananmen Square, carrying a banner identifying them as Gugong staff (this was not unusual, as many demonstrators carried flags of their work units or *danwei*). In addition to marching and participating in the demonstrations, Gugong staff arranged for thirty thousand renminbi in gate receipts to be donated to the demonstrator's cause.[52]

Two days after the violent crackdown on the night of June 3–4, Gugong director Zhang Zhongpei was visited by a commander of the martial law troops, who requested that some of his units be permitted to encamp on museum grounds, in front of the Hall of Supreme Harmony. Director Zhang refused the request and told the officer, "The Palace Museum is a World Heritage Site, it is a national treasure. If you want to authorize it, go ahead, but I will oppose it with my resignation."[53] Subsequently, the PLA and other security units swept into and interrogated staff in various institutions known to have participated in the demonstrations. Staff members who marched in the demonstrations were also under a political cloud, and made to reflect (*fanci*) on their actions and confess them. Some faced intensive interrogations (*xingzhi shenpan*). On August 2, Zhang was suspended from the directorship while an investigation was conducted.

During a three-day hearing, he was accused of malfeasance and of having benefited himself. In the absence of evidence, Zhang was left to do his research at home. Director Zhang finally resigned in 1991, no doubt under political pressure, but he continues to do archeological research and works part-time at the museum (through 2004). Yang Xin was also

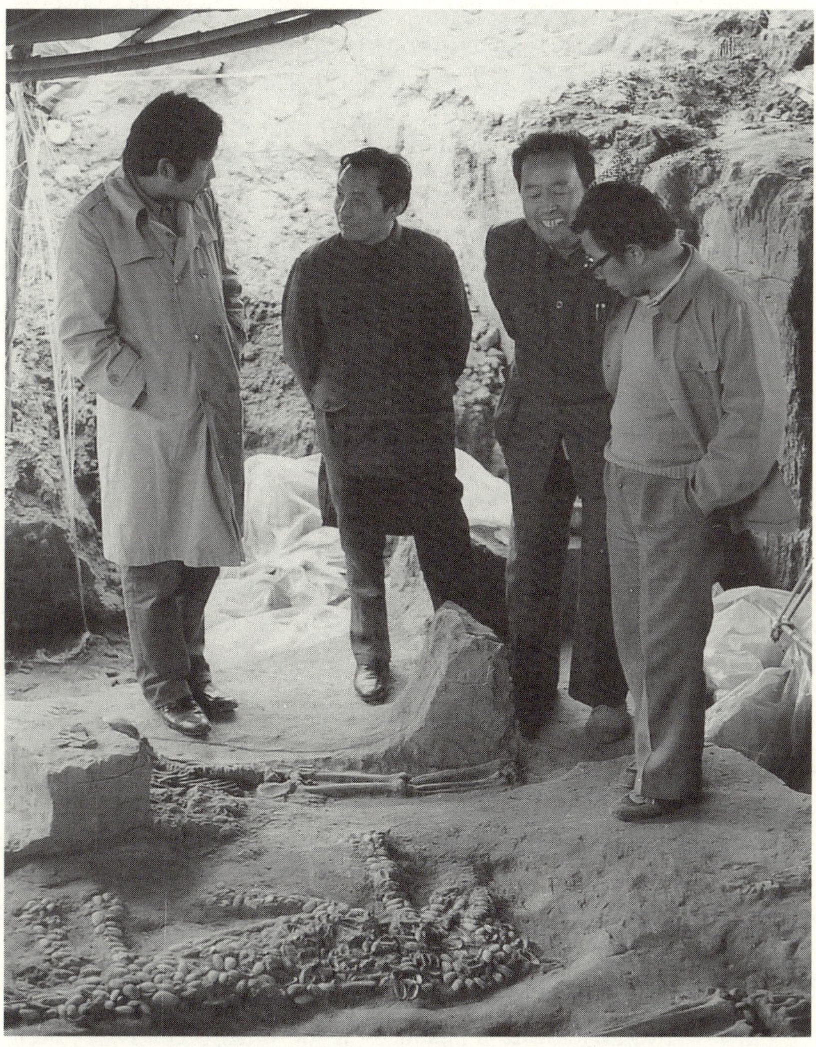

Palace Museum director Zhang Zhongpei visiting archeological site in Henan province, January 29, 1988. Xinhua News Agency Photo Archive, Beijing.

interrogated, put on a two-year leave, but was eventually allowed to return to work and served as vice-director until 2001.

After 1989, a number of former military officers were assigned to the senior administrative staff of the Gugong. This included Pei Huanlu, a retired air force general, who served as acting director from 1993 to 1997.

Tan Bin, son of former CCP intelligence and public security official Tan Zhengwen, was also appointed to a senior administrative post. He was transferred to the Gugong in 1997 (from the National Library) and became Communist Party secretary of the Gugong. During the Cultural Revolution, Tan Bin had been a Red Guard leader, then named Tan Lifu. He was very active in the early stages of the Cultural Revolution in Beijing, but then became caught up in factional in-fighting and was arrested and imprisoned. He was incarcerated in prison and at a military labor reform camp until 1970, when he was transferred to work on an army base until 1979, when he was politically rehabilitated and returned to the capital. He was eventually assigned work in the National Library. He changed his name to Tan Bin in 1970, to dissociate himself from his past.[54]

Organizational Structure

As of 2003 the Gugong employed approximately two thousand staff members, divided into three broad types/divisions (*san da lei*): administration, professional and research, and services.[55] Each division was composed of between five and nine numerous sections/offices, totaling twenty departments in all.

The Administration Division (Guanli Jigou) included the Director's Office, Personnel Office, Security Office, Ancient Buildings Department, a Communist Party branch office (Dangwei), and a (Communist Party) Discipline Inspection Department (Jiwei). The Director's Office was subdivided into four sections, each of which was managed by a vice-director: art; security, logistics, and repairs; publications and tourism; and professional affairs. The second division was the Professional and Research Division (Yewu Keyan Jigou) and included the following sections: research, exhibition and publicity, ancient books and printing, bronze and jewelry, the Palace Department (Gu Qing Bu), science and technology, a library, and an information center. The third division, the Services Division (*Fuwu Jigou*), included the General Services Center, Development Office (for fundraising), Engineering Department, Finance Department, and the Tourism Office.

Directors

Ma Heng continued to serve as director of the Gugong until early 1952, when he was reassigned as a member of the Cultural Relics Inventory Committee of the Bureau of Cultural Relics.[56] After Ma's transfer there was a hiatus of two years before a new director was appointed. In late 1954, Wu Zhongchao succeeded Ma, and his tenure proved remarkably long; Wu served as Gugong director for three decades until 1984 (although he was hospitalized in 1980). He was not an art historian or a man of museums prior to his appointment, although he became a very effective administrator and did much to improve the museum and its collection. Wu had been a Chinese Communist Party activist and was involved in the training of party cadres. Wu joined the CCP in 1928 and worked in the underground workers movement in Shanghai and Wuxi. This was a very dangerous time, as it came just after the 1927 Shanghai massacre and the white terror unleashed by Chiang Kai-shek's troops and paramilitary gangs. Wu survived and went on to join the New Fourth Army, serving as a deputy regiment commander. After 1949, Wu returned to the Shanghai and Jiangsu region and served in a series of CCP administrative positions, culminating in his appointment as secretary-general of the CCP's East China Bureau and vice president of the East China Party School. Wu was thus a loyal and dedicated communist apparatchik. But he was also apparently a collector of cultural artifacts. Wu's reign as Gugong director was marked by physical rehabilitation of the facilities, the growth of the collection (through donations and reacquiring much of the art that had been sold or lost), numerous reorganizations of the administrative structure, the hiring of many new staff members, and an atmosphere relatively free from politics.

When Wu fell ill and was hospitalized in 1980, he left a leadership void. At first the museum was codirected by vice-directors Yang Boda and Peng

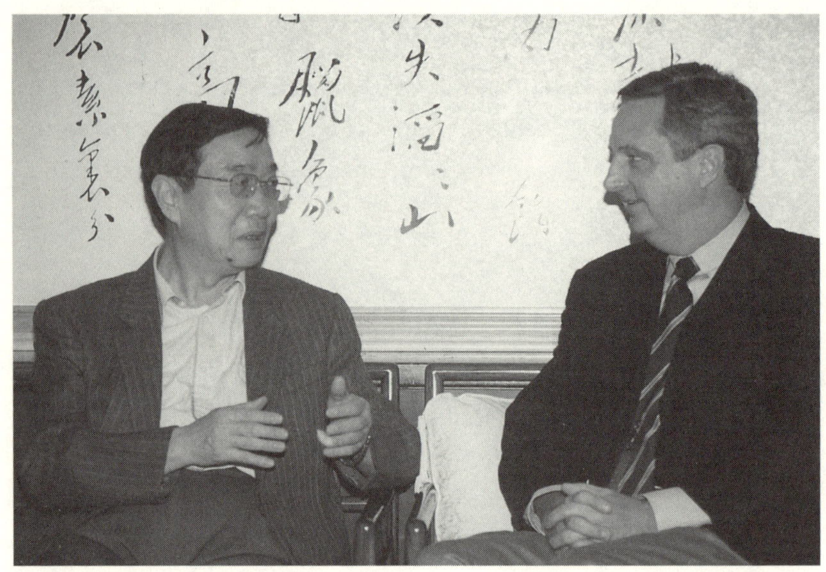

David Shambaugh with Palace Museum Director Zheng Xinmiao, September 2004.
Author's photo.

Yan (although it seems that Peng was given the title of director in 1983). From 1982 to 2002, with the exception of the period 1987–1991 when Zhang Zhongpei was full director, the Gugong was managed by a "leadership committee" (*lingdao weiyuanhui*) made up of vice-directors, one of whom served as acting director: Peng Yan from 1980 to 1982, Xu Li from 1982 to 1984, Yu Jian from 1984 to 1987, Yu Jimin from 1991 to 1993, Pei Huanlu from 1993 to 1997, Tan Bin from 1997 to 1998, and Zhu Chengru from 1998 to 2002. In October 2002 Deputy Minister of Culture Zheng Xinmiao was appointed full director. Zheng was assisted by an expanded group of vice-directors: Tan Bin, Li Wenru, Zhang Zhizhu, Xie Fangkai, Xiao Yanyi, Jin Hongkui, and Ji Tianbin. It is striking that three possessed military backgrounds (Zhang Zhizhu, Xie Fangkai, and Ji Tianbin). Two came from editing and publishing (Li Wenru and Xiao Yanyi). Thus, in addition to Director Zheng, among the seven vice-directors only one—Jin Hongkui—had a background in art history or connoisseurship. Obviously, the authorities in the State Council's Ministry of Personnel and in the CCP's Organization Department who determined leading appointments to the Gugong's staff placed a higher priority on political reliability, even military experience, than on training in art history or museum management. In October 2003, as Tan Bin retired, a museum specialist, Li Ji, was appointed executive vice-director.

As noted above, Zhang Zhongpei served as director from 1987 through 1991, although his was a tumultuous tenure owing to the events of 1989. Unlike many previous and subsequent directors and vice-directors, Zhang was a scholar; he had previously taught archeology at Jilin University. Zhang was appointed by the State Council during Zhao Ziyang's tenure as premier. During Zhang's time as director, there were four vice-directors, each of whom managed different aspects of the museum: Wei Wenzao was responsible for architecture and facilities; Wang Shuqing for security and protocol; Ma Zishu for finance and tourism; and Yang Xin for education, research, publications, exhibitions, and storage.

Finances

Until the 1980s, the Gugong was run like all other institutions in China—according to fixed plans and operating with the provision of fixed government subsidies. But the museum was also touched by Deng Xiaoping's financial and management reforms. In 1984, it was decided that the museum should also adopt a "responsibility system" (zi ren zhi) to increase accountability, improve efficiency and performance, and to provide incentives and disincentives for work. This involved devolution of management, with performance and fiscal responsibility being assigned to department heads. As a result, selective bonuses were to be paid to staff for good work or overtime, while various penalties were imposed for shoddy performance. Workers could still not be fired (and therefore the "iron rice bowl" could not be broken), but much more discretion in personnel management was the goal.

Yet, these intended reforms never really took hold, as there was considerable resistance among the staff. It was not until Zhang Zhongpei took over as director that there was real movement to reform the pay system. Zhang began his efforts in 1988, against substantial opposition. He pushed though a series of initiatives that in effect replaced the longstanding flat pay scale—in which everyone from guards to curators received more or less equal compensation of about 40 renminbi (RMB) per month—with a new sliding scale. The plan dictated that professional staff (administrators and curators) be paid RMB145–180 per month and receive bonuses for extra or special work, while guards and ordinary workers' salaries were raised to a flat RMB70 per month. Department heads (*chuzhang*) were paid RMB120 per month, while vice-directors received RMB150–180 monthly, depending on their responsibilities and performance. Also during Zhang's tenure, the Gugong was permitted for the first time to keep a portion of admission ticket receipts.

Even though it is a national museum and a central-level institution, the Gugong surprisingly does not receive large subsidies from the central government. According to Vice-director Pei Huanlu, the annual operating budget by the late-1990s was approximately RMB80 million (US$9.75 million). This is precisely the amount of annual ticket receipts that the museum was permitted to retain by the Bureau of Cultural Relics (out of RMB180 million, or US$21.9 million, in total receipts).[57] Thus, in fiscal year 1999 at least, the Gugong operated right at the margin, with no profit and no loss. It seems that the Gugong is entirely dependent on revenue generated by ticket receipts, although it also receives income from foreign exhibitions.[58] Surely, the Gugong must receive additional fiscal subsidies from the central government, but it appears that the museum is more or less financially on its own. In addition to paying staff salaries and benefits, Vice-director Pei indicated that the Gugong annually pays on average RMB8 million (US$975,609) for building repairs, and RMB20 million (US$2,439,024) for its water system.

Sometimes special projects require special funds. The construction of a 21,000 square meter state-of-the-art underground storage facility (*dixia kufang*), to keep the 650,000 artworks in appropriate climate-controlled conditions, took six years to build (1987–1990, expanded 1994–1997) and cost RMB1.17 billion altogether (US$1,342,310). The dredging of the canal around the Forbidden City (1997–1999) cost RMB600 million (US$73,170,730), but this was underwritten by the Beijing municipal government. Funds have been raised from Hong Kong's China Heritage Fund for the authentic restoration of the nine Qianfugong halls in the northwest corner of the Gugong, a project that is supposed to be complete for the Gugong's eightieth anniversary in 2005. Another ambitious project in the northeast corner of the Gugong is the restoration of Emperor Qianlong's garden and retirement villa, the Palace of Repose and Longevity. This project is supported by the World Monument Fund (a U.S.-based foundation). A new Information Center, with digital photography, was completed in 2002 at a cost of RMB30 million (US$3.65 million) and was jointly funded by the Gugong and the Japanese printing firm, Toppan.

The 2008 Olympic Games, to be held in Beijing, will benefit the Gugong; additional funds will be provided to improve exhibition spaces and other elements of the museum. One source claims that RMB100 million (US$9.75 million) has been allocated over six years (2002–2008) for the upgrading and restoration of the Gugong's infrastructure—including communications, electricity lines, heating and temperature control systems, fire control, and security.[59] While substantial efforts are being made to ready the Gugong for the 2008 Olympics, the restoration plan envisions continuing to 2020.

Security

Security for the Gugong continues to rest with the Central Guards Bureau (Zhongyang Jingwei Ju) of the Beijing Garrison Command of the PLA's Beijing Military Region. For many years this regiment was known as the 8341 Unit. While the Central Military Commission (CMC) has direct command of this unit and the CMC General Office oversees it on a daily basis, the Beijing Garrison Command and the Security Bureau of the PLA General Staff Department apparently share some command authority and provide funds, equipment, training, and barracks for the elite guards.[60] The Central Guards Bureau certainly does more than protect the Gugong, as it also provides all the security for China's leaders and the Zhongnanhai leadership compound.

The units protecting the museum are now rotated regularly, but this has not always been the case. The policy change came about in part when some members of the Central Guards were found in 1992 to be stealing antiques from the Gugong and transferring them to the Chaoyang An-

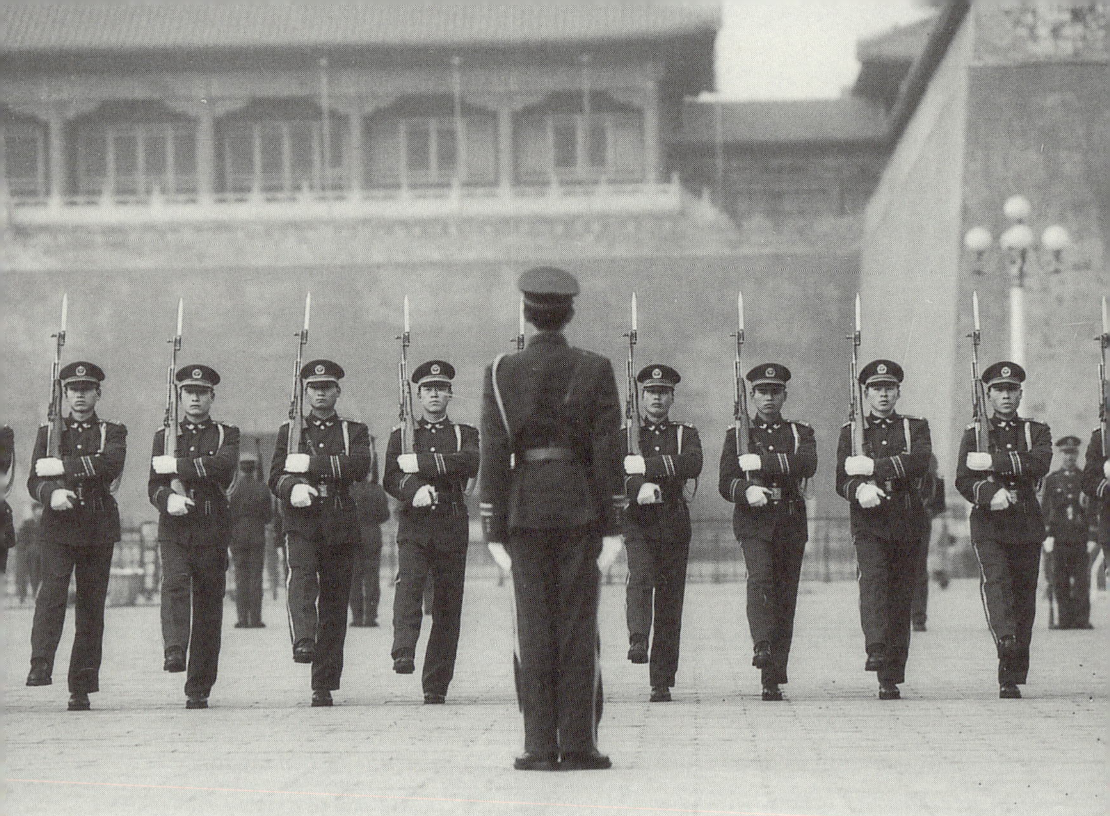

People's Liberation Army Central Guards Bureau drilling in Wumen Square outside of the Palace Museum entrance, March 28, 1992. Xinhua News Agency Photo Arch ive, Beijing.

tique Market for sale to foreigners.[61] The individual soldiers involved were remanded and court-martialed, and thereafter the Central Guards Bureau has been closely monitored and regularly rotated.

EXHIBITIONS AND ACTIVITIES

Since the late 1970s and recovery after the Cultural Revolution, the Gugong has been active in a variety of areas. In 1979 a monthly scholarly journal focusing on the history of Chinese art was inaugurated (*Gugong Bowuyuan Yuekan*), a bimonthly journal entitled *Forbidden City* was begun in 1980, and the Forbidden City Publishing House was established in 1983. The latter has published a large number of high-quality books. Beginning in the early 1980s, the Gugong Library was reorganized and its rich collection of imperial books and tablets were made available for scholarly use (although it took until 2004 for such access to actually be granted). A photo archive was also opened in the 1980s, which contains photos and slides not only of objects in the Gugong, but also of those in other museums around China.

The sixtieth and sixty-fifth anniversaries of the Gugong, in 1985 and 1990, were each celebrated with a special exhibition, with a ceremony attended by China's leaders, and with an international scholarly conference. These conferences—"Wu School Style of Painting during the Ming Dynasty" and "Ancient Architecture in the Forbidden City," respectively—produced important volumes. A major celebration is planned for the museum's 80th anniversary in 2005.

Various exhibitions have been held in the Gugong and sent abroad over the years. Yet the museum itself is severely constrained by a lack of exhibition space (to say nothing about the quality of the space). Some sources indicate that with the existing available physical exhibition space, less than one-tenth of the approximately one million objects in the permanent collection can be displayed at any given time;[62] but even this estimate seems high.

The museum's chronic shortage of exhibit space, and the constraints imposed by the requirement not to disturb the architectural plan of the Forbidden City, have led to years of consideration and heated debate over the possibility of building modern underground exhibition halls. In 1998 a plan was approved and work almost began on two levels of underground exhibit space totaling 20,000 square meters, near the Donghua (East China) Gate beneath the area that used to house the imperial riding stables.[63] But this plan was halted before construction could begin, falling prey to arguments about safety and worries that it could not be done without affecting the existing buildings. Another plan has been to build a new hall under the Shangsiyuan Courtyard in the southeast corner of the Gugong, covering 10,900 square meters and to include exhibition galleries, projection rooms, meeting facilities, rest rooms, and a book and souvenir shop. But this plan also has not been implemented. Despite a decade of planning and preparation, no new underground exhibition halls have been started and the plans seem to have been permanently shelved. Construction of a new aboveground exhibition hall has also been considered, but the idea has been rejected for aesthetic, architectural, and safety reasons. In 2004, however, the museum succeeded in gaining some new underground space from the adjacent (No.1) Ming-Qing Archives, which museum director Zheng Xinmiao has indicated will be used for expanded exhibition space.[64]

While the Gugong can display its possessions in ten exhibit halls, these aboveground spaces (mostly the Hall of Paintings, Hall of Treasures, and Hall of Clocks and Watches) are in old palace buildings made of wood, which are deemed too dangerous to install modern lighting, audiovisual, and security equipment, for fear of electrical short-circuiting and fire.[65] While there is some air conditioning in the aboveground halls, it remains very difficult to control humidity and temperature fluctuations—which is crucial for the preservation of paintings and other objects. Each October many of the most valuable original paintings in the collection are put on view, as the autumn weather offers the optimal climate for the scrolls. Nevertheless, the aboveground exhibition halls remain dismal and in very poor condition by international standards. As the *China Daily* newspaper observed, "The Palace Museum is known throughout the world, but cries out for modernization."[66]

In terms of foreign exhibitions, during the 1950s they were limited entirely to countries of the Soviet bloc. The first post–Cultural Revolution exhibit—arts and crafts of the Ming and Qing—was sent to Japan in 1974. During the 1980s, exhibitions were sent to various Western countries, including the United States, West Germany, Canada, France, Holland, Austria, and Portugal.[67] Within the Asia-Pacific region, exhibits were sent to Singapore, Australia, Japan, South Korea, and Hong Kong.[68]

TIES TO THE PAST, LEGITIMACY FOR THE PRESENT

For more than a half century, the Palace Museum in Beijing has played an important political role for the Chinese Communist Party and the People's Republic of China. It has represented the party and state's tie to its national past and has helped to thereby bestow contemporary legitimacy on the regime. The government has also used the museum and its collection to bolster the PRC's international legitimacy and profile. Right from the outset in 1949, China's Communist Party leadership recognized this symbolic value, but they also seemed to genuinely want to preserve and rebuild the collection as a national treasure. Extraordinary efforts were made during difficult times to reacquire art and artifacts lost from the imperial collection, to physically restore and improve the museum and its grounds in the Forbidden City, and to protect it during turbulent political times. Unfortunately, the Palace Museum and its staff were subjected to the full range of political campaigns that punctuated the Maoist era, including the dramatic demonstrations and their military suppression in 1989. Many of these were very trying experiences, decimating individual careers and lives and casting a shadow over the Palace Museum as an institution.

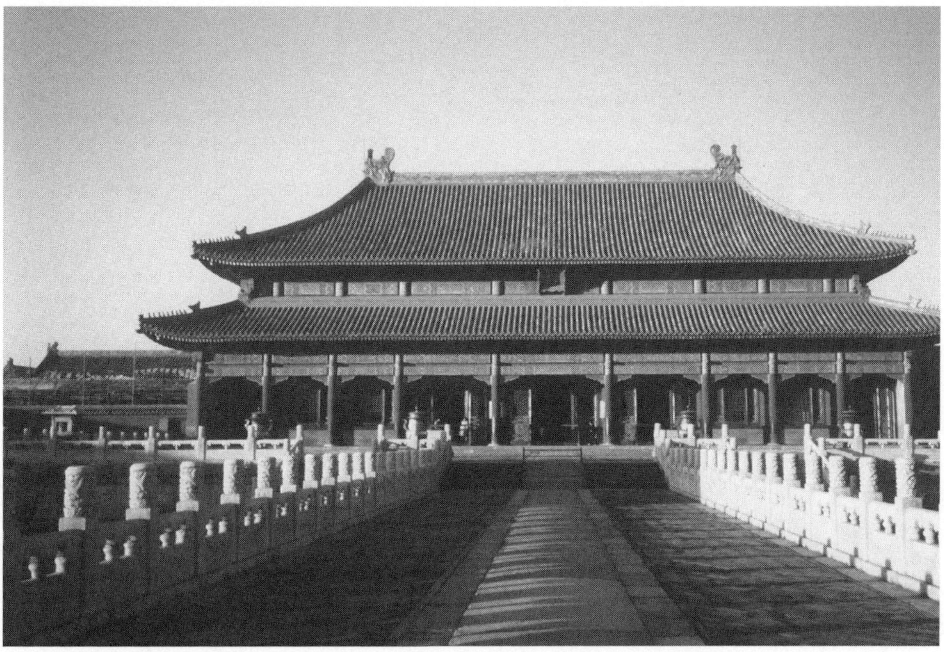

Palace Museum, Beijing. Courtesy Alfreda Murck.

Today, as China enters the twenty-first century, the Palace Museum continues to be a tremendous source of pride for the nation. It remains a symbolic link to China's past—an era of national greatness that haunts collective memories and inspires future aspirations. Yet, as it has for several hundred years, the imperial art collection remains an object of political value and symbolism for the government. Some things do not change.

7

Epilogue:
The Politics of China's Imperial Art

This book has chronicled the extraordinary saga of China's imperial art treasures over three thousand years, from the Bronze Age to the early twenty-first century. The history of the imperial art collection mirrors the turbulent history of China itself. While the collection grew in quantity and quality over time, it was also subjected to repeated fracturing as a result of natural calamities, invasions, war, revolution, theft, dynastic transitions, regime change, political movements, and other phenomena.

Throughout this long and complicated history, the imperial collection was inextricably intertwined with the politics of the time. Indeed, the central argument of this study has been that the imperial collection has been a key source of legitimacy for successive Chinese rulers, regardless of the dynasty or government in power. As such, each new emperor or ruler has sought to associate himself personally, and his dynasty/government, with the imperial collection as a means of conferring contemporary legitimacy through continuity with the past. This was certainly true for the long line of emperors and empresses during China's imperial period, but it was equally true for the Nationalist and Communist governments of the twentieth century.

Today, the continued division of the collection symbolizes the continued division of the Chinese nation. The imperial collection has now been split between the Palace Museum (Gugong) in Beijing and the National Palace Museum in Taipei for more than a half century. Will the two collections ever again be united into a single and truly "National" Palace Museum? This question is, of course, a subset of the more than eighty-year rivalry between the Chinese Communists and Nationalists, the more than fifty-year rivalry between the People's Republic of China (PRC) and the Republic of China (ROC), and the more recent indigenous movement towards independence on the island of Taiwan. It is a question of politics, identity, and sovereignty.

Since 1949, the two Palace Museums have played important politically symbolic roles for the governments on the mainland and on Taiwan. Each government has used the imperial collection to enhance its political legitimacy, right to rule, and historical legacy. Each museum has criticized the other, yet they have had little direct contact. In some periods, the bad feelings between the two sides have been thinly masked. In 1972 Chuang Yen, then director of the National Palace Museum on Taiwan, displayed his annoyance during an interview, claiming that "the Communists had tried to spread the idea that we (the Republic of China) intended to sell the palace treasures in the United States."[1] Chuang's indignation was compounded by Beijing's accusation that the National Palace Museum's staff had helped to "steal" imperial art from the mainland. In the view of the museum staff in Taiwan, however, they had saved the great national treasures from the "Communists bandits" (*gong fei*), as they were often called.

In more recent times, there have actually been some instances of collaboration between the two museums. In 1992, for the first time, the National Palace Museum in Taipei and the Gugong in Beijing were both represented in the same exhibition, "Circa 1492: Art in the Age of Exploration," presented only at the National Gallery of Art in Washington D.C.

Despite the political/diplomatic struggle between Beijing and Taipei, the PRC has real reason to be tolerant of the divided collection. That is, from Beijing's perspective, the very fact that much of the collection remains on Taiwan and is housed in an institution still called the National Palace Museum gives the island and the ROC government an important tie to the mainland and its Chinese past. This is not unimportant given the drift on the island farther and farther away from a common identity with the Chinese mainland in recent years—although Beijing is disturbed by recent moves (described in chapter 5) by the Chen Shui-bian government to possibly change the name of the museum and to introduce more native Taiwanese art into the collection.

Perhaps someday the two Palace Museums will have direct exchanges and exhibitions, thus serving as a cultural bridge to some form of political union. This would open the door for the two Palace Museums to maybe once again merge their collections. If this occurred, it would be a refreshing instance in the imperial collection's history of politics serving art rather than vice versa.

The saga of China's imperial art collection fuses past, present, and future. The authors of this study hope to have contributed to an enriched understanding of this history, but also to have stimulated others to take up the story. There remain many gaps in the historical record and numerous future episodes to be written.

Notes

Foreword

1. The Qianlong Emperor's degree of connoisseurship is a subject of continuing discussion. For example, see Kohara Hironobu, "Kenryû Kôtei no Gagaku ni tsuite" and "Qianlong Emperor's Skill."

2. Pu Yi had mixed opinions of both Shaoying and Luo Zhenyu, regardless of their efforts on his behalf. See Aisin-Gioro, _From Emperor to Citizen_, 78–79, 106, 125, 140, 142, 146–48, 150, 163, 173–79.

Chapter 1. China's Imperial Art Treasures from Early Times to the Twelfth Century

1. Ledderose, "Some Observations on the Imperial Art Collection," 33–46.

2. Quoted in Murowchick, _China: Ancient Culture, Modern Land_, 74. A scholar-official, Wang Yirong, ordered a package of dragon bones from his apothecary in 1898, and prior to grinding them up (for medicinal purposes) he recognized the incised graphs to be an earlier form of writing than anything known.

3. Sullivan, _Arts of China_ (1999), 23–24.

4. Ledderose, "Some Observations on the Imperial Art Collection," 35.

5. Wu Hung, _Wu Liang Shrine_, 95.

6. Cheng, "Ding Tripods," 46–47.

7. Wu Hung, _Wu Liang Shrine_, 90–93.

8. Chiang, "Masterpieces of Chinese Seals." The National Palace Museum on Taiwan possesses the five chests of ancient seals collected by Emperor Qianlong, including more than twelve hundred pieces from the Han dynasty.

9. Sima Qian, *Records of the Grand Historian*, vol. 1, 125–26. Xiao was the emperor's close friend and chief officer, and is credited with organization of the Han administration.

10. Ibid. The Chinese term for painting, *hua*, usually did not include charts and maps, *tu*, which were usually kept in scroll form.

11. Vinograd, *Boundaries of the Self*, 20.

12. Wu Hung, *Wu Liang Shrine*, 197–99.

13. Ibid.

14. Quoted in Bush and Shih, *Early Chinese Texts on Painting*, 26.

15. Quoted in Jing, "Portraits of Kublai Khan and Chabi," 77.

16. Acker, *Some T'ang and Pre-T'ang Texts* (1974), 108.

17. At a conference at the Palace Museum in Beijing on October 15, 2003, former Gugong deputy director Yang Xin questioned the attribution of these paintings to Gu Kaizhi.

18. The painting was the subject of an international symposium held at the British Museum in June 2001. See McCausland, *Gu Kaizhi and the Admonitions Scroll*, and McCausland, *First Masterpiece of Chinese Painting*.

19. Wu Hung, *Wu Liang Shrine*, 172–73.

20. Acker, *Some T'ang and Pre-T'ang Texts* (1974), 120–21.

21. Ibid., 123. Yang Renkai, in his overview of art lost from imperial collections considers this the greatest such calamity on historical record (see Yang Renkai, *Guobao Chenfu Lu*).

22. Acker, *Some T'ang and Pre-T'ang Texts* (1974), 24.

23. Cohn, *Chinese Painting*, 40.

24. Acker, *Some T'ang and Pre-T'ang Texts* (1974).

25. Ibid.

26. Sickman and Soper, *Art and Architecture of China*, 161.

27. Cahill, *Chinese Painting*, 14, 20–22, 28, 56, 57.

28. Calligraphic styles were transmitted more successfully than painting because the most admired texts were inscribed from time to time on stone or wood. Tang emperor Gaozu (r. 618–626) and the first emperor of the Northern Song, Taizu (r. 960–976), frequently ordered calligraphy they liked engraved on wood or stone.

29. Ledderose, *Mi Fu and the Classical Tradition*.

30. Ibid.

31. Chang, "National Palace Museum," 5.

32. Ferguson, "Emperor Hui Tsung"; Ebrey, "Taoism and Art at the Court of Song Huizong."

33. Tseng, *Emperor Tsung Hui-tsung*, 10.

34. Siren, *Chinese Painting*, 2, 79.

35. Sturman, *Cranes Above Kaifeng*, 36.

36. Keswick, *Chinese Garden*, 53–56.

37. A useful summary of these catalogues is provided by Lawton in "Mo-yuan Hui-kuan," 15.

38. Lawton, "Mo-yuan Hui-kuan," 15.

39. Fong, *Beyond Representation*, 178–86.

40. Quoted in Sturman, *Cranes Above Kaifeng*, 40.

41. Chao, "The Day Northern Sung Fell," 144–56.

42. Ibid., 150–51.

43. See Murray, "Southern Song Painting."

44. Chang, "National Palace Museum," 6.

45. Rudolph, "Dynastic Booty," 176–77. Professor Robert Gimello reminded the authors that the Jin also took the Imperial Library.

46. There they remained until 1932, when they were carefully wrapped and taken south with other Palace Museum treasures in the wake of the Japanese invasion. They were returned to Beijing after 1949 and remained in the Beijing Palace Museum. For more information see Mattos, "Stone Drums of Ch'in."

47. MacFarquhar, *Forbidden City*, 43, 46.

48. Toyama, "Kin Shoso shuzo," 531–40, lists all the known collection of Jin Zhangzong.

49. There are numerous alternate spellings, including Genghis Khan. Khan means universal chief.

50. Murray, "Role of Art in the Southern Sung Revival," 41–59.

51. Murray, "Sung Kao-tsung as Artist and Patron," 28.

52. Ibid., 47n17.

53. Ibid., 44–45.

54. Rossabi, *Kublai Kahn*, 122.

55. Ibid., 169.

56. Fu, "Princess Sengge Ragi," 71n8.

57. Fu, ibid., and "History of the Yuan Imperial Collections," part IV, 2.

58. Weidner, "Aspects of Painting and Patronage," 42. Lu Yuan was invited by Kublai Khan to execute images for the newly established Temple of the Lokopalas in 1270.

59. Fu, "History of the Yuan Imperial Collections," part IV, 9.

60. Fong and Fu, *Kao-tsung and Dynastic Revival*, 85.

61. Weidner, "Aspects of Painting and Patronage," 38.

62. The Tang dynasty painters Han Gan (active c. 756) and Yan Liben (d. 673) and the Song painter Li Gonglin (c. 1041–1104) are considered the supreme Chinese painters of horses.

63. Three of these paintings are now in the National Palace Museum in Taipei, and three are in the Gugong in Beijing. See Fu, "Princess Sengge Ragi," 63–64.

64. Fu, "History of the Yuan Imperial Collections," part II, 2.

Chapter 2. Imperial Treasures under the Ming and Qing Dynasties

1. Levathes, *When China Ruled the Seas*, 59.

2. Story recounted in Siren, *Chinese Painting*, vol. 4, 112.

3. Loehr, "Chinese Painting with Sung-Dated Inscriptions," 224; and Owyang, "Formation of the Family Collection," 119n19.

4. Owyang, "Formation of the Family Collection," 117.

5. Barnhart, "Streams and Hills," 228–30.

6. Barnhart, *Painters of the Great Ming*, 129.

7. Levathes, *When China Ruled the Seas*, 72.

8. Ibid., 70.

9. Ibid., 88, 89.

10. Zheng He led seven maritime expeditions in all, the last one under Emperor Xuanzong. Their dates were 1405–07, 1407–09, 1409–11, 1413–15, 1417–19, 1421–22, 1431–33. See Gernet, *History of Chinese Civilization*, 401.

11. Gernet, *History of Chinese Civilization*, 407.

12. Weng and Yang, *Palace Museum*, 78. Thanks to Alfreda Murck for this information.

13. Steinhardt, *Chinese Imperial City Planning*, 168. The Forbidden City is correctly called a Ming-Qing complex because it was not fundamentally altered by the Manchus (the Qing rulers) when they took possession in 1644.

14. Barnhart, *Painters of the Great Ming*, 57.

15. Ibid., 61–62.

16. Quoted in ibid., 70.

17. Ibid., 74.

18. Ibid., 57, 60–61. Bian Wenjin, active in the first three Ming courts, was dismissed by Emperor Xuanzong in 1426, charged with selling influence and accepting bribes from men seeking employment at court. The seventy-year-old artist, who specialized in bird and flower themes, continued to produce handsome compositions.

19. Barnhart, *Painters of the Great Ming*, 66.

20. Ibid., 56–57.

21. Ibid., 139.

22. Ibid., 56.

23. Ibid., 123.

24. Hummel, *Eminent Chinese of the Ch'ing Period*, vol. 2, 669–70.

25. Yang Renkai, interview by Jeannette Shambaugh Elliott and Ingrid Larsen, October 1992, Beijing.

26. Gernet, *History of Chinese Civilization*, 464–65.

27. Beurdeley, *Chinese Collector through the Centuries*, 174.

28. Siren, *Chinese Painting*, vol. 5, 82.

29. Kahn, "A Matter of Taste," 302.

30. Spence, *Ts'ao Yin and the K'ang-hsi Emperor*, 145–46.

31. Zou Yigui, quoted in Sullivan, *Symbols of Eternity*, 228.

32. Rogers, "Court Painting Under the Qianlong Emperor," 310.

33. She, "Overview of Stylistic Development," 75.

34. Yang, "Development of the Ch'ien-lung Academy," 349.

35. Ibid., 333–55.

36. Ibid.

37. Kohara, "Qianlong Emperor's Skill," 60–61.

38. Mote, "Intellectual Climate in Eighteenth Century China," 53.

39. This is compared with the total number published in the catalogues of paintings and calligraphies in the Song dynasty imperial collection of the Huizong Emperor. Huizong's catalogue of paintings (the *Xuanhe Huapu*, dated 1120) lists 6,396 paintings by 231 artists. See Lawton, "Mo-yuan Hui-kuan," 15.

40. Rogers, "Court Painting Under the Qianlong Emperor," 303–5.

41. Ibid. Rogers explains that it was permissible to offer a poem, painting, or calligraphy to the emperor as an indirect way of requesting a favor, since a direct written request for a favor was proscribed. This function may explain the disproportionate number of paintings from officials, compared with the number by artists from the painting academy.

42. Kohara, "Qianlong Emperor's Skill," 60–61.

43. Sullivan, *Symbols of Eternity*, 140, 142.

Chapter 3. From Private to Public Treasures: The Early Republican Era, 1911–1930

1. Brackman, *Prisoner of Peking*.

2. For a complete list of the Articles for Favorable Treatment (Youdaitiaojian), see Qin, *Xun Qinghuang Shiyishi*, 7–8.

3. Johnston, *Twilight in the Forbidden City*, 300–2. Johnston reproduces the original agreement in full and provides a chart with the appraiser's 1914 estimated value of these objects.

4. Fairbank, *Liang and Lin*, 49–50. In supervising renovation work at the Forbidden City, Zhu associated with master craftsmen who had been keeping the imperial buildings in repair throughout their lifetimes, and from whom he gained an interest in preserving traditional Chinese architecture.

5. Chang, "National Palace Museum," 1.

6. Gernet, *History of Chinese Civilization*, 627–28. In January 1915, the Japanese embassy in Beijing presented Yuan Shikai with a list of twenty-one demands aimed at making China into a Japanese protectorate.

7. Johnston, *Twilight in the Forbidden City*, 367–68.

8. *Beijing Bowuguan Nianjian* (1916), 69–70.

9. Johnston, *Twilight in the Forbidden City*.

10. Ibid., 227–28.

11. Ibid., 103, 216–25.

12. Ibid., 334.

13. Qin, *Xun Qinghuang Shiyishi*, 77–78; Johnston, *Twilight in the Forbidden City*, 322–24. In 1922, the Household Department set up rules for auctioning items from the palace.

When Johnston complained that only inside bidders were allowed, he was correct; a bidder had to pay thirty thousand yuan to gain a permit to bid.

14. Johnston, *Twilight in the Forbidden City*, 323–24.

15. The banks involved in loans to the imperial household were the Salt Industry Bank (Yanye Yinhang); the Golden City Bank (Jincheng Yinhang); the Mainland Bank (Dalu Yinhang); and the Central-South Bank (Zhong'nan Yinhang). See also Na, *Gugong Sishinian*, 10.

16. Charles Lang Freer directly purchased some paintings from Pang Yuanji in 1919. In the 1940s, some of Pang's collection was sold through a New York dealer to the Freer Gallery in Washington, D.C., as well as to Chinese-American collector C. C. Wang. After 1949, Pang's widow sold items to the Shanghai Museum and the Palace Museum in Beijing.

17. The question arises as to how to distinguish between treasures from the Qing household that became part of the Palace Museum collection and ordinary household items. There was no distinction; everything was inventoried and absorbed into the Palace Museum when it was established in 1925. Moreover, any painting commissioned by an emperor, if retained in the imperial household, became ipso facto part of the imperial art collection.

18. Chang, "National Palace Museum," 24. Also see chapter 6 on the rebuilding of the palace compound.

19. Johnston, *Twilight in the Forbidden City*, 336.

20. Ibid., 140–41, 339.

21. Aisin-Gioro, *Emperor to Citizen*, vol. 1, 129.

22. Quoted in Yang, *Guobao Chenfu Lu*, 68–69.

23. Ibid., 74.

24. Chang, "National Palace Museum," 24.

25. They were not well packed according to later historians.

26. Yang, *Guobao Chenfu Lu*, 67–68.

27. *Shuntian Shibao*, June 8, 1922; quoted in Yang, *Guobao Chenfu Lu*, 293.

28. Johnston, *Twilight in the Forbidden City*, 354–58.

29. Ibid., 356–57.

30. Ibid., 390–91.

31. Ibid., 391.

32. Ibid., 393.

33. During his years in Tianjin, Pu Yi occasionally sold paintings to raise cash. A few items were sold to Laurence Sickman. For more information on these transactions, see Churchman, "Laurence Sickman," 50–56.

34. Yang Renkai published an exhaustive study of the Dongbeihuo paintings and calligraphies in 1991; see his *Guobao Chenfu Lu*.

35. Johnston, *Twilight in the Forbidden City*, 393.

36. John King Fairbank, *Great Chinese Revolution*, 138–92. In retribution for the siege of the foreign legations in Beijing in 1900, the Boxer Protocol of 1901 imposed on the Manchu government an indemnity of $333 million to be paid over forty years. In 1908

the United States voted to apply half of its share of $25 million to the education of Chinese in America; in 1925, the remainder of the French, British, and American funds were remanded to China to support the China Foundation for Promotion of Education and Culture.

37. Na, *Gugong Sishinian*, 17.

38. The eight Nationalist representatives were Wang Zhaoming, Cai Yuanpei, Lu Zhonglin, Fan Yuanlian, Yu Tongkui, Shen Jianshi, Ge Wenrui, and Chen Yuan. Representing the Qing household were Xiaoying (head of the Household Department), Zairun, Qiling, Baoxi, and Luo Zhenyu. Luo had been one of the outside experts who supervised the 1923–1924 inventory of the palace collection for Pu Yi. He remained a loyal adviser, following Pu Yi to Manchuria in 1931.

39. Na, *Gugong Bowuyuan Sanshinian*, 11; Wu, *Gugong Bowuyuan Chuangshi Wunianji*, 29.

40. Jiang, "Jinian Yi Peiji," 40–48.

41. Na, *Gugong Bowuyuan Sanshinian*, 18, and *Gugong Sishinian*, 4–5.

42. Langlois, "Chuang Yen and the National Palace Museum," 16–17.

43. This was a rubbing of a calligraphy by Wang Xizhi, fourth century AD, from the collection of the Qianlong Emperor, one of his greatest treasures.

44. Li Chu-tsing, "Recent History of the Palace Collection," 65–66.

45. Langlois, "Chuang Yen and the National Palace Museum," 16–17.

46. Ma, *Fifteen Different Classes of Measures*, 9–12.

47. Yang, *Guobao Chenfu Lu*, 74. Yang later discovered that these lists of articles taken out of the palace in 1924 were incomplete. As director of the Liaoning Provincial Museum in later years, he spearheaded the search for these treasures.

48. *Beijing Bowuguan Nianjian* (1988), 5.

49. Doty, "Joy Morton and the Forbidden City," 35, 41–42, 44.

50. Ferguson became a trusted advisor to the Palace Museum in the 1930s and was eventually made an honorary member of the Palace Museum board. Some of his own collection was donated to Nanjing University. Ferguson also compiled comprehensive indexes on bronzes and paintings, organized by artist, date, and subject. "Ferguson's Lists" have helped to develop a modern system of indexing Chinese art.

51. As reported in "Peking Museum Restored: Forbidden City Palaces Hold a Vast Treasure; 100 Rooms Fitted for Exhibition," *North China Daily News*, October 23, 1930.

52. The Double Tenth refers to October 10, the anniversary of the founding of the Republic of China.

53. Jiang, "Jinian Yi Peiji," 15.

Chapter 4. The Treasures through Times of War, 1931–1947

1. Chuang Yen, interview by Jeannette Shambaugh Elliott, National Palace Museum in Taipei, Taiwan, 1970. The Stone Drums and their original twelfth century AD move to Beijing are described in chapter 1.

2. Chuang, "National Palace Museum."

3. Mattos, *Stone Drums of Ch'in*.

4. Nelson Wu, "Meaning of the Chinese Treasures," 27–28, 56–57.

5. Timperley, "Future of the Peiping Palace Treasures."

6. Quoted in Jiang, "Jinian Yi Peiji," 47.

7. Quoted in Wu, *Gugong Dabaoan Zhenxiang* , 189–92.

8. Pu Yi had described seeing the replacement of real jewels with fakes.

9. Wu Jingzhou has included this article verbatim in his book, *Gugong Dabaoan Zhenxiang*, 112.

10. See Jiang, "Jinian Yi Peiji." Yi Peiji had first fled in 1920 from capture by Zhang Jingyao, the Changsha, Hunan province, warlord; in 1926 he fled from arrest in Beijing after participating in a protest march, accused of being a Communist agitator; and in 1933, he fled to escape arrest by court order.

11. Van Gulik, *Chinese Pictorial Art*, 396. The two volumes presented in court were entitled, *I-P'ei-Chi teng ch'in-chan-ku-kung-wu-an chien-ting-shu*. Volume 1 described 2,145 scrolls checked in Shanghai, 478 in Beijing, and 516 in the second investigation in Shanghai. Volume 2 described 1,029 scrolls in Nanjing, 327 items in Nanjing, and 109 items in the Nanjing secretariat. Van Gulik mistakenly records that Yi Peiji and other museum officials were indicted for having stolen and "smuggled abroad" a number of antiquities belonging to the imperial collection.

12. Quoted in Zhu, "Huiyi Ma Heng Yuanzhang," 1, 3–5.

13. Jiang, "Jinian Yi Peiji," 40–48.

14. *Zhongguo Dabaike Quanshu: Kaoguxue*, 300.

15. Zhu, "Huiyi Ma Heng Yuanzhang."

16. This *jia liang* is on display in the National Palace Museum, Taiwan. Other *jia liang* have been found of square or oblong shape.

17. Ma, *Fifteen Different Classes of Measures*. Each dynastic founder was to establish standard weights, measures, coinage, axels, dress, and the corrected calendar. In the West, most units of measure had been based on human proportions and there was little uniformity of measures between countries until 1804, when the Napoleonic code imposed the metric system as a universal standard.

18. Li Chu-tsing, "Recent History of the Palace Collection," 61–74. The lack of a predetermined destination for the treasures does not imply that Yi Peiji was irresponsible. He was never free from the problem of raising adequate funds for the move, and by late 1932 and early 1933 he had already been accused of misappropriating those funds that had been raised.

19. Ibid., 61–64.

20. Na, *Gugong Sishinian*, 67–69.

21. Preface to part 1 in *Jiaoyubu Dierci Quanguo Meishu Zhanlanhui Zhuanji*.

22. Na, *Gugong Bowuyuan Sanshinian*, 157–59. Thirteen persons were appointed special members of these committees, among them Guo Baochang, John C. Ferguson, and Tan Lan. Fifty-two persons were appointed corresponding members at this time, including Zhu Jiqian, Fu Shinian, and Liang Shicheng.

23. Ferguson, "Reflections on the London Exhibition," 433–42.

24. The French Sinologist and art historian Paul Pelliot has suggested that the painting was probably a Tang copy of the fourth century original by Gu Kaizhi. R. L. Hobson of the British Museum's Asian Antiquities section rejected this suggestion (interview by Jeannette Shambaugh Elliott, 1971, London).

25. British Organizing Committee, *International Exhibition of Chinese Art*, rear jacket.

26. Basil Gray, interview by Jeannette Shambaugh Elliott, 1985, London.

27. Ferguson, "Reflections on the London Exhibition," 433–42.

28. Cohen, *East Asian Art*, 112–16.

29. Hobson, "Chinese Exhibition," 313–17.

30. Interview with Chinese resident by Jeannette Shambaugh Elliott, 1971, London.

31. Cohen, *East Asian Art*, 123.

32. The Metropolitan Museum of Art repeated its invitation in 1948, when Horace Jayne of the museum recognized the eighty cases from the London exhibition, still crated, in Chongqing. The Chinese Nationalist government, then in the midst of a civil war with the Communists, was again willing to loan that group of objects to the Metropolitan, especially since it would have helped assure their safety during the war and the exhibit might have had a positive influence on American public opinion at a critical time. However, Chiang Kai-shek's forces collapsed too rapidly in the face of the Communist advance and the eighty cases of art objects, along with almost all the palace treasures then in southern China, were taken to Taiwan in late 1948 and early 1949.

33. Cohen, *East Asian Art*, 123–25.

34. Li Lin-ts'an, curator of the National Palace Museum, interview by Jeannette Shambaugh Elliott, 1971, Taipei.

35. Chang, "National Palace Museum."

36. For details of the travels of the cases of treasures to western China and back, the best account in English is Li Chu-tsing, "Recent History of the Palace Collection." In Chinese, see also Na Chih-liang's accounts in Na, *Gugong Bowuyuan Sanshinian* and also *Gugong Sishinian*.

37. Na, *Gugong Bowuyuan Sanshinian*.

38. This part of the journey has been memorably described in John Hersey's novel *Single Pebble*.

39. Na, *Gugong Sishinian*, 88–92.

40. Chiang, "Transfer of the National Palace Museum."

41. *Beijing Bowuguan Nianjian*, 11.

42. Ibid., 30.

43. Ibid., 12–13.

44. Ibid., 39.

45. Shen Shiyuan, interview by Jeannette Shambaugh Elliott, 1993, Taiwan. Shen had been at the Palace Museum since its founding.

46. *Beijing Bowuguan Nianjian*, 12.

47. Yang Boda, senior research curator, interview with Jeannette Shambaugh Elliott and Ingrid Larsen, October 1992, Beijing.

48. *Beijing Bowuguan Nianjian*, 12–13, 32.

49. Na, *Gugong Bowuyuan Sanshinian.*

50. Na, *Gugong Sishinian*, 65.

51. Yang Renkai, *Guobao Chenfu Lu*, 145.

52. The *Beijing Bowuguan Nianjian* lists many retrievals made for the Palace Museum before December 1949 that were not taken to Taiwan. These include records like the following:

1945– Han dynasty seal donated.

1946– The ceramic collection of Guo Shiwu (purchase).

1946– Jannings collection of bronzes.

1946– 741 library relics from Frankfurt Chinese Institute Friendship Association.

1947– Sets of books, Yuan Dynasty edition.

1948– John Ferguson's collection stored in the Antiquities Hall.

53. The secretary said the list was being prepared for a student named Max Loehr, who went on to become a professor of Chinese art at the University of Michigan and at Harvard University.

Chapter 5. Relocating and Rebuilding the Palace Museum on Taiwan

1. Zhu, "Huiyi Ma Heng Yuanzhang," 3–4.

2. Ibid., 2–6.

3. Interviewed many years later (1972) in Taipei, Chuang Yen told Jeannette Shambaugh Elliott that he believed the Communists had been forcibly holding Ma Heng in Beijing against his will.

4. Na, *Gugong Bowuguan Sanshinian*, and *Gugong Sishinian.*

5. Chang, "National Palace Museum," 4.

6. Chuang Yen, interview by Jeannette Shambaugh Elliott, 1971, Taipei.

7. In 1946, Hang Liwu recovered 117 trunks of books that had been seized by the Japanese in Hong Kong and sent to Japan. A group of scholars went to Japan to recover this shipment from the Ministry of Culture, along with many items removed from private owners. Another recovery, 102 cases of rare old books from the National Central Museum and Library, had been secretly shipped to the United States in 1941 for safekeeping at the Library of Congress. Although the subsequent civil war prevented their timely return to China, the books were sent to the Republic of China on Taiwan in the 1960s. See Tsien, "How Chinese Rare Books Crossed the Pacific," 359–72.

8. Na, interview by Jeannette Shambaugh Elliott, June 1972, Taipei. The persistent rumor that U.S. naval transport was used for this operation and that some naval personnel received gifts from the Palace Museum was categorically denied by Na.

9. For a complete list of figures on relics moved to Taiwan compared with rel-

ics moved south in 1933, see Na, *Gugong bowuguan sanshinian*, 110–11, 207. See also Chuang, *Shantang Qinghua*, 137–38.

10. James Cahill, interview by Jeannette Shambaugh Elliott, November 1994, Berkeley, California.

11. Thanks to James Cahill for this insight.

12. See the beginning of chapter 4 for a description of how the Stone Drums were prepared in 1933 for their move to southern China.

13. In October 1985, to commemorate the sixtieth anniversary of the founding of the Palace Museum, the drums were moved to the Famous Carvings Hall (Mingkeguan) in the museum. Curator Yang Boda praised Chuang Yen's job of preparing them for travel in 1933, for they had suffered no damage.

14. Hang, *Zhonghua Wenwu Bojian Ji*.

15. Na, *Gugong Bowuguan Sanshinian*.

16. Cahill, interview.

17. Cohen, *East Asian Art*, 138–45.

18. There does not seem to have been the same degree of concern over the selection of bronzes, ceramics, and other works.

19. Li Lin-ts'an, "Five Hundred and Thirty Days," 2–3. Many of this chapter's details are taken from Li's dairy.

20. National Gallery of Art, *Chinese Art Treasures*.

21. Introduction to catalogue, National Gallery of Art, *Chinese Art Treasures*, 8.

22. Ibid.

23. Sullivan, *Arts of China* (1977), 45–56.

24. Li Lin-ts'an, "Five Hundred and Thirty Days," 231 and concluding section.

25. The dating of this anonymous painting was controversial. Takashi Sugiura, the mounter, noted that the silk fibers still had a lot of strength and did not appear to date back to the Tang dynasty.

26. In a 1971 interview by Jeannette Shambaugh Elliott in Taipei, Chuang Yen said that the wave of American interest in China engendered by the Chinese Art Treasures exhibition of 1961–62 was related to the gift to build the art museum in Taipei.

27. The Federal Republic of Germany dealt with the same problem in a similar fashion in 2003. Interview by David Shambaugh with German Foreign Ministry official, February 21, 2003, Berlin.

28. Solomon, "Don't Mess with Our Cultural Patrimony!" This article contains an excellent overview of the controversies surrounding, and the saga of, the exhibition. Also see Murck, "Art and Politics," and "Elections and Art Loans," *New York Times*, January 26, 1996.

29. Solomon, "Don't Mess with Our Cultural Patrimony!" 32.

30. Ibid., 33.

31. Ibid., 44.

32. Chang, "National Palace Museum," 25.

33. Tu, "Five Goals for the New Century."

34. Ibid.

Chapter 6. The Gugong in Beijing:
National Treasure and Political Object

1. Quoted in Fairbank, *Liang and Lin*, 169.

2. Yu, "Gugong Bowuyuan de Lishi he Fazhan," 7–8.

3. Quoted in Wang and Deng, *Gugong Bowuyuan Licheng*, 70.

4. Ibid., 70–72.

5. Much of this paragraph is drawn from the account in Wang and Deng, *Gugong Bowuyuan Licheng*, 65–66.

6. The museum on Taiwan would continue to identify itself as the National Palace Museum.

7. We are indebted to James Cahill for this information about Bureau of Cultural Relics activities and the people involved. Zhang Congyu, Xu Bangda, and C. C. Wang were members of an artist's group in 1930s Shanghai that was centered on Wu Hufan, an artist, connoisseur, and teacher.

8. Gugong Bowuyuan, *Gugong Bowuyuan Wushinian*, 16.

9. Ibid., 12.

10. Ibid., 13.

11. Xu Bangda, interview by Jeannette Shambaugh Elliott, October 1992, Beijing.

12. Gugong Bowuyuan, *Gugong Bowuyuan Wushinian*, 16.

13. Ibid., 13. Altogether, Pu Yi left 1,010 items with the bank as collateral. Only in 1952 were the remaining items returned to the Gugong.

14. They were bought by Guo Shiwu, a collector of fine porcelains. Guo had promised to give these scrolls to the National Palace Museum in Taiwan on his death, but his son said he could not afford to give them as gifts and mortgaged them instead to an unidentified Hong Kong bank. *Beijing Bowuguan Nianjian* (1951), 13.

15. The *Night Revels of Han Xizai* handscroll was sold to the Beijing Gugong by Zhang Daqian, the same painter and art dealer who shipped many of his paintings to Taiwan on the last plane out of Chengdu in 1948. Zhang may have acquired this scroll from Pu Yi's treasures in Beijing or Manchuria, and he is credited with selling it to the museum at a price far below its worth so that it would not go to a foreign collection.

16. Pei Huanlu, Gugong vice-director, interview by David Shambaugh, September 13, 2000, Beijing.

17. Wang Shanshan, "Mourned Art Collector Himself a Treasure," *China Daily*, October 21, 2003, 9.

18. Jiang, *Zijincheng Mijian*, 326.

19. Ibid., 324–25, 328; and Pei Huanlu, interview.

20. Gugong Bowuyuan, *Gugong Bowuyuan Wushinian*, 15.

21. Ibid.

22. Ibid., 14.

23. Ibid.

24. *Beijing Bowuguan Nianjian*. An inventory at the Gugong listed seven hundred thousand items found in the palaces after 1949.

25. Pei Huanlu, interview.

26. Interview by David Shambaugh with Palace Museum director Zheng Xinmiao in Beijing, September 29, 2004.

27. Gugong Bowuyuan, *Gugong Bowuyuan Wushinian*, 13–14.

28. Wang and Deng, *Gugong Bowuyuan Licheng*, 78.

29. Ibid.

30. Yang, *Guobao Chenfu Lu*.

31. Ibid. This account is disputed by other art historians who claim that the handscroll survived the war and is in a private collection in Japan.

32. Andrews, *Politics and Painters*.

33. Yun Baocheng, former Gugong staff member, interview by David Shambaugh, September 13, 2000, Beijing. Yun himself was "capped" and sent to Jilin province for manual labor.

34. Lawton, "Jin Futing," 45.

35. Yun Baocheng, interview; and Wang and Deng, *Gugong Bowuyuan Licheng*, 68.

36. Wang and Deng, *Gugong Bowuyuan Licheng*, 72.

37. Yun Baocheng, interview.

38. Jiang, *Zijincheng Mijian*, 327.

39. Yun Baocheng, interview.

40. Jiang, *Zijincheng Mijian*, 327.

41. Yun Baocheng, interview.

42. Ibid.

43. Yu, "Gugong Bowuyuan de Lishi he Fazhan," 5.

44. Pei Huanlu, interview.

45. Yun Baocheng, interview.

46. Ibid; and Jiang, *Zijincheng Mijian*, 327.

47. Xu Bangda, interview.

48. Jiang, *Zijincheng Mijian*, 327.

49. Ibid., 328.

50. Yun Baocheng was appointed as a guide for Henry Kissinger and President Richard Nixon. Yun escorted Kissinger on several of his subsequent visits, as well as U.S. presidents Gerald Ford, Jimmy Carter, and Japanese prime minister Tanaka Kakuei.

51. Wang and Deng, *Gugong Bowuyuan Licheng*, chapters 3 and 4.

52. Zhang Zhongpei, interview by Alfreda Murck, December 17, 2003, Beijing.

53. Ibid.

54. For a thorough analysis of Tan Lifu's life and activities, see Andrew Walder, "Tan Lifu: A 'Reactionary' Red Guard in Historical Perspective," *The China Quarterly*, no. 180 (Dec. 2004), pp. 965–88.

55. Pei Huanlu, interview. The following information derives largely from information provided by Pei, although much of it is confirmed in published sources.

56. Wang and Deng, *Gugong Bowuyuan Licheng*, 66.

57. In fact, all ticket receipts went to the Ministry of Culture's Bureau of Cultural Relics, which then reallocated a portion back to the Gugong. According to former

director Zhang Zhongpei the ministry/bureau is supposed to return two-thirds to the museum, although it regularly falls short. Zhang Zhongpei, interview.

58. In 2003 the admission ticket price was RMB60 (US$7.20) during peak tourist season and RMB40 (US$4.80) during the off-season.

59. Li Chang, "Gugong Xiugai" [Restoring the Gugong], http://book.sina.com.cn/2003-04-23/3/5208.shtml (accessed May 10, 2004).

60. See Shambaugh, *Modernizing China's Military*, 120–21.

61. Interview by David Shambaugh with a German diplomat who served in Beijing at the time, February 21, 2003, Berlin.

62. Li Xudong, "Modern Hall to Better Protect Museum's Relics," *China Daily*, October 5, 1998, 9.

63. Yang Ruichun, "Pohuai Bainian Geju? Gugong Da Xiu Fang'an Yinfa Zhengyi" [Destroying One Hundred Years of Structure? The Gugong's Renovation Project Invites Controversy], *Nanfang Zhoumuo* [*Southern Weekend*], April 25, 2002, http://www.china.com.cn/chinese/2002/Apr/137997.htm (accessed May 2, 2004).

64. Shambaugh's interview with Zheng Xinmiao in Beijing, September 29, 2004.

65. Ibid.

66. Li Xudong, "Modern Hall to Better Protect Museum's Relics."

67. Wang and Deng, *Gugong Bowuyuan Licheng*, 112

68. Ibid.

Chapter 7. Epilogue: The Politics of China's Imperial Art

1. Chuang Yen, interview by Jeannette Shambaugh Elliott, June 1972, Taipei.

Bibliography

English-Language Sources

Acker, William Reynolds Beal. *Some T'ang and Pre-T'ang Texts on Chinese Painting.* 1954. Reprint, Leiden: The Netherlands: E. J. Brill, 1974.

Aisin-Gioro, Pu Yi. *From Emperor to Citizen: The Autobiography of Aisin-Gioro Pu Yi.* 2 vols. Translated by W. J. F. Jenner. 1965. Reprint, Beijing: Foreign Language Press, 1986.

Ancient Chinese Calligraphy and Painting Authentication Group, eds. *Masterpieces of Chinese Calligraphy and Painting.* Vol. 1. Beijing: Wenwu Publishers, 1984.

Andrews, Julia F. *Painters and Politics in the People's Republic of China, 1949–1979.* Berkeley and London: University of California Press, 1994.

Barnhart, Richard M. "Streams and Hills under Fresh Snow Attributed to Kao K'o-ming." In Murck and Fong, *Words and Images,* 223–46.

Barnhart, Richard M., ed. *Painters of the Great Ming: The Imperial Court and the Zhe School.* Dallas: Dallas Museum of Art, 1993.

Beurdeley, Michel. *The Chinese Collector through the Centuries, from Han to the 20th Century.* Translated by Diane Imber. Rutland, VT: Charles E. Tuttle Publishers, 1966.

Brackman, Arnold C. *The Prisoner of Peking.* New York: Van Nostrand Reinhold Company, 1980. Reissued as *The Last Emperor.* New York: Carroll and Graf, Inc., 1991.

British Organizing Committee. *International Exhibition of Chinese Art: Catalogue and Supplement.* London: Royal Academy of Arts, 1935–36.

Bush, Susan, and Hsio-yen Shih. *Early Chinese Texts on Painting.* Cambridge, MA: Harvard University Press, 1985.

Cahill, James. *Chinese Painting.* Geneva: Skira, 1960.

Chang Lin-sheng. "The National Palace Museum: A History of the Collection." In *Possessing the Past,* edited by Wen Fong and James C. Y. Watt. New York: The Metropolitan Museum of Art, 1996.

Cheng Qinhua. "The Ding Tripods." *China Reconstructs* (May 1986).

Chiang Fu-tsung. "Masterpieces of Seals in the National Palace Museum." *National Palace Museum Quarterly* (March 1974).

———. "The Transfer of the Palace Museum Collection to Taiwan and Its Subsequent Installation." *National Palace Museum Quarterly* 14, no. 1 (August 1979).

Chou Ju-hsi and Claudia Brown, eds. *The Elegant Brush: Chinese Painting Under the Qianlong Emperor*. Phoenix, AZ: Phoenix Art Museum, 1985.

———. "Chinese Painting Under the Qianlong Emperor: The Symposium Papers in Two Volumes." *Phoebus* 6, nos. 1 and 2 (1988).

Churchman, Michael S. "Laurence Sickman and the Formation of the Chinese Collection at the Nelson-Atkins Museum of Art." *Orientations* (April 1995).

Cohen, Warren I. *East Asian Art and American Culture: A Study in International Relations*. New York: Columbia University Press, 1992.

Cohn, William. *Chinese Painting*. 2d ed. London: Phaidon Press, Ltd., 1950.

Doty, Carol. "Joy Morton and the Forbidden City: A Mystery Solved?" *The Morton Arboretum Quarterly* 25, no. 3 (Autumn 1989).

Ebrey, Patricia. "Taoism and Art at the Court of Song Huizong." In *Taoism and the Arts of China*, exhibition catalogue, 95–111. Chicago and Berkeley: The Art Institute Press in association with the University of California Press, 2000.

Fairbank, John King. *The Great Chinese Revolution: 1800–1985*. New York: Harper and Row Publishers, 1986.

Fairbank, Wilma C. *Liang and Lin: Partners in Exploring China's Past*. Philadelphia: University of Pennsylvania Press, 1994.

Ferguson, John C. "Reflections on the London Exhibition of Chinese Art." *T'ien Hsia Monthly* (May 1936).

Fong, Wen C. *Beyond Representation: Chinese Painting and Calligraphy, 8-14th Centuries*. New York: The Metropolitan Museum of Art, 1992.

Fong, Wen C., ed. *The Great Bronze Age of China: An Exhibition from the People's Republic of China*. New York: The Metropolitan Museum or Art and Alfred A. Knopf, Inc., 1980.

Fong, Wen C., and Marilyn Fu. *Sung and Yuan Paintings*. New York: The Metropolitan Museum of Art, 1973.

Fu, Shen C. Y. "A History of the Yuan Imperial Collections." *National Palace Museum Quarterly* 13, no. 1 (Autumn 1978); no. 4 (Summer 1979).

———. "Princess Sengge Ragi: Collector of Painting and Calligraphy." In Weidner, *Flowering in the Shadows*.

Gernet, Jacques. *A History of Chinese Civilization*. Translated by J. R. Foster. 1982. Reprint, Cambridge: Cambridge University Press, 1990.

Hersey, John. *A Single Pebble*. Thorndike, ME: Thorndike Press, 1992.

Hobson, R. L. "The Chinese Exhibition." *Apollo* (December 1935).

Hummel, Arthur W. *Eminent Chinese of the Ch'ing Period*. 2 vols. Washington, D.C.: U.S. Government Printing Office, 1943.

Jing, Anning. "The Portraits of Kublai Khan and Chabi by Anige (1245–1306), a Nepali Artist at the Yuan Court." *Artibus Asiae* 54 (1994).

Johnston, Reginald F. *Twilight in the Forbidden City*. London: Victor Gollanz Ltd., 1934.

Kahn, Harold L. "A Matter of Taste: The Monumental and the Exotic in the Qianlong Reign." In Chou and Brown, *The Elegant Brush*, 288–302.

Keightley, David N. *Sources of Shang History: The Oracle Bone Inscriptions of Bronze Age China*. Berkeley: University of California Press, 1978.

Keswick, Maggie. *The Chinese Garden: History, Art, and Architecture*. New York: Rizzoli International Publications, 1980.

Kohara Hironobu. "The Qianlong Emperor's Skill in the Connoisseurship of Chinese Painting." In Chou and Brown, "Chinese Painting Under the Qianlong Emperor," *Phoebus* 6, no. 1: 67–83.

Langlois, John D., Jr. "Chuang Yen and the National Palace Museum." *Echo of Things Chinese* (March 1972).

Lawton, Thomas. "Jin Futing: A 19th Century Chinese Collector-Connoisseur." *Transactions of the Oriental Ceramics Society* 54 (1989–90): 35–61.

———. "The Mo-yuan Hui-kuan by An Ch'i." *National Palace Museum Quarterly* (1969): 13–35.

Ledderose, Lothar. *Mi Fu and the Classical Tradition of Chinese Calligraphy*. Princeton: Princeton University Press, 1979.

———. "Some Observations on the Imperial Art Collection of China." *Transactions of the Oriental Ceramic Society* 43 (1978–79): 33–46.

Levathes, Louise. *When China Ruled the Seas: The Treasure Fleet of the Dragon Throne, 1405–33*. New York: Simon and Schuster, 1994.

Li Chu-tsing. "Recent History of the Palace Collection." *Archives of Chinese Art Society of America* 12 (1958): 61–75.

Li Chu-tsing, ed. *Artists and Patrons: Some Social and Economic Aspects of Chinese Painting*. Lawrence: Kress Foundation and the Department of Art History, University of Kansas, 1989.

Li Lin-ts'an. "Five Hundred and Thirty Days." (Li's diary of travels with the 1960–61 Loan Exhibition from the National Palace Museum, Taipei, to museums in the United States.)

Loehr, Max. "Chinese Painting with Sung-Dated Inscriptions." *Ars Orientalis* 4 (1961): 219–84.

MacFarquhar, Roderick, ed. *The Forbidden City*. New York: Newsweek Publishers, 1972.

Ma Heng. *Fifteen Different Classes of Measures as Given in the Lu Li Chih of the Sui Dynasty History*. Translated by John C. Ferguson. Peiping: N.p., 1932.

Mattos, Gilbert L. "The Stone Drums of Ch'in." *Monumenta Serica Monograph Series* XIX. Nettetal: Steyler Verlag-Wort und Werk, 1988.

McCausland, Shane. *First Masterpiece of Chinese Painting: The Admonitions Scroll*. London: The British Museum Press, 2003.

McCausland, Shane, ed. *Gu Kaizhi and the Admonitions Scroll*. London: The British Museum and the Perceival David Foundation, 2003.

Mote, F. W. "The Intellectual Climate in Eighteenth Century China: Glimpses of

Beijing, Suzhou and Yangzhou in the Qianlong Period." In Chou and Brown,*The Elegant Brush*.

Murck, Alfreda. "Art and Politics." *Orientations* (March 1996).

Murck, Alfreda, and Wen C. Fong. *Words and Images: Chinese Poetry, Calligraphy and Painting*. Princeton: Princeton University Press, 1991.

Murowchick, Robert E., ed. *China: Ancient Culture, Modern Land*. Norman: University of Oklahoma Press, 1994.

Murray, Julia K. "The Role of Art in the Southern Sung Dynastic Revival." *Bulletin of Sung-Yuan Studies*, no. 18 (1986).

———. "A Southern Song Painting Regains its Memory: *Welcoming the Imperial Carriage* (*Ying-luan t'u*) and its Colophon." *Sung-Yuan Studies* 22 (1990–92): 109–24.

———. "Sung Kao-tsung as Artist and Patron." In Li Chu-tsing, *Artists and Patrons*.

National Gallery of Art. *Chinese Art Treasures*. Washington, D.C.: National Gallery of Art, 1960.

National Palace Museum. *Chinese Art Treasures: A Selected Group of Objects from the Chinese National Palace Museum and the Chinese National Central Museum, Taichung, Taiwan, Exhibited in the United States*. Geneva: Skira, 1961.

Owyang, Steven D. "The Formation of the Family Collection of Huang Tz'u and Huang Lin." In Li Chu-tsing, *Artists and Patrons*.

Rogers, Howard. "Court Painting Under the Qianlong Emperor." In Chou and Brown, *The Elegant Brush*, 303–17.

Rossabi, Morris. *Kublai Khan: His Life and Times*. Berkeley: University of California Press, 1987.

Rudolph, Richard C. "Dynastic Booty: An Altered Chinese Bronze." *Harvard Journal of Asiatic Studies* 11 (1948).

Shambaugh, David. *Modernizing China's Military: Progress, Problems and Prospects*. Berkeley and London: University of California Press, 2002.

She, Cheng. "An Overview of Stylistic Development in the Qianlong Painting Academy." In Chou and Brown, "Chinese Painting Under the Qianlong Emperor," *Phoebus* 6, no. 1: 74–90.

Sickman, Laurence, and Alexander Soper. *The Art and Architecture of China*. Harmondsworth, Middlesex, UK: Penguin Books Ltd., 1956.

Sima Qian (Ssu-ma Ch'ien). *Records of the Grand Historian: Translated from the Shih chi of Ssu-ma Ch'ien*. 2 vols. Translated by Burton Watson. New York: Columbia University Press, 1961.

Siren, Osvald. *Chinese Painting: Leading Masters and Principles*. 7 vols. New York: Ronald Press, 1956–58.

Solomon, Andrew. "Don't Mess with Our Patrimony!" *New York Times Magazine*, March 17, 1996.

Spence, Jonathan D. *Ts'ao Yin and the K'ang-hsi Emperor: Bondservant and Master*. New Haven: Yale University Press, 1988.

Spendlove, F. St. George. *Catalogue of the International Exhibition of Chinese Art, 1935–36*. London: Royal Academy of Arts, 1935.

Steinhardt, Nancy Shatzman. *Chinese Imperial City Planning*. Honolulu: University of Hawaii Press, 1990.

Sturman, Peter C. "Cranes Above Kaifeng: The Auspicious Image at the Court of Huizong." Ph.D. dissertation, Department of Art History, Yale University, 1989.

Sullivan, Michael. *The Arts of China*. Revised ed. 1977; 4th ed, Berkeley: University of California Press, 1999.

———. *Symbols of Eternity: The Art of Landscape Painting in China*. Stanford, CA: Stanford University Press, 1978.

Thorp, Robert L., and Richard Ellis Vinograd. *Chinese Art and Culture*. New York: Harry Abrams Publishers, 2001.

Timperley, H. J. "The Future of the Peiping Palace Treasures." *China Weekly Review*, January 13, 1934.

Tseng Yu-ho (Ecke). "Emperor Tsung Hui-tsung, the Artist: 1082–1136." PhD dissertation, New York University, 1972.

Tsien, Tsuen-hsuin. "How Chinese Rare Books Crossed the Pacific at the Outbreak of the World War II: Some Reminiscences." Association for Asian Studies, *Committee on East Asian Libraries Bulletin*, no. 101 (December 1993): 109–12.

Tu Cheng-sheng. "Five Goals for the New Century." *National Palace Museum Newsletter* 33, no. 1 (January-February 2001).

Van Gulik, R. H. *Chinese Pictorial Art*. Roma: Instituto italiano per il Medio ed Estremo Oriente, 1958.

Vinograd, Richard. *Boundaries of the Self: Chinese Portraits 1600–1900*. Cambridge: Cambridge University Press, 1992.

Walder, Andrew. "Tan Lifu: A 'Reactionary' Red Guard in Historical Perspective." *The China Quarterly*, no. 180, December 2004.

Weidner, Marsha. "Aspects of Painting and Patronage at the Mongol Court, 1260–1368." In Li Chu-tsing, *Artists and Patrons*.

Weidner, Marsha, ed. *Flowering in the Shadows: Women in the History of Chinese and Japanese Painting*. Honolulu: University of Hawaii Press, 1990.

Weng, Wang-go, and Yang Boda. *The Palace Museum: Peking, Treasurers of the Forbidden City*. New York: Abrams, 1982.

Wu Hung. *The Wu Liang Shrine: The Ideology of Early Chinese Pictorial Art*. Stanford, CA: Stanford University Press, 1989.

Wu, Nelson. "The Meaning of the Chinese Treasures." *Art News* 60, no. 4 (1961): 26–29, 56–57.

Yang Boda. "The Development of the Ch'ien-lung Academy." In Murck and Fong, *Words and Images*.

Yu Jian. "Treasures of the Palace Museum." *China Reconstructs* (December 1985).

Yu Zhaoyun. *Palaces of the Forbidden City*. New York and London: Viking Press, 1984.

Zhou, Shacen. *Beijing Old and New: A Historical Guide to Places of Interest*. Beijing: New World Press, 1984.

Chinese- and Other-Language Sources

Beijing Bowuguan Nianjian [The Yearbook of Beijing Museums]. Beijing: Yanshan chubanshe, 1912–1987.

Chavannes, Edouard. *Mission Archaeologique dans la Chine Septentrionale*. Paris: E. Leroux, 1913.

Chuang Yen, ed. *Shantang Qinghua* [Idle Talk in a Mountain Pavilion]. Taipei: National Palace Museum, 1980.

Gugong Bowuyuan, ed. *Gugong Bowuyuan Wushinian Rucang Wenwu Jingpingji* [Selected Gems of Cultural Relics Newly Collected in the Palace Museum in the Last Fifty Years]. Beijing: Forbidden City Publishing House, 1999.

Gugong Zhoukan, no. 3 (October 26, 1929); no. 28 (April 19, 1930).

Hang Liwu. *Zhonghua Wenwu Bojian Ji* [The Record of the Transfer of the Chinese Antiquities]. 1980. Reprint, Taipei: Shangwu yinshuguan, 1983.

Jiang Shunyuan. "Jinian Yi Peiji" [In Memory of Yi Peiji]. *Gugong Bowuyuan Yuekan*, no. 4 (1987).

———. *Zijincheng Mijian* [Secret History of the Forbidden City]. Beijing: Guoji wenhua chubanshe, 1994.

Jiaoyubu Dierci Quanguo Meishu Zhanlanhui Zhuanji [A Special Collection of the Second National Exhibition of Chinese Art under the Auspices of the Ministry of Education]. Nanjing exhibition catalogue. Nanjing: Shangwu yinshuguan, 1937.

Kohara Hironobu. "Kenryû Kôtei no Gagaku ni tsuite [On the Qianlong Emperor's Connoisseurship]." *Kokka*, no. 1079 (January 1985): 9–25; no. 1081 (March 1985): 35–43; no. 1082 (April 1985): 33–41.

Kokka, no. 380 (January 1922).

Liu Beisi and Xu Qixian, eds. *Gu gong zhen cang ren wu zhao pian hui cui* [Exquisite Figure-Pictures from the Palace Museum]. Beijing: Forbidden City Publishing House, 1994.

Lo Chen-yu. *Yin-hsu shu-ch'I ching-hua*. N.p., 1914.

Na Chih-liang. *Fujin Yiwanghua Guobao: Gugong Wushinian* [Fifty Years of the Palace Museum: Recalling the Past and Comparing it with the Present; Talks about the National Treasures]. Hong Kong: Liren Shuju, 1984.

———. *Gugong Bowuyuan Sanshinian Zhi Jingguo* [Thirty Years of the Palace Museum]. Taipei: Zhonghua congshu bianshen weiyuanhui, 1957.

———. *Gugong Sishinian* [Forty Years of the Palace Museum]. Taipei: Shangwu yinshuguan, 1966.

Pu Yi. *Wode Qian Bansheng* [The First Half of My Life]. Beijing: Dongfang Publishers, 1999.

Qin, Guojing. *Xun Qinghuang Shiyishi* [Concerning the Expulsion of the Qing Emperor]. Beijing: Forbidden City Publishing House, 1985.

Shan Shiyuan. *Gugong Shihua* [Historical Narrative of the Gugong]. Beijing: Zhonghua Shuju, 1964.

Siku quanshu (Ssu-k'u ch'uan-shu) [Comprehensive Library of the Four Treasuries]. Compiled 1773–1782. Reprint, Taipei: Shangwu yinshuguan, 1983.

Toyama, Gunji. "Kin Shoso shuzo no shoga ni tsuite" [The Art Collection of Jin Zhangzong]. In *Kanda hakushi kanreki kinen shoshigagaku ronshu*. Kyoto: N.p., 1957.

Wang Shuqing and Deng Wenlin. *Gugong Bowuyuan Licheng, 1925–1995* [The Course of the Palace Museum, 1925–1995]. Beijing: Forbidden City Publishing House, 1995.

Wu Jingzhou. *Gugong Bowuyuan Chuangshi Wunianji* [The First Five Years]. Taipei: Shijie Shuju, 1971.

———. *Gugong Dabaoan Zhenxiang* [Truth About the Theft of the Palace Treasures]. Beijing: Wenshi Zilao, 1983.

Yang Renkai. *Guobao Chenfu Lu: Gugong Sanyi Shuhua Jianwen Kaolue* [Record of the Vicissitudes of National Treasures: Investigation of the Dispersed and Lost Calligraphy and Paintings from the Former Palace Museum]. Shanghai: People's Publishing House, 1991.

Yu Jian. "Gugong Bowuyuan de Lishi he Fazhan." *Gugong Bowuyuan Yuekan*, no. 1 (1986): 5–6.

Zhongguo Dabaike Quanshu: Kaoguxue [China's Complete Encyclopedia: Archaeology]. Beijing: Zhongguo dabaike quanshu chubanshe, 1982.

Zhu Jiajin. "Huiyi Ma Heng Yuanzhang" [Reminiscences of Curator Ma Heng]. *Wenwu Tiandi*, no. 1 (1987): 2–3.

Index